MANCHESTER UNITED

The Betrayal Of A Legend

MANCHESTER UNITED

The Betrayal Of A Legend

Michael Crick & David Smith

PELHAM BOOKS
Stephen Greene Press

PELHAM BOOKS/Stephen Greene Press

Published by the Penguin Group
27 Wrights Lane, London W8 5TZ, England
Viking Penguin Inc., 40 West 23rd Street, New York, New York 10010, USA
The Stephen Greene Press Inc., 15 Muzzey Street, Lexington, Massachusetts 02173, USA
Penguin Books Australia Ltd, Ringwood, Victoria, Australia
Penguin Books Canada Ltd, 2801 John Street, Markham, Ontario, Canada L3R 1B4
Penguin Books (NZ) Ltd, 182–190 Wairau Road, Auckland 10, New Zealand

Penguin Books Ltd, Registered Offices: Harmondsworth, Middlesex, England

First published 1989
Copyright © Michael Crick & David Smith 1989

Printed and bound in Great Britain by Richard Clay Ltd, Bungay
Typeset in Linotron 10½ on 12½pt Meridian by
Cambrian Typesetters, Frimley, Surrey

A CIP catalogue record for this book is available from the British Library.

ISBN 0 7207 1783 3

CONTENTS

ACKNOWLEDGEMENTS

IN THE course of research for this book the authors spoke to over a hundred people involved with Manchester United. Many preferred to remain anonymous, but those whom we can thank publicly (in alphabetical order) are: Tommy Appleby, John Aston Junior, John Aston Senior, Ron Atkinson, Alan Ball, Michael Berisford, Alec Bird, Jackie Blanchflower, Alan Brazil, Laurie Brown, Mick Brown, Martin Buchan, Bill Burke, Nigel Burrows, Sir Matt Busby, Mary Carroll, Bobby Charlton, Steve Coppell, Pat Crerand, Jack Crompton, Dick Donald, Ian Donald, Tommy Docherty, Derek Dougan, Tony Dunne, Martin Edwards, Alex Ferguson, John Fletcher, Alan Gowling, Brian Greenhoff, Richard Greenwood, Harry Gregg, Magi Haroun, Sam Holt, Jim Holton, Stewart Houston, Brian Kidd, Louis Kilcoyle, Denis Law, John Lillie, Lou Macari, John McCabe, Paddy McGrath, Paul McGrath, Danny McGregor, Wilf McGuinness, Andrew McHutchon, Laurie McMenemy, Tony Metcalfe, Barry Moorhouse, Willie Morgan, Malcolm Musgrove, Frank O'Farrell, John Parncutt, Peter Raymond, Jimmy Rimmer, Dennis Roach, David Sadler, Paul Satinoff, Ron Saunders, Dave Sexton, Alex Stepney, Ian Storey-Moore, Rick Taylor and Harvey Wilde Senior.

We are grateful to staff at Companies House, the Football Association, Central Library, Manchester, the *Manchester Evening News*, St Katherine's House and Somerset House for guiding us through our research requests. John Edwards, Chris Ingram and Nick Pitt were extremely helpful in providing detailed information on press coverage of Manchester United for the years 1987–89.

Paul Greengrass, formerly of Granada TV's *World in Action*, kindly lent his extensive research material from the 1980 programme on United. David Sadler, secretary of the Association of Former Manchester United Players, helped us contact many of his members. We would also like to thank Nicholas Mills and Ron Lyle of Cokethorpe School; Michael Fennell of stockbrokers A. J. Bekhor;

Graham Endicott of Littlewoods Pools; Stan Royle, the *Manchester Evening News* picture editor; Dave Appleton of Salford City Council; Hugh Adam of Rangers Football Club; and David and Winnie Blakemore of the Warwickshire Supporters' Association. The staff of News Information at ITN were particularly helpful and sympathetic.

Margaret Crick was marvellous in tolerating her husband's behaviour over the past two years during the writing of this book, as were Anne and Gregg Smith who had to endure what was a traumatic period in their family life. Our agent Bill Hamilton saw us through two contracts. We are grateful to Dick Douglas-Boyd at Pelham for accepting the idea originally, and to Roger Houghton and Hilary Foakes for seeing it through its rocky course. John Crick, Margaret Crick, Andrew Curry, Chris Fiddler, Alec Fraser, Nick Pitt, Anne Smith and Nigel Stephenson provided useful comments on various drafts of the text.

INTRODUCTION

THE FATEFUL summons to see the chairman of Manchester United came at thirteen minutes to five on Thursday, 12 March 1987. David Smith, chairman of the Manchester United Supporters' Club, had been working in his offices below K stand at Old Trafford. It was a brisk three-minute walk – underneath the stand on to the Scoreboard End terraces, along the front of the Panini-sponsored family section and out through the staff entrance, before crossing the concourse to United's modern administration block next to the railway.

The receptionist nodded him through the electronic glass security doors without a thought, for Smith was a regular visitor. Rather than take the private lifts, the supporters' chairman climbed the fifty-one carpeted stairs with their gleaming chrome bannisters. At the top was a luxury suite of offices, rooms that seemed more appropriate to a City merchant banker than the boss of a northern football club.

Martin Edwards put the phone down and seated his visitor in one of the brown swivel chairs at the oblong conference table which stood to one side of the L-shaped room.

'David, it's a bit of a delicate problem I'm going to talk to you about.'

As soon as Edwards mentioned the words 'delicate problem', David Smith knew his instincts had been correct.

'You know this Government guideline where we go for 50 per cent membership?' Edwards continued. 'Well, we're going to go for it.'

The prime minister, Margaret Thatcher, had for some months been arguing for identity cards as a way of tackling football hooliganism. As a first step the Government wanted half of each club stadium to be listed as a 'designated area' for members only. Most clubs had resisted this. Few in football believed that registered members would make any difference to the problem of violence. The fear was, though, that if clubs did not comply with the Government's demands, identity cards would be forced on them by law.

'We could pussyfoot about,' the United chairman went on, 'but I think the more clubs pussyfoot about, eventually the Government might make us do what they say.'

Smith was not surprised. Indeed, he had already written to United suggesting how free identity cards might be distributed to supporters at a future home game. Moreover, he had discussed with Martin Edwards plans for developing the supporters' organisation with a view to it becoming linked more directly with the football club.

The two men who sat talking in the top-floor office that afternoon had much in common. Martin Edwards was forty-one, David Smith fifteen months older. Both had been watching United since they were boys: Edwards had occasionally come to Old Trafford with his parents and sat in the United directors' box; the young David Smith, in contrast, had watched the same '50s team from the terraces of the Stretford End. At the time Martin Edwards joined his father on the United board in 1970, David Smith was already an active official of the Manchester United Supporters' Club. And by the 1980s Manchester United had become a full-time occupation for both of them, as Martin Edwards became one of the first full-time chief executives of a football club, while David Smith was spending most waking hours on work for the club's supporters.

Martin Edwards went on to explain to the supporters' chairman a few details of the membership scheme he now envisaged. It would start the following August, just five months away. But obviously there would be something of a clash between the new official Manchester United membership, and the supporters' club that Smith had run for most of his adult life. It was soon clear that Edwards wanted to swallow up the supporters' body within the official club scheme.

'Now,' Edwards continued, 'this is going to make your role completely surplus to club requirements. I realise you haven't got a contract with the club and, in a way, you're a bit in limbo, but we'll take account of that.'

So, for David Smith, this was the outcome of nearly twenty years' work for the cause of Manchester United. Since the early 1970s, Manchester United had been a full-time job for him, even though he was not actually employed by the club. It had meant fifteen- or sixteen-hour days, often seven days a week. He was not just organising the biggest football supporters' club in the country, but also arranging coach and train trips to away matches. The profits from this travel work provided an income to keep him and his family. The work had also involved Smith drawing up measures with United, the Government and the police to combat football hooliganism. And, perhaps in a small way due to those efforts, United fans had, by the end of the '70s, largely lost their reputation as the most troublesome supporters in the land.

Smith was involved in more direct work for the football club too. On Saturday afternoons and weekday evenings, for every first-team match and countless reserve and youth games, he had been down by the touchline, always behind the opposition goalkeeper, taking photographs for the *United Review*. For this work he received no more than an occasional ex-gratia payment. It all meant a lot of effort, and long hours. But Smith had achieved what few people manage – combining a hobby with a job. Manchester United was his whole life. Now, though, he was apparently 'surplus to club requirements'.

'You've given us years of service,' the United chairman admitted, 'which is appreciated, and it's obviously going to come as a blow to you. We realise that, and we will look to compensate you in some way.

'You're not a club employee and you don't work under a contract. Whatever we do, hopefully we're going to be able to give you an ex-gratia payment.'

Edwards talked of making a 'clean break', but of 'cushioning' Smith. The United boss suggested that Smith should go away, think about things and meet him again in a day or two.

In the weeks ahead there were in fact several meetings, all of them in the chairman's suite, and each initiated by Smith. Edwards wanted to get the United membership scheme going before the season ended. He asked for the membership lists from Smith's club, and he was looking for the supporters' club's cooperation and goodwill towards the venture. At first David Smith wasn't in principle opposed to Edwards' plans: he felt it was inevitable that some kind of identity card scheme would be brought in. Smith was, of course, upset about the way he was being pushed out, but tried to see if he could maintain a link with the club and protect his family financially. Yet when Edwards tried to discuss money, Smith found it difficult to evaluate the vast amount of work he had done for the club over the years. Nearly all of it had been unpaid.

However, Smith's attitude changed radically when it became clear what kind of membership scheme Martin Edwards was actually planning. One day, while visiting the general office at Old Trafford, he spotted on top of a tray of papers the minutes of a United senior management meeting. These revealed that membership would cost £5 per person. Smith thought that was a bit expensive, but there was far worse to follow. The minutes also revealed an estimated profit of £2.63 per member. In other words he and his club were being sacrificed to make way for a money-making operation. Yet when Martin Edwards announced the scheme at a press conference and later met officials from supporters' club branches, he said that it was 'not designed as a money-making exercise'.

The final showdown came at noon on Thursday, 16 April. This time David Smith, who by now had decided he could not endorse the club's plans, was accompanied by his wife, Anne, herself a founder member and former secretary of the supporters' club. Martin Edwards had his fellow director and club solicitor, Maurice Watkins, at his side. Smith asked whether the club would allow him to continue taking photos for the United programme.

'We didn't visualise that, to be honest,' Edwards replied, and proceeded to ask if Smith would give back the equipment he used as club photographer.

'That is mine, chairman, and there are letters to the club to that effect.'

'Oh, are there?' Martin Edwards obviously knew very little about the situation. 'Well, what we propose to do is offer you £15,000.'

To Smith the offer only served to confirm that he had made the right decision. The directors had already approved a compensation payment of £20,000. Now Edwards was trying to reduce that by £5,000 because of the photographic equipment which he had not known actually belonged to Smith.

Anne Smith reasoned that surely Edwards could find a job for her husband supervising the membership scheme, saying that he knew best how to deal with all the supporters' branches. Edwards replied that United were worried that several branches had not affiliated to Smith's club, and he wanted to be sure that every branch would accept the new proposals. Privately Smith himself was not too happy about his wife's idea.

After half an hour, David Smith refused to continue the discussion. 'You've broken my life,' he sobbed and stormed from the room.

His wife Anne was left to carry on talking with the United chairman.

David Smith had one further meeting with Edwards, but there was still no chance of being offered further work with the club. The United senior management had vetoed the idea, and seemed determined to get rid of him altogether.

For some months the supporters' chairman had anticipated his demise. Various members of the United staff disliked Smith's independent supporters' operations and saw his work as an obstacle to further commercial expansion. Relations had become difficult a year earlier when Smith helped defend a friend who had been incorrectly accused of fraud within the United Development Association. Smith was also aware of certain malpractices within the Association which had been sanctioned by the United management.

Some weeks before he was finally due to leave Old Trafford, Smith dropped into a room on the first floor of the administration block. Small and without windows, the office was much more spartan than Edwards' large suite situated directly above. Behind the desk sat the man who, more than anyone, was responsible for the legend of Manchester United.

'Boss, I'd just like you to know, before hearing it from anybody else. They've done it, they've got rid of me.'

Sir Matt Busby, the seventy-eight-year-old former United manager, looked puzzled.

'They're kicking me out for the membership scheme,' explained Smith.

The president of Manchester United shook his head in dismay: 'I'm sorry.' Having sat powerless over the years while the club he had built was transformed into a profit-orientated business, Sir Matt understood precisely.

As time passed Smith's initial disappointment turned to anger. He was angry that United supporters were, as he saw it, being exploited by the membership scheme for the benefit of Martin Edwards and his family, who, in salary, bonuses and dividends, were already taking more than £100,000 a year from the club. The supporters' chairman felt that the United legend established by Sir Matt Busby – the great teams of 1948, 1958 and 1968; Duncan Edwards and the Busby Babes who died at Munich; and the family football club – was all being betrayed in the name of profit. Above all he felt the fans, and his members, were being let down by a man who simply wanted to make money from this great club.

Smith gradually cleared the supporters' club files from his office at the ground. Soon the organisers of the official membership scheme would occupy the same rooms. But Martin Edwards never got the membership lists. His £15,000 offer was rejected, and there was certainly no 'goodwill' towards the new scheme. Smith had decided to carry on running the Manchester United Supporters' Club even if it no longer had the football club's backing. He was encouraged by the

5

depth of support he had received, and by the hostility towards Edwards shown in the meeting the United chairman held with branch officials. Being realistic, though, he knew that many of his members would eventually be forced to join the official scheme.

To continue his club, Smith rented a box number from the Post Office with an Old Trafford address. The phone number of the supporters' club office was quickly transferred to an office near Old Trafford lent by a friendly businessman. United were particularly annoyed about that.

David Smith gradually decided that the full story of the Edwards family's betrayal of United now had to be told. Over the years he had, of course, learnt a vast amount about the club. Helping Geoffrey Green in the late 1970s research his history of United had enabled Smith to read United minute books, though the club had stopped Green himself from using much of the material. He had also enjoyed a long friendship with the late United director Denzil Haroun who had taken a close interest in supporters' club activities. In addition, working at the Old Trafford ground every day, in close contact with United players and officials, Smith could not help hearing things the press and the fans never knew. The time had come to tell the true story of life at Old Trafford.

This book is that story. It describes how Matt Busby built Manchester United from the ruins of the Second World War into one of the greatest teams in football history, only to see his ambitions devastated in the snow of Munich airport. It was with the 1958 crash when eight players died, that the legend was born – the extra ingredient that makes Manchester United that bit special.

Yet the week of the Munich crash also saw the entry on to the United scene of Louis Edwards, a Manchester butcher who had been encouraged to join the United board by Matt Busby himself. It was the beginning of the transfer of power from Busby, the man who built the modern United, to the Edwards family who bought it. Now the legend that the family own is being used for profit.

A journalist, Michael Crick, happened to visit Martin Edwards' office a few days after Smith's traumatic meeting in March 1987, though he was largely unaware of what was going on. A devoted United supporter since his schooldays in the early 1970s, he was visiting the United chairman while researching a book he also planned about the club. What interested him most was the politics and economics of Britain's most famous football club. His research brought him into contact with David Smith, but it was not until the corrected proofs of Crick's book were about to go back to the publishers that the two agreed to combine their work and Crick's first draft was abandoned.

What follows is based on facts, not opinion, and has the private support of many people involved with the club over the years. It is the work of two United fanatics, whose sincere hope is that the club will be reformed and restored to its former glory; that one day Manchester United will regain its reputation for entertainment rather than money; that lucrative dividends will give way to glittering trophies.

1 THE BEGINNINGS OF A LEGEND

'This was a first division club – but, to be frank, in name only.'

Sir Matt Busby on United in 1945.

FOR THE German *Luftwaffe* in the early months of the Second World War, Trafford Park, the large industrial area around the docks at the end of the Manchester Ship Canal, was an obvious target. In the skies of north-west England on the evening of 11 March 1941 there were, according to the *Manchester Guardian*, 'seldom more than a few minutes during which planes could not be heard'. Trafford Park was showered with bombs aimed at the wharves and warehouses, at General Electric, Metro Vickers and the other large works. Some of the bombs went slightly off target and hit a small patch of green next to the great factories, wedged between the Manchester to Liverpool railway and the Bridgewater Canal.

In the local press the following day this particular target got only vague mentions. For security reasons newspapers at the time could not be specific about which particular sites the Germans had hit. 'Slight outbreaks of fire were reported from a football ground,' wrote the *Guardian*, which could only locate it in an inland town in the North-west. The next day saw a little more detail: 'Incendiaries fell on the main stand, and the dressing rooms were damaged by high explosive.' Yet neither readers of the *Manchester Guardian* nor the German *Luftwaffe* were to know until much later that the ground concerned was in fact the famous home of Manchester United.

The stadium that had once staged FA Cup finals and internationals was now in ruins. The main stand next to the railway tracks was reduced to a heap of rubble and twisted metal. So too were the dressing rooms and the offices, which meant that many of the club records were destroyed. The pitch upon which United had beaten

Bury 7–3 in a wartime game only three days earlier had been scorched by the fire and heat.

Yet before the war Manchester United's stadium had a more impressive history than its team. It would have been difficult to argue that United were one of the big names in English football. Back in 1888 six Lancashire sides had been among the original twelve founders of the Football League, but Manchester United were not one of them. Nor had United enjoyed the long, consistent successes of historic sides like Arsenal, Everton, Aston Villa, Sunderland and Newcastle United. Manchester United's only significant trophies – two league titles in 1908 and 1911, and the FA Cup in 1909 – had been followed by a long period of mediocrity. Since joining the Football League in 1892 United had spent almost as many seasons in division two as division one.

The German raids over Old Trafford in 1941 – worse than the war damage inflicted at any other League ground – were only the final episode in what had been a wretched decade for Manchester United Football Club. In the early 1930s the club had very nearly gone bankrupt, and, at one point, United had come within a game of being relegated to join clubs like Accrington, New Brighton and Tranmere in the northern section of division three. It would have been so easy for United to go out of existence during these years, and for the city of Manchester today to be sustaining one league soccer club, not two.

The 1931 season had seen United relegated with the club's worst ever record in division one. At the start of November 1930 the team had not one single league point, after a run of twelve consecutive defeats and forty-nine goals conceded since the start of the campaign. In December 1930 came the club's worst ever loss, 7–0 at Aston Villa. The drop to division two was the inevitable outcome after a league season that saw twenty-seven defeats, 115 goals conceded and just seven victories. The club finished nine points below the safety level.

As early as October 1930 the supporters had been in revolt. Three thousand fans met at Hulme Town Hall, where it was agreed to boycott the next day's game at home to Arsenal. There was even an extraordinary scene where one leader of the supporters' club, a man called Greenhough, stood on a soap-box outside Old Trafford and implored people not to go in. The boycott for that particular game failed – 23,000 went through the turnstiles – but for less attractive visitors in that disastrous season, home gates often fell below 10,000.

Indeed, barely 3,500 came to Old Trafford for United's first home game in division two. In what were depressing times for the economy as a whole, the club was feeling the chill wind of unemployment. Interest payments on the club mortgage were delayed, along with debts to the local council, and income tax was long overdue. A week before Christmas 1931 the club secretary, Walter Crickmer, went to the bank to collect the players' wages. He was refused. Manchester United was £30,000 in debt.

It was at this point that the club was rescued by a wealthy businessman. James W. Gibson, a director of a major local clothing firm, Biggs, Jones and Gibson Ltd, paid the players' wages, and gave the club a further £2,000. But Gibson initially pledged his support for only three weeks, saying further assistance depended on there being sufficient public backing for the team.

The crowd for the next game, on Christmas Day against Wolves, was 33,000, bigger than the gates for the previous four home matches put together, and James Gibson continued his rescue operation. He quickly installed himself as chairman and president of United. The existing directors willingly resigned, and four new men joined Gibson on the board. A public appeal was made for £20,000, earmarked 'solely for transfer fees', and new shares were issued in the company. And, not for the last time in their history, United were aided by their neighbours and rivals, Manchester City, whose chairman urged the Manchester public to support Gibson's efforts. In the months ahead Old Trafford attendances did improve a little. Twenty thousand pounds was indeed spent on new players. A promising new manager, Scott Duncan, was appointed. But the results were still not good enough.

In early May 1934 the United team travelled south for the last game of the season, with division three looking an almost certain prospect for the coming autumn. The men who drew up the league fixture list happened, for this final match, to have pitted United against Millwall, the club just a point above them in the table. If the reds beat Millwall, the London club would go down to the third division instead. A draw would save Millwall.

United won 2–0.

Two years later, in 1936, United returned to division one, having won the second division championship, and after having been unbeaten in the last nineteen games of the season. But the success didn't last long: Manchester United spent just one season in division one before going back down again.

After several unsuccessful months back in division two the manager, Scott Duncan, left to look after Ipswich Town, then a non-league club. From then until 1945 United had no full-time manager. Instead, team matters were looked after by the club secretary, Walter Crickmer, and the long-serving chief scout, Louis Rocca.

Manchester United in the inter-war years had been one of those sides, like Leicester City, Birmingham City and West Bromwich Albion in the '70s and '80s, who are not quite good enough to be among the elite, but are often too good for the second division. What made the reds' position particularly bleak at that time was that the '20s and '30s era was the heyday of their sky-blue rivals from Maine Road, Manchester City.

The City side of Frank Swift, Sam Cowan, Fred Tilson, Alec Herd and Eric Brook brought the FA Cup back to Manchester in 1934, having been beaten at Wembley by Everton only the previous year. And they carried off the league championship title in 1937, the same season in which United were relegated again. Among the big-name sky-blue footballers, perhaps the leading playing influence in the City side, was the right-half, a Scot from a Lanarkshire mining family. His name was Matt Busby.

When war broke out in 1939, the league programme was suspended, but there were already signs of how the post-war pattern of Manchester football would be very different. Not only had United bounced back again to division one, but City's run of success had suddenly ended with relegation the very season after they won the title – the only time that has ever occurred. One reason for City's remarkable change of fortune might have been that their Scottish right-half had now moved on, to Liverpool.

At Old Trafford, meanwhile, James Gibson and Walter Crickmer had already taken the first steps in developing a youth programme for United. For years the club had been spending thousands of pounds on transfers, few of which were ever successful. As early as March 1932 Altrincham Football Club agreed to let United use their ground on alternate Saturdays for the reds' new third team, the 'A' side, consisting of teenage players, to play in the Manchester League. Later, soccer clubs in Newton Heath and Denton also allowed United's junior teams to use their grounds.

In February 1938 the board minutes record how the United directors decided that 'with reference to the formation of a Junior Athletic Club for cultivating young players after they leave school, a scheme as submit [sic] was approved, and the matter was left with the Secretary.' So began the famous MUJACs, the players of the Manchester United Junior Athletic Club, an idea of Gibson and

Crickmer. The MUJACs were coached and trained by local teachers, and instructors from Manchester University. According to James Gibson, the club's attitude towards the young boys was not that they would necessarily join United: 'We only tell them that we hope that if as a result of what the club has done they rise to anything like fame they will bear the club in mind.' The United chairman had high ambitions for the junior scheme: 'It is from these unusually comprehensive nurseries that the club hopes an all-Manchester team at some distant period might be produced.' Of the MUJAC's early players, however, only one achieved great success – John Aston.

In these dark years before the outbreak of war, the club were gathering together some of the players who would serve them so well in the distant future. Johnny Carey was signed from St James's Gate in Dublin for a fee of £200 in November 1936, after being spotted by Louis Rocca on a trip to watch a different player. He made his United debut a year later, having already played for Ireland. Jack Rowley joined from Bournemouth in 1937, after James Gibson had seen him play during a weekend spent in the south-coast resort. Another young forward, Stan Pearson, came to Old Trafford from local junior soccer. And a young wing-half, Allenby Chilton, arrived from the North-east in 1938.

James Gibson hoped that United's great Old Trafford ground might one day take over from Wembley as the venue for Cup finals, and he talked of extending the stadium to hold 120,000. The FA Cup final had indeed been played at Old Trafford in 1911, a year after the ground opened, and a final replay had taken place there in 1915. During the inter-war years the stadium was a frequent venue for FA Cup semi-finals – 77,000 crammed in to see Wolves beat Grimsby in 1939 – and internationals such as the 1926 England v. Scotland game and England's 7–0 victory over Ireland in 1938. In the late '30s £35,000 was spent on ground improvements, including new roofing over part of the terracing. In 1936 Gibson arranged for a special railway station to be opened alongside the main entrance to the ground.

So, as United entered the Second World War there were glimmers of hope for the future. The reserves won the Central League in 1939 and the first team took the Manchester Senior Cup, a competition contested by league sides in the area.

Yet the club still had no full-time manager; Walter Crickmer carried on looking after playing matters during wartime football. In spite of modest profits in the late '30s, earlier transfer deals had left debts of more than £70,000. And then, suddenly, in 1941 the club no longer had a ground to play on.

Manchester City agreed to lend United their Maine Road ground for the rest of the war. As for the question of a manager, the chief scout, Louis Rocca, had an idea about a future prospect. In December 1944 he wrote a letter to an old friend who was a former City player:

> I don't know if you have considered what you are going to do when the war is over, but I have a great job for you if you are willing to take it on. Will you get in touch with me at the above address and when you do I can explain things to you better.

The recipient, Matthew Busby, was born in May 1909 in Orbiston, a tiny mining village near Motherwell, east of Glasgow. His father was shot dead in the First World War, and for his mother, raising four children in a two-room cottage, times were difficult. The Busbys decided to follow many of their relations to America, and while waiting for a visa the teenage Matt Busby worked as a miner.

Saturdays, however, were spent playing inside-forward in local junior soccer teams. Matt Busby was quickly spotted by a scout for Manchester City, who in 1928 lured him south, to England. Ideas of America were abandoned as City persuaded him to go professional, much to the annoyance of his local side, Glasgow Celtic, who also had their eye on him.

Initially things did not go well for Busby at City, since the club was overrun with forward players. 'I feel I am out of my sphere in football,' Busby wrote to Jean, the girlfriend he would eventually marry. 'I actually dreaded the approach of each football season,' he wrote later. Returning to the pits in Scotland was a serious possibility.

The young player stuck things out, however, and indeed at one point was very nearly signed by Manchester United. A United director watched Busby playing for City reserves several times; so did Louis Rocca. A transfer fee of £150, a large sum for a reserve player at that time, was mentioned, but the deal fell through because, Busby says, United could not afford it. Shortly afterwards, Busby was moved to wing-half. There his career progressed rapidly and he became captain of the side. In 1933 he won his only cap for Scotland in peacetime football, though many believe he should have been a Scottish regular.

Busby's move to Liverpool for £7,000 in 1937 marked the final period of his playing career. And indeed, after he had spent the later war years as an instructor in the Army Physical Training Corps, Liverpool was the logical club to return to when hostilities ended.

Anfield offered him a five-year contract as a coach. Ayr United thought he would make a good manager. Reading were interested too. Verbally he accepted the job at Anfield, but then came the letter from Louis Rocca.

It led to an interview with James Gibson, who was impressed by Busby's 'ideas and honesty of purpose', and offered him a three-year contract at £750 a year. Busby insisted on five years and Gibson conceded. The Busby family's affection for Manchester, and the fact that they still had many old friends in the city, probably made the difference between Old Trafford and Anfield. The choice had historic consequences.

The nineteenth of February 1945 was the day on which Matt Busby signed for Manchester United. He was still in sergeant-major's uniform and not officially able to start work until October, after he had been demobbed.

The United players soon learnt that Busby's style of management was very different from what they were used to. Before the war football managers had usually been administrators in pin-stripe suits who spent most of the day in their offices, and the former manager Scott Duncan typified this. Matt Busby was still young enough to be playing football himself and was determined to be one of the first tracksuit managers. He would be out training with his players whatever the weather, talking to them and showing by example how he wanted the game played.

The new manager had only taken the Old Trafford job on the understanding that it was on his terms:

> Call it confidence, conceit, arrogance, or ignorance, but I was unequivocal about it. At the advanced age of thirty-five I would accept only if they would let me have all my own way. As the manager I would want to manage. I would be the boss.

Such an attitude, which of course is quite normal today, was highly unusual in 1945. The fact that United had continued since 1937 with the secretary, Walter Crickmer, as the part-time manager was some indication of how the directors saw the job. Team selection was officially the responsibility of the directors, and for many years after Busby's arrival the first item on the weekly board agenda was the selection of club sides for forthcoming fixtures. Indeed, until 1947 Busby would attend board meetings solely to discuss playing matters and then, the minutes often record, 'The manager having conducted his business retired from the meeting.' Only then, with Busby absent, would the directors discuss the minutes of the previous meeting and the club's financial affairs. Slowly, however, Busby gained power and influence. He was soon present throughout the whole of each board meeting, and while team selections were still mentioned, the item became more of a formality on each week's agenda.

Matt Busby fought several early battles with his board. During one match, for example, while sitting in the directors' box at Maine Road, one board member, Harold Hardman, remarked loudly about Johnny Carey: 'How he can keep picking him, God only knows!'

'Never dare to say anything like that to me when other people can hear you,' Busby blasted when he met Hardman later in the gents. And Busby made his feelings clear at the next board meeting.

Busby says the chairman, James Gibson, could also be difficult to deal with. 'You are always telling me "No",' Gibson complained when Busby had turned down the chairman's latest suggestion of a new player to sign. 'Well, I'm telling you now,' Gibson said, 'go and sign him.'

Busby recalled the occasion:

'No,' I said, 'and I will remind you of two things, Mr Gibson. I am here to manage the club and part of management is giving you advice. And the second is that I lived long before I ever saw you.'

Gibson apologised. Busby gained his independence. And Manchester United flourished.

Matt Busby set out to end any divisions among the players, remembering his own unhappy experience at Manchester City:

As a youngster, I felt that there was too much class distinction at Maine Road, and in most other clubs as well, too large a gap between the established first-team players and the rest of the playing staff. Team spirit and pride in the club – two most valuable assets – suffered accordingly. . . . I learned a lesson at Maine Road – the lesson that team snobbery has no place in a happy club; and what unhappy club could possibly enjoy any consistent run of success?

Busby also decided to try to emulate some of the better practices he had seen during his brief stay at Liverpool. The Merseyside club, he says, 'treated everyone on the staff as human beings should be treated, with kindness, consideration and understanding . . . Liverpool were always prepared to reward good service, even when they could so easily have evaded their obligations to players whose first XI days were ended.' He was particularly impressed by the way in which Liverpool had given one of their former star players, Jimmy McDougal, full pay long after he had been dropped from the first team.

For the first four years after the war United carried on playing at Maine Road, and by now bushes were growing through what was left of the Old Trafford stand. In the post-war reconstruction, a football stadium was not a priority for a building licence and permission was needed even for exterior painting work. City and United played home league games on alternate Saturdays and all their reserve matches at United's training ground, The Cliff, in Salford. The club's administration had been moved to one of James Gibson's business premises, the Cornbrook Cold Stores, about a mile from Old Trafford. One small office was occupied by Walter Crickmer, his teenage clerk, Les Olive, and a typist loaned by Gibson from his firm. It also hosted weekly board meetings.

The players would often train on a patch of concrete at the back of Old Trafford, while any medical treatment or indoor practice was carried out in a small second-hand Nissen hut bought by Walter Crickmer for £85 in 1947.

If the club lacked many basic resources, at least Busby had inherited several promising players. Along with Carey, Pearson, Rowley, Aston and Chilton, who had all joined the club before fighting began, several others had been recruited by Crickmer and Rocca during the war. Left-winger Charlie Mitten joined the staff in 1940; wing-halves Henry Cockburn and John Anderson arrived as junior players in 1944. Forward Johnny Morris and goalkeeper Jack Crompton had also been spotted in Manchester youth teams. While nearly all the important ingredients were already there when the new manager arrived, it was left to Busby to devise the right recipe for success.

His club captain, Johnny Carey, is widely regarded as one of the greatest players Ireland has ever produced, and indeed he played regularly for both Irish international teams – on one occasion within the space of three days. Carey could play in any position, and during his time at United he wore every shirt except number eleven, including the goalkeeper's jersey for one whole match. Calm, thoughtful and with a perfect understanding of the game, Carey was the obvious team leader. Before the war the Irishman had usually played at inside-forward, but, in a typically inspired move, Busby moved him further back and mainly played him at right-back. There he organised the defence brilliantly.

16

Carey was just one example of the way Busby experimented with players in new positions, remembering how he himself had been successful at Manchester City only after moving from inside-forward to wing-half. A second change involved John Aston, the former MUJACs player, who was switched from the forward line to left-back. The two ball-playing forwards-turned-defenders created a new phenomenon in football – attacking, creative full-backs.

The post-war Manchester United side is best remembered for its forward line – Delaney, Morris, Rowley, Pearson and Mitten. Jimmy Delaney was the only major player whom Busby bought for United in those years. A fast Scottish right-winger, Delaney had already won a Scottish Cup medal with Celtic in 1937. When Busby bought him for £4,000, many observers considered him to be past his best and injury-prone. They were totally wrong: Delaney went on to play nearly 200 games for United and was recalled by Scotland.

Johnny Morris, at inside-right, was known for his individual touches and nutmegging – putting the ball through an opponent's legs. The centre-forward, Jack Rowley, was known as 'the Gunner' for his powerful shot, and could be depended on for goals – in five of the six post-war seasons he scored more than twenty in the league alone. Stan Pearson also hit the net regularly, while Charlie Mitten, at outside-left, who was skilled at crossing, hit the ball hard and rarely failed with a penalty.

In the half-back line Henry Cockburn was still working five days a week in a Lancashire mill when he won his first England cap in 1946, after just six league games for the reds. The 6-foot Allenby Chilton was switched from wing-half to the centre of defence.

It has been said that Matt Busby inherited his first great team. Players like Johnny Carey and Stan Pearson disagree. 'He had some talent,' says Pearson, 'but it definitely needed sorting out.' That was certainly what he did.

'Every good general needs good lieutenants,' Busby, the former army PT instructor, argued. Shrewdly he chose as his main assistant a Welshman with an Irish name, Jimmy Murphy, who joined United in 1946. Busby had known Murphy through his footballing career, and when they met again in the summer of 1945 Busby asked Murphy to come to Old Trafford. A cheerful, smiling character, yet firm, Murphy was Busby's first and perhaps most important signing. Like many successful partners they rarely mixed socially. Murphy would be much tougher with the players than the manager himself, and often kept them from bothering Busby.

17

It could be that what either Jimmy Murphy or I lacked the other had. He would always give a straightforward opinion. He was no yes-man. But once having made a point he would accept that mine was the decision. He was forthright with never a suggestion of usurping my position. In fact he turned down many managerial jobs offered him at other clubs. If he judged a player I found that his judgements almost always confirmed mine. He was invaluable in handling boys but his value did not rest there. He could tackle the established players with the same conviction and enthusiasm.

Below Busby and Murphy, everyday training sessions were run by Bert Whalley, a former United centre-half who had been forced to retire early through injury. The other trainer, Tom Curry, was an old-fashioned sponge man who had been with United before the war. He would never allow swearing in the dressing room and protected the players like his own children.

On Sunday mornings Matt Busby, the coaching staff and players would come to the ground for a regular ritual – some after they had been to church. It was a chance for treatment, to discuss what had happened the day before, and for a light kick-about. One morning two first-team players were in a bad state after the previous night, and as Busby was arriving Curry hid them in the toilets. Busby was not fooled. He carried on as normal, apparently oblivious to their absence. But as he passed Curry on his way out of the changing rooms he said quietly, 'You can tell those two to come out of the toilets now.' He had the ability to know when something was going on behind his back and to handle it without making a great fuss.

Louis Rocca carried on looking for new players right up until his death in 1950. As successor to his great friend, Busby appointed as his main scout Joe Armstrong, a GPO engineer who had previously scouted for Manchester City. Armstrong had spent all his spare time scouring park and schools pitches before becoming United's chief scout full-time. When other scouts were knocking on a youngster's front door, it was said, Armstrong would be there in the kitchen, drinking tea with his parents, having already struck a deal. Armstrong was assisted by three superb Irish scouts, Bob Bishop and Bob Harper in Northern Ireland and Billy Behan in Dublin. Together they served the club for several decades and found dozens of stars for United and the two Irish international sides.

The highly efficient Walter Crickmer continued as club secretary behind the scenes. He was 'a wise little man', says Busby, who gave 'invaluable' advice about procedures. Crickmer was prepared to recognise, however, who was now in charge of the club.

Matt Busby's philosophy was a simple one. Les Olive, a United servant for more than forty years, recalls that 'Matt was a great example to anybody by the way he treated people he met. He always used to tell me that if you can't say a good word about anybody then don't say anything.'

It was this attitude, as much as Busby's knowledge of the game, that endeared him not only to those he dealt with every day, but also to complete strangers. Never one to seek the limelight or personal glory, he was always quick to praise the assistance of others. He possessed the knack of never forgetting people, and many who had met him just once found that Busby would remember their names or faces many years later.

When league football resumed in August 1946 United got off to a brilliant start with five wins in five games. In spite of having to play at Maine Road the fans flocked to see them, as indeed they turned up everywhere in those post-war boom years for soccer. United were soon attracting bigger attendances than City, their second-division hosts. City did not mind much at first: United were paying £5,000 a year rent as well as a percentage of each gate.

United came second in the league in 1946–47, just a point behind the champions, Liverpool: it was their highest position since winning the title in 1911. The 1947–48 season saw them runners-up again, and even playing home games at City's ground they chalked up one of their highest-ever attendance figures. An average of 54,890 went through the turnstiles.

Soon Busby's team had some silverware to reward their followers. United's 1948 FA Cup run must be one of the most impressive of all time. In every round the reds beat top-ranking first-division opponents – Aston Villa, Liverpool, Charlton Athletic, Preston North End, Derby County and Blackpool. Every tie was won by a margin of at least two goals, without any replays. And, of course, every game had to be played away from home: because of City's own Cup run even Maine Road was available on only one occasion, and other 'home' matches had to be played at Goodison Park and Huddersfield.

One of the most remarkable games in United's history occurred at the start of that Cup run, in front of 65,000 at Villa Park in January 1948. The Birmingham side were ahead within fourteen seconds, with a goal direct from the kick-off. Yet by half-time Morris with two goals and Pearson, Rowley and Delaney with one each had put United 5–1 up. Surely the tie was now beyond doubt. Bit by bit, through the second half Villa chipped away at the Manchester lead: 5–2, 5–3 and then Villa made it 5–4 with still nine minutes left in which to grab what everybody must have thought would be the inevitable equaliser. It was not to be. Two minutes from the end, Stan Pearson put the game beyond doubt and United returned home with a remarkable 6–4 scoreline.

The final against Blackpool at Wembley that April was almost as dramatic – indeed it is regarded by many as the finest Cup final of all time, a masterful display of attacking football. Blackpool may have languished in divisions three and four in modern times, but they were then a major force in English soccer, boasting both Stan Mortensen and the great Stanley Matthews. The seaside club took the lead with a controversial penalty. Rowley equalised, but Blackpool went in at half-time 2–1 ahead from Mortensen. It was only in the sixty-ninth minute, after a long period of pressure from Blackpool, that United could equalise again, when Rowley headed in Morris's free kick. Then John Anderson, who until recently had been in the reserves, set up a goal for Pearson, and later scored himself from 30 yards to make the final result 4–2.

The players shared out a bonus of £550 for their Cup success, and a further £440 for coming second in the league. Today such successes would earn players thousands of pounds each – a vast increase, even allowing for inflation.

The debts United had inherited from the dismal pre-war and wartime years were quickly wiped out by Busby's run of success. With vast crowds bringing in the cash, and United restricted first by FA rules in the wages they could pay players, and second by the Government's refusal to grant a building licence, annual profits piled up: £10,215 in 1946; £13,393 in 1947; £22,329 in 1948 and £50,810 in 1949. By the end of the decade the club's bank balance was more than £50,000 in credit.

In spite of the Cup success, the league championship would still elude Matt Busby's side. The reds came second for a third successive year in 1949, this time five points behind Portsmouth. But the crowds continued to pour on to the high Maine Road terraces. Eighty-two thousand nine hundred and fifty saw the reds draw 1–1 with the champions Arsenal on New Year's Day 1949 – the all-time record gate for a league match – while 81,500 turned up to see non-league giant-killers Yeovil beaten 8–0 in the fifth round of the FA Cup.

United were enjoying the most successful period in the club's history and Matt Busby's work was well rewarded. In October 1947 his salary was increased from £750 to £1,750, and for the 1948 Cup win he got a bonus of another £1,750. In March 1949 the directors gave him a three-year contract on an annual salary of £3,250, a vast amount at that time. It was more than five times the maximum earnings for players, who received £12 a week in the playing season and £10 in summer, and more than four times Busby's starting salary in 1945. No wonder Busby turned down an offer from Spurs of £3,000 a year, and an approach to return to Manchester City.

There are few players who speak ill of United's, and arguably football's, greatest manager. Even those who departed Old Trafford under protest retain the greatest respect for the man they still refer to as 'Boss'.

Busby was determined to develop a family atmosphere around him. At Christmas the team members were each given National Savings certificates. The players would be taken to fights at Belle Vue or to the theatre. There were annual summer outings for both players and staff to Blackpool or Colwyn Bay. And on one occasion Busby organised a trip to see England in a mid-week match at Wembley when three United players were included in the side. A large party went, from first-team players down to the third team.

In August 1949 United at last returned to Old Trafford, marking the first game back with a 3–0 win over Bolton. City had long been making it clear that United could not go on sharing their ground forever, and finally, in November 1948, served notice to quit at the end of the season. 'My board feel that your directors will appreciate that existing conditions cannot be expected to continue indefinitely,' wrote the City chairman. This put United in a bit of difficulty, since they had hardly been able to carry out any repairs at Old Trafford since the 1941 blitz. It was not lack of money, but simply that successive applications to the Ministry of Works, including a delegation to London, had failed. A building licence was eventually issued in January 1949, but when Old Trafford reopened, the main stand still had no roof, and even the directors had to sit without cover, hoping it would not rain.

Back at Old Trafford crowds were in fact smaller than they had been at Maine Road, and the move failed to give the extra push the club needed to win the league. They dropped to fourth in 1950 before coming second once again in 1951, for the fourth time in five years.

After further five-figure profits – £35,604 in 1950 and £22,677 in

1951 – the club finally wiped out the last of the debts hanging over from the inter-war years. The chairman since 1931, James Gibson, had for many months been absent from board meetings through illness. He did, however, live just long enough to hear the news that the club had returned to the black. Gibson, the man who rescued United, was replaced as chairman by Harold Hardman, who had sat on the board almost continuously since 1912. Small in stature, Hardman was a Manchester solicitor and, unlike Gibson, was not particularly wealthy. He had once played football himself, for Everton, England and United briefly, after winning an Olympic medal in 1908 as an amateur player for Great Britain.

In spite of the successful results on both pitch and balance sheet, things did not always go smoothly for Busby. The players briefly went on strike after the 1948 Cup final, while Johnny Morris was transferred to Derby County after clashing with Busby on a matter of principle. And, as in recent times, United crowds had become accustomed to a high level of entertaining football, yet were impatient for the ultimate success in trophies. In January 1951, after three successive defeats, and not having won at Old Trafford for three months, there was even talk of Busby going.

'I'm not getting the sack,' Busby told the magazine *All Football*:

> Let me scotch first those rumours which, I am told, go the rounds – I am not resigning. I am not being sacked and there is neither trouble nor panic in our camp.
>
> These rumours seem to have started because we are not quite the glamour team we used to be. Maybe we are not. You cannot stay on top all the time and we had a longer run than usual. . . . There is nothing to panic about. Before long you will see Manchester United back on top, beating the best.

Fifteen months later, when United met Arsenal at Old Trafford in the last game of the 1951–52 season, they finally made it to the summit. The 6–1 victory over the Londoners, their nearest rivals, secured the first of Matt Busby's five league titles. United's success had not been a foregone conclusion, however. No fewer than six different clubs headed the table at one point or another, but for much of the campaign Arsenal themselves had looked the most likely title winners, having been unbeaten from the end of December until late April.

Seven members of the 1952 championship side – Carey, Cockburn, Chilton, Pearson, Rowley, Aston and Crompton – had helped lift the

22

FA Cup in 1948, but an era was drawing to a close. It was clear that new blood would have to be injected. Busby was keen on continuing the youth policies developed by James Gibson and Walter Crickmer in the 1930s. The transfer market would only be used as a last resort. 'Jerry builders' Busby called those clubs who sank all their cash into expensive, glamorous first teams; 'Costly imports of temperamental stars, and the acquisition of expensive cast-offs from other clubs, did not fit in with my plans.' What Busby proposed was quite natural today, yet pioneering at the time.

> In 1946 it was revolutionary even to think about getting boys straight from school. Get them early enough, I thought, and they would be trained according to some sort of pattern: in my case, the pattern I was trying constantly to create at Manchester United, in the first team and any other team, was that if a boy came through as far as his ability, courage, speed and character were concerned, he would fit into the pattern without feeling like a stranger among people, painting pretty pictures he did not understand and had never seen before.

Manchester United's pre-war junior scheme, the MUJACs, had been closed down in 1941, and it was not until 1947 that Busby was able to get it going again. Joe Armstrong, together with no more than seven or so other paid scouts, was sent off to discover the Manchester United players of tomorrow. Busby himself was also closely involved in the work:

> With a railway timetable my constant companion, I travelled the length and breadth of the British Isles to watch school teams, youth teams, works teams, and even Water Board teams. As soon as a tip arrived from one of my scouts, I followed it up regardless of the distance involved or the inconvenience suffered. . . . Yes, the hunt was on – and I was first in the field, knowing that before long the competition would become fiercer, and well aware that you cannot discover footballers if you sit in the manager's chair all day.

As other clubs began to copy United, there were stories of boys' parents being offered illegal payments to clinch their signatures. Five hundred pounds or £1,000 might be handed over in banknotes. Alternatively, the father of a promising young player might be employed as a part-time scout, though of course he was not expected to do anything for this. But such inducements were rarely the deciding factor in joining United. The club's growing prestige was more important.

Once taken on as apprentices the teenage boys were housed with the club's special team of landladies, and they were sent on training courses and fixed up with part-time jobs in case they never made it as footballers. Their previous junior clubs would be given grants in gratitude. The minutes in March 1949 record, for instance, how Ryder Brow, the north Manchester junior club that had just provided United with a young player called Roger Byrne, were sent a cheque for £25. 'It has never been my entire and complete aim to build a Manchester United team capable of winning the League or the Cup,' Busby wrote, 'but rather to concentrate on a system which will produce a number of first-class Manchester United teams, from fifteen-year-olds upwards.'

Buying players through transfers was only the 'last resort' for Matt Busby. 'If my club decide to buy a player, we do so only because every other method of filling a place in the United team has failed,' he said. Between 1951 and 1958 the United manager acquired only one player through the transfer market. And through careful sales the United transfer account remained in healthy surplus from his arrival in 1945 until 1958.

Within a few months of the 1952 title win United had fallen to fourth from bottom of the first division, only just above Manchester City. They had lost six of the opening eleven matches. When the shareholders began asking questions at the Annual General Meeting, Busby promised that there was '£200,000 worth of skill in the youth and reserve sides ... in another couple of years we shall have wonderful young material when it is needed most.' His estimate would be the equivalent of £12 million worth of talent today. And Busby was right. Within twelve months several of these young players would be brought into action.

Busby's promising teenagers soon distinguished themselves in the Football Association's new knockout competition for club youth sides, the FA Youth Cup. It was a measure of the excitement generated by the young players that more than 20,000 turned up on a Monday afternoon in May 1953 to see them beat Wolves 7–1 in the first leg of the final. Eddie Colman, Duncan Edwards, Billy Whelan, David Pegg and Albert Scanlon helped the reds win 9–3 on aggregate.

Duncan Edwards had been spotted in Dudley, under the eye of the local Wolves scouts – recommended by the former Arsenal captain and future City manager, Joe Mercer. The deciding factor was that

Edwards wanted to play for Manchester United more than any other club. In his brief career in football Edwards achieved a reputation as one of the greatest players the world has ever known. There was little on which he could be faulted. Physically he was large and powerful, but he was also fast and tireless. He was strong with either foot, a good header of the ball, an accurate passer, a keen tackler and a superb defender, yet he regularly scored goals too and had a powerful shot. No one could agree on whether it was best to play him in defence, midfield or attack. One interesting side point is that, strangely, Edwards rarely kicked the ball with the inside of the foot but nearly always with the instep, whether he was passing or shooting.

Eddie Colman was another exciting prospect, snapped up from local Salford football. He had superb ball control and was known for his swerving hips and for sending even his own players the wrong way. In time he formed a brilliant wing-half partnership with Edwards.

The youth team's triumph made up for the stumblings of the first team who, having finished the 1952–53 season in eighth place, by far their lowest position since the war, began the following campaign without a victory in the first eight matches. For a midweek friendly game at Kilmarnock in October 1953 Busby decided to experiment with some of the talent he was nurturing. Stan Pearson and Jack Rowley made way for Irish centre-half Jackie Blanchflower and the forward Dennis Viollet, and half-way through the first half Henry Cockburn went off injured and was replaced by the seventeen-year-old Duncan Edwards.

It seemed to work. Kilmarnock were beaten 3–0 and Busby decided to keep the changes for the following league match at Huddersfield. Viollet, Blanchflower and Edwards kept their places for the rest of the season. Stan Pearson never played for United again.

The Kilmarnock and Huddersfield games have gone down in United's history as the beginning of the 'Busby Babes', though the process of bringing in the new blood was in fact a very gradual one. Blanchflower had actually made his debut eighteen months before, and both Viollet and Edwards had played odd first-team games at the end of the previous season. Duncan Edwards' first appearance had been against Cardiff that spring, at the age of sixteen.

Other changes had already occurred. Johnny Carey had left to become manager of Blackburn in the summer of 1953, having turned down a coaching job under Busby. In March 1953 the United manager had crossed the Pennines to sign Barnsley's young centre-forward, Tommy Taylor, for £29,999. He and Jimmy Murphy spent four days in a local hotel waiting to pounce, and the final pound had been knocked off to prevent the record fee going to the player's head. Another forward, Johnny Berry, had been signed from Birmingham in 1951.

Slowly the pieces of Busby's new team were being gathered together. Left-back Roger Byrne had been in the side continuously since 1951, while two other 'Babes', Mark Jones and Bill Foulkes, had made their first-team debuts in 1950 and 1952. It was a while, however, before the new blend matured sufficiently. In 1954 and 1955 the reds had to be content with fourth and then fifth in the league table.

The youth team had turned into a conveyor belt of talent, and could not be faulted. A further victory over Wolves secured a second Youth Cup in 1954. Playing at centre-forward was another hot prospect, Bobby Charlton, who had been spotted in the North-east. This time 28,651 turned up for United's win in the second leg at Molyneux, a crowd Wolves would rarely expect for first-team games nowadays. West Bromwich Albion were the beaten finalists as the youths claimed their third Cup victory in 1955, this time winning 7–1 on aggregate.

The stream of young players progressing to the first team was soon attracting the international selectors. Tommy Taylor first appeared for England in 1953; the two full-backs, Roger Byrne and Bill Foulkes, made their England debuts in 1954, and though Foulkes never appeared again, Byrne went on to win thirty-three consecutive caps. Taylor and Byrne were joined against Scotland in 1955 by the eighteen-year-old Duncan Edwards; he was the youngest man ever to play for England and was rarely out of the national team thereafter.

Everything was now in place for the 1955–56 season. It was to be the most outstanding league campaign in United's history. At Old Trafford the team went unbeaten, winning eighteen matches and drawing the remaining three. The championship was clinched with a 2–1 win at home to Blackpool on 7 April.

For a championship-winning team Matt Busby used a remarkably high number of players during the course of the season – twenty-four. Tommy Taylor was out through injury early in the year, but it was also an indication of how many good players there were to choose from. The team got off to a poor start, but once a settled side had been chosen, round about November, they lost only three times between then and the end of the season. The side's youth has often been exaggerated: the average age was actually twenty-three, but it was one of the youngest championship teams in history.

Ray Wood, a goalkeeper signed from Darlington for £5,000, was said to live on a diet of tea and cigarettes. Bill Foulkes and Roger Byrne worked successfully at full-back. Eddie Colman, Mark Jones and Duncan Edwards filled the half-back positions. Johnny Berry and the speedy David Pegg were the outside-forwards; Billy Whelan, a player said to be like oil because of the way he slipped past opponents, shared the inside-right shirt with Jackie Blanchflower and Johnny Doherty; Tommy Taylor was centre-forward and Dennis Viollet, with his lightning pace and superb dribbling ability, played at inside-left.

Roger Byrne and Johnny Berry were all that remained from the team that had won the title four years earlier. Only three of the players had cost the club transfer fees. 'One of the secrets of Manchester United's success,' said Roger Byrne, 'is that nearly all of us grew up together as boy footballers. We were knitted into a football family. Apart from Johnny Berry – formerly with Birmingham City, Tommy Taylor and Ray Wood, who quickly fitted into the Old Trafford set-up – the Manchester United way is the only way we know.'

The great collection of players in reserve had also won the Central League title for the first time since 1947. Largely through his clever youth policies, and with only selective use of the cheque book, Matt Busby had produced his second great United side. Now the Busby Babes would look for those wider horizons that in such tragic circumstances would establish the United legend.

2   INTO EUROPE

'I asked a nurse which hospital we should go to next, to see the other lads. She looked puzzled. I asked again where the other people were, and she said there were no others. She said the only survivors were in the hospital in which we were standing. That was when the whole thing really hit me.'

Bill Foulkes on the day of Munich.

WHEN UNITED'S directors met at Old Trafford on 22 May 1956 for their regular board meeting, they had in front of them a letter from Sir Stanley Rous, the Secretary of the Football Association. He invited the club to take part in the new European Champion Clubs Cup Competition, United having qualified by winning the Football League Championship. The European Cup, as it became known, had been initiated only the year before by the French sports magazine *L'Equipe*. The idea of a competition for the top European sides had first been mooted before the war, but had only been made a realistic possibility by the advent of floodlights and regular air travel. Just sixteen teams had taken part in the first year, though not all of them had been national champions. For the first final, which at the time of Rous' letter, was yet to take place, Real Madrid were due to play the French side, Stade de Rheims.

The three United directors present at the board meeting unanimously agreed to enter the 1956–57 contest. It was a momentous decision in the history of the club, one that in time would bring both disaster and triumph, and transform Manchester United, a successful English football club, into a world legend.

Matt Busby was extremely keen on entering the new competition. Always a pioneer, he believed that the contact with foreign club sides could only help British football. The 1950s had been a dismal period for the English national side. The first World Cup that England entered, in 1950, after boycotting the competition in the 1930s, led to humiliating defeat by the United States. Then came an even greater upset to national pride – the Hungarians' surprise 6–3 defeat of England at Wembley in 1953. The following spring England's inferiority was confirmed when the Hungarians won 7–1 in Budapest. Busby was among those who believed that the nation which had invented football would never overcome its two recent World Cup failures if it remained isolated. 'Prestige alone demanded that the Continental challenge should be met, not avoided,' he stated.

The United manager also felt the experience of European competition against the best clubs in Europe would be invaluable to his young players. And it would boost the United bank balance with money from television rights as well as gate receipts.

Taking part in the European Cup was not an easy decision, though. Chelsea, the 1955 league champions, had been persuaded to withdraw from the previous contest by the League Management Committee, who argued that the club would not be able to cope with the extra fixtures on top of the English league and FA Cup competitions. More cynical observers suggested that the football authorities were frightened that crowds would be impressed by Continental skills and demand higher standards at home. It was thus left to the Scottish club, Hibernian, to defend British interests in the first year of the European Cup. They reached the semi-finals and made £25,000 in the process.

Matt Busby accepted that the League's arguments against entering the Cup might have carried some weight for some sides. Participation would mean fifty or sixty first-team matches over a nine-month season:

> An 'ordinary' club, boasting no more than thirteen or fourteen players of the required first team strength, would most certainly find the European Cup a burden; I have thought for a long time that, without considering such distractions, the League programme is already too congested for comfort. At Old Trafford, however, I have at least eighteen players, maybe twenty, who could be played in the first team in the place of the regulars without any noticeable reduction in the strength of the team as a whole. Other managers, no doubt, have similar ideas about their reserves, but how many of them would feel confident about playing seven or eight members of the reserve side in the first XI? . . . Many clubs have the quantity, but few the quality.

However, only a few weeks after United had accepted the FA's invitation, the Football League, the lower authority, were expressing doubts. In August 1956 their objections grew louder. They wrote to say that United's 'participation was not in the best interests of the League, having regard to the possible effect on League match attendances', and they asked the board to reconsider.

By now United had been drawn against the Belgian champions, Anderlecht, in the first round, and the opening game was only three weeks away. The Old Trafford directors stuck to their decision, but to placate the League they decided to pay the usual 4 per cent levy for European Cup matches, as if they were league games. The era of English clubs playing in Europe had begun. 'Some people called me a visionary,' said Busby of this venture on to the Continent, 'others a reactionary, while a few called me awkward and stubborn.'

Yet there was another problem to overcome. European Cup matches were played in the middle of the week, and United had not yet installed floodlights at Old Trafford. They could never expect high attendances if games were played on Wednesday afternoons, while local employers would be angry about people taking the afternoon off work. The General Electric Company told the club that there would be an eight-to-fourteen-month delay for the delivery of steel for the towers on which the lights would be mounted. So Matt Busby approached Manchester City to see if they would again let United use Maine Road, which already had lights. The City chairman, though, was not convinced that United's venture would be worthwhile, and predicted no more than 10,000 would come to the first home game. City's terms – £300 or 15 per cent of the gate – reflected his pessimism.

Many observers regarded United's opening tie against Anderlecht as an easy one since the Brussels side consisted of amateurs and part-timers. Yet their opponents had been Belgian champions seven times in the previous ten years, and in 1953 had beaten the league champions Arsenal at Highbury.

In the first leg, in Brussels, the Belgians hit a penalty against the post, before Viollet and Taylor gave United a 2–0 lead for the return trip to Manchester. Matt Busby told shareholders at the AGM the following week that he was keen to win the European Cup and thought the team had a 'very good chance'.

A crowd of 43,635 assembled at Maine Road for the second game, fourteen days after the first. It was many more than the City chairman had expected, though not an unusual attendance by any means – but then Manchester did suffer torrential rain and the overall result of the tie already looked beyond much doubt. However, those wise enough to go that night were treated to an extraordinary spectacle amid the pools of water, possibly the greatest game in United's distinguished history.

Anderlecht had made several changes in the team that lost in Brussels and suffered for them. United were ahead after nine minutes with a header from Tommy Taylor. He toe-poked a second goal shortly afterwards. Then Taylor's scoring partner, Dennis Viollet, got in on the act with a hat-trick before half-time. Two of these goals were the result of mistakes by the Anderlecht defence; the third a powerful shot from the edge of the penalty area. United went in 5–0 ahead at the interval, 7–0 up on aggregate.

In such a position most sides would enjoy their lead and relax, yet the second period proved just as exciting. A goalmouth scramble allowed Taylor to complete his hat-trick. Whelan made it 7–0 and Byrne passed to Viollet for his fourth goal and the reds' eighth. Johnny Berry got the ninth and Whelan scored a second to create United's all-time record score – 10–0. It might have been even higher had not the players been trying desperately to get a goal for David Pegg; he had made five of the goals, but was the only member of the forward line not to score himself.

Over the years many sides have achieved double-figure scores in European competitions, but invariably against much weaker sides from countries such as Iceland, Malta, Norway and Luxembourg. United had marked their first European game on English soil by beating a top Continental team. 'Why don't they pick this team for England?' the Anderlecht captain wanted to know. Matt Busby called it 'the finest exhibition of teamwork I had ever seen from any side either at club or international level'.

No wonder 75,598 turned up for the next European game United played at Maine Road, against the West German champions, Borussia Dortmund. At first United seemed to be carrying on where they had finished only three weeks before, with another brilliant display of precise, zestful, entertaining, attacking football. Dennis Viollet's two goals, and an own goal by the Germans, sent the reds in 3–0 up at the interval. But then United became cocky. The Germans meanwhile raised their game considerably, fought back fiercely and scored two goals in reply.

After Borussia's second-half performance in Manchester, the 3–2 lead the reds took to Germany looked precarious. But it proved sufficient as, on a hard, frosty pitch United held out in the second

31

game, urged on by several thousand British servicemen stationed nearby, to draw 0–0.

Before the next round in the New Year, United asked the Football League for permission to increase bonus payments for European games. They turned the request down, but the League secretary, Alan Hardaker, did say that if United progressed further in the competition they might look upon the request more favourably.

The club's next opponents looked like being the toughest so far. Atletico Bilbao had won both the Spanish Championship and the Spanish Cup in spite of their rivals, the European champions Real Madrid. Moreover, in the previous round Bilbao had defeated the Hungarian side Honved. First, though, United had to get to Spain.

The club had decided to go by aeroplane to the away games of the European ties. For distant matches there was simply no alternative if United was not going to disrupt its normal league match programme. Most European venues were too distant for the team to contemplate travelling by boat and train. Air travel, of course, did involve greater risks. In 1949 the great Italian side Torino, winners of four successive Italian championships, had been completely wiped out in an air crash on the Superga mountainside outside Turin. And indeed, when United had visited the United States the following year, the club's directors had insisted that the players should not travel by air in America.

The two planes that took the United party to Bilbao went through some terrible weather, and had to stop at Bordeaux to refuel. Then on arrival, Bill Foulkes recalled, it was far from sunny Spain:

> We evidently circled over Bilbao for some time, and because the clouds rolled back from time to time I could see that there was snow on the ground below. I wondered why we did not go in to land, and I soon found out. The steward . . . asked us to keep our eyes skinned, and to let him know if we saw an airport . . . Imagine the scene, as the Manchester United party glued their heads to the windows to look for Bilbao airport. Every time someone spotted a wide road they would sing out – there it is – but eventually the pilot got us down on a deserted field. There were no airport buildings, just a landing strip and an old shed where the customs men lurked.

In fact it had not been until the British assistant consul heard the Dakota circling overhead that he had rushed off to get the airfield reopened!

Bilbao's ground was just as unwelcoming. It had suffered heavy rain for several days and then a snowstorm just before United arrived. The reds conceded three goals before half-time. Taylor and Viollet got two back within eight minutes of the second half, before Bilbao scored two more to make it 5–2. Finally, five minutes from time, Billy Whelan took the ball more than half the length of the field, through the mud, past several Spanish players before placing it in the top corner of the net. Most of those who witnessed the goal regard it as one of the best they have ever seen. Having lost 5–3, United were only two goals down, and had some faint hope for the game in Manchester.

Meanwhile United had a league match at Sheffield Wednesday the following Saturday. The pressure was on the party to get home quickly from what was their longest European journey so far. 'In view of the League's suggestion that United should have nothing to do with the European Cup,' Busby commented later, 'I could well imagine the repercussions if we failed to turn up at Hillsborough.' But Bilbao was still under a snowstorm. The next day at the airfield, players, officials, supporters and journalists all had to help clear the snow and ice from the wings of the plane.

Then, according to Bill Foulkes, it was another rough journey back to England:

> When the crew condescended to fly us home, the trip became every bit as ghastly as the outward journey had been. This time we were tossed about in a fearsome gale.
>
> As we came in to land at Jersey airport, which was on a cliff top, the plane dipped below the cliff, and then shot over the top to bounce in on the runway. Taking off again, the plane seemed to be whisked 60 feet into the air, bumped down again, and then we were away.

Manchester United had certainly learnt about the hazards of winter air travel in Europe. Yet it was typical of the attitude of the club in that era that a few days afterwards the United directors presented the pilot with an inscribed silver cigar box, and his navigator with a pen set, in appreciation of the 'skilful and safe handling of the private aircraft . . . in very difficult weather conditions'.

The team did get to Hillsborough but, with exactly the same side that had played in Spain, not surprisingly they lost 2–1.

By now the European Cup had truly captured the British public's interest. In the second leg at Maine Road, Bilbao understandably went on the defensive. United missed several good chances before Dennis

Viollet made it 1–0 at half-time. Two United goals were disallowed for offside before Tommy Taylor made it 2–0 with nineteen minutes to go. Taylor's cross to Berry five minutes from the end gave United the tie 6–5 on aggregate. In three European ties Maine Road had enjoyed three superb displays of football. Even the Football League had to acknowledge United's achievement, and it now granted permission for United to pay the players bonuses.

Great games and great goals against great sides had put United through to the semi-finals, where they had the biggest challenge of all, the European champions Real Madrid. Fortunately the away game was not due to take place until April, by which time Spain would be rather sunnier. By then the team was on target to perform a remarkable football treble – the European Cup, the league championship and the FA Cup. No team since Preston North End and Aston Villa in the late nineteenth century had achieved the double of the League and FA Cup. Now Manchester United were on the way to adding the European trophy as well.

In the FA Cup, the third round had taken them to third-division Hartlepool on the north-east coast. United threw away a three-goal lead, but a late winner saved any embarrassment. Wrexham were easier opponents in the fourth round, with the reds triumphing 5–0. Everton were defeated 1–0 at Old Trafford, and the sixth round provided the most difficult opposition so far. Third-division Bournemouth had already slain two giants, Wolves and Spurs. By half-time at Dean Court, a third looked to be in deep trouble: the home side were 1–0 ahead and Mark Jones had gone off injured. Two goals by Johnny Berry, however, ensured United's place in the semi-final against Birmingham City. The match at Hillsborough was a fairly easy game. United scored two early goals from Berry and Bobby Charlton, who was that day making his debut in the FA Cup. United were at Wembley for the first time since 1948. The treble was getting closer.

United's second journey to Spain was somewhat easier than the first, and snow had given way to sun. But the match itself was so much harder. One hundred and thirty-four thousand people filled Madrid's vast Bernabeu stadium, almost certainly the largest crowd ever to watch Manchester United. For Matt Busby this was the big test. He had already travelled to France to see the Madrid side beat Nice, and by all accounts came back somewhat in awe of them and particularly of their Argentine centre-forward, Di Stefano.

The 3–1 defeat in Spain was not a disastrous score – the Bilbao matches had proved that it was possible to wipe out a two-goal lead.

United's attack had been ragged and below form, while Madrid had not looked invincible in defence, and Di Stefano had been dogged by Jackie Blanchflower and Eddie Colman. Back in Manchester new floodlights at Old Trafford meant United could now play on their own pitch, and the new local ITV station, Granada, paid £2,500 for transmission rights.

Though the score was 2–2 this time, Real Madrid's superiority was obvious. The Spaniards first let United exhaust themselves, then took a two-goal lead through Kopa and Di Stefano. Charlton and Taylor scored two in reply but the Spaniards deservedly went through 5–3 on aggregate. In Busby's words: 'A great, experienced side will always triumph over a great, inexperienced side.' Yet coming back from two goals down to draw the match was some achievement, and towards the end Real Madrid had anxiously been kicking the ball out of play.

The treble was now out of United's grasp, but the rare FA Cup and League double looked almost certain. United had clinched a second successive league championship with a 4–0 win over Sunderland five days before the Madrid game. The points total, sixty-four, was the best since Arsenal's sixty-six in 1931, and the second highest of all time, yet had been achieved after the busiest fixture list yet tackled by an English club. The runners-up, Spurs, were eight points behind, and few thought United could lose against Aston Villa in the final. Matt Busby felt certain of victory. Yet, as so often in cup finals, form was cast aside. Manchester's chances were gravely reduced when the goalkeeper, Ray Wood, was charged by Villa's Peter MacParland. Wood went off with a broken jaw. Jackie Blanchflower took over in goal and did well. But Villa went on to win 2–1.

Busby now had gathered around him almost enough players to field two top-class sides. Though the team was so young, seven of them – Byrne, Berry, Edwards, Foulkes, Pegg, Taylor and Wood – had played for England, while Blanchflower, Webster and Whelan had also won international caps. To the players who had won the league the year before had been added a nineteen-year-old inside-forward, Bobby Charlton, who scored ten goals in just fourteen games – half of them, appropriately, in two games against Charlton Athletic!

Matt Busby's ambition of three league championships in a row, emulating Huddersfield and Arsenal in the inter-war years, got off to a good start in 1957, with five wins and twenty-two goals in the first six matches. But then several players hit bad form, and the side suffered too many silly defeats. Meanwhile Stan Cullis' emerging Wolves side quickly raced ahead and by January their lead over United was six points. The reds were confident of catching them but, as it turned out, to have done so would have required winning every game from mid-January until the end of the season.

Hopes were still alive in the cup competitions, however. Perhaps this year his more experienced side would achieve glory in the competition that Busby told the 1957 AGM had made United 'a household word throughout the universe'. In preparation Busby had played two games in Copenhagen the previous May, and then in Berlin and Hanover before the new season started. The preliminary round draw was kind to United. The reds triumphed 6–0 over Shamrock Rovers in Dublin, though the second leg at Old Trafford was a much more embarrassing affair, with United winning, perhaps rather fortunately, 3–2. The Czech champions, Dukla Prague, were United's next opponents. A 3–0 victory in Manchester in November was more than enough to allow for a 1–0 defeat in Prague in the second leg.

Again United experienced the problems of winter air travel. The players were due to play at Birmingham City the following Saturday, but fog in Britain meant that United could not catch their intended flight. A new route was worked out. The team flew back via Amsterdam and made the rest of the journey to Manchester by boat and coach. The press did not get home until the Friday. Jimmy Murphy wrote later:

> How we wished there was more elasticity to give an English club more breathing space to go into Europe and win the European Cup as a gigantic boost to the prestige of British football. That's what we were hoping to do. But always there was this mad dash to leave England on a Monday after a hard league match the previous Saturday: a European Cup game in mid-week, then another hectic scramble to get home, usually on the Thursday, so that the lads could be in trim for another tough league match on the Saturday.

For the quarter-finals United again met East European opposition – Red Star Belgrade from Yugoslavia. The first match was at Old Trafford in mid-January. Though they deserved to win, United were sloppy and the final score was only 2–1.

Before setting off for Yugoslavia the Busby Babes were to give what was perhaps their greatest ever performance against an English side. A massive crowd of 63,578 crammed into Highbury on 1 February 1958.

Exploiting a frail Arsenal defence, United had shot into a 3–0 lead before half-time, with goals from Edwards, Charlton and Taylor. In the dressing room at the interval the players were euphoric, but Johnny Berry warned that the game was not over yet. And, sure enough, in a remarkable three-minute spell fifteen minutes into the second half, Arsenal scored three times to level the scores. While most sides might have been destroyed by such a sudden setback, the babes remained calm and continued playing as before. Soon Viollet and Taylor pushed the reds into the lead again. A late Arsenal strike narrowed United's lead to one goal, but the Londoners were unable to pull off another comeback. The programme for the historic game at Highbury costs more than £12 from dealers nowadays. Five of the United team – Byrne, Colman, Jones, Edwards and Taylor – would never play on English soil again.

For the trip to Yugoslavia United had chartered their own special plane so as to avoid any problems with scheduled flights. But the trip from Ringway to Belgrade was another troublesome winter journey. Fog in Manchester had made it doubtful whether the plane would ever take off in the first place. Munich in southern Germany was just over half-way on the 1,150-mile journey and a logical spot for the Elizabethan aircraft, *Lord Burghley*, to refuel. By the time the party reached Yugoslavia, it was snowing.

The match in Belgrade was yet another of those dramatic European Cup games. Just as at Highbury, United were 3–0 ahead by half-time. And just as at Highbury the three-goal lead was thrown away. Taking advantage of United's injuries, the Yugoslavs struck back to make the final result 3–3. The reds, however, were through to the semi-finals again by virtue of the victory in Manchester. Again the result was 5–4, though this time over two matches.

The Elizabethan began the long journey back to Manchester the following morning. Once again there was pressure to get home. United had a home league match on the Saturday, and their opponents were Wolves who were six points ahead of United at the top of the table. So a victory was vital if United were to maintain their ambitions of three successive championships, and Busby hoped to get back for a day's rest on the Friday.

The plane's departure from Belgrade was delayed by an hour when Johnny Berry mislaid his passport. Then the Elizabethan stopped again to refuel in Munich. It was wet and cold in the Bavarian capital, but United had overcome bad flying conditions before. The players settled into their seats and began their usual card schools. Twice the aircraft tried to take off. Twice it sped along the runway, twice it could not get off the ground, and twice the pilot quickly brought it to a halt and taxied back to the start. The party went back to the airport building while checks were made, then quickly returned to the aircraft. For a third time the plane raced through the snow down the runway. It took off slightly, but hit a house at the end of the runway and crashed.

There had been one important absentee from the plane. Jimmy Murphy, who had been appointed manager of the Welsh national team the year before, had gone to Cardiff instead, for a World Cup qualifying match against Israel on the Tuesday night. Murphy had arrived back at Old Trafford just before 4 p.m. on the afternoon of 6 February. Matt Busby's secretary told him the news. He recalls:

> The numbing horror of that moment will live with me till I die. I dashed into my office and picked up the phone . . . and put calls through to the police . . . newspapers . . . BBC, asking for news. Then it started to come in.
>
> Roger Byrne . . . Eddie Colman . . . Mark Jones . . . Tommy Taylor . . . Billy Whelan . . . Geoff Bent . . . and David Pegg were dead, killed in a snowstorm at Munich airport. So was Bert Whalley, one of my closest friends and one of the greatest soccer coaches I ever met. Tom Curry, dear patient Tom, the club trainer, and the club secretary, Walter Crickmer, they too had been killed and Matt Busby was fighting for his life.

Eleven more had died too, including eight journalists and three other passengers.

The airline, BEA, flew relatives of the survivors out to Munich, and Jimmy Murphy joined them on the plane. Busby's wife Jean and his children Sandy and Sheena were in the hospital when a priest gave him the last rites. Duncan Edwards also lay dangerously ill nearby, with injuries that meant he would never play again even if he lived. Busby beckoned Murphy to his side with a slight flicker of his hand. 'Keep the flag flying, Jimmy,' he murmured.

Slowly the United manager recovered. Another of the injured, Johnny Berry, came to Busby's bedside, complaining how his best friend Tommy Taylor had not been to see him yet. Berry did not know Taylor was dead. It was Busby's lowest point.

United's league match at home to Wolves was, of course, postponed. So too was the following week's FA Cup tie against Sheffield Wednesday, but Murphy, with no other coaching staff to help, would eventually have to come to terms with the club's crisis. United boasted strength in reserve. But in addition to the seven dead, eight other players were injured, three of whom would never play again.

The Football Association gave United special consideration, and agreed to suspend the rule whereby players could only appear for one club in the FA Cup competition in one year. This eased Murphy's problems only slightly. It was impossible to know how much the survivors had really recovered from the crash, and how the injuries and trauma would affect their game in the long term.

United had great reserves of wealth but, though people were sympathetic, clubs would not sell their players at bargain prices. Only Liverpool and Nottingham Forest came forward to offer players. When Murphy looked down the list of remaining fit staff at Old Trafford, he was in despair: 'It read like a team of schoolboys. There was plenty of talent which might – and indeed did – show itself in two, three or four years' time. But I needed players, top-class players with first-division experience, immediately.'

A week after the crash Jimmy Murphy reported to the directors on his search for new talent. He had thought of two Swansea players from his own Welsh side. Mel Charles, the versatile wing-half, was 'not available', while the Welsh club wanted £35,000 for their winger, Cliff Jones. Murphy thought that was too much, and Spurs snapped up Jones instead. Ernie Taylor of Blackpool was coming for an interview. Jimmy Murphy was considering several other players, though few were up to United's usual standards – Bobby Mitchell, the Newcastle winger; Sunderland's Colin Grainger and Billy Elliott; Jim Iley of Spurs; Joe Haverty of Arsenal; Preston's forward, Bob Foster; Laurie Hughes of Liverpool and Brian Pilkington of Burnley. The board minutes record the acting manager's plight: 'The following team was chosen provisionally for the match v. Sheffield Wednesday: Gregg or Gaskell, Foulkes, Greaves or P. Jones, Goodwin, Cope, ——, Webster, Taylor, Dawson, Pearson, ——.' Possible players from other clubs to fill the blanks would be watched on the coming Saturday.

The Sheffield Wednesday match was rearranged for Wednesday, 19 February, thirteen days after the crash. When the programme went to press the final selection was so uncertain that every place in the United line-up was left blank in what became probably the most historic English football programme of all time.

In the end Murphy bought only two major players. Ernie Taylor, the tiny inside forward who had won the FA Cup with both Newcastle and Blackpool, came to United with the help of Paddy McGrath, a

United supporter who owned nightclubs in Blackpool and Manchester and who was a close friend of both Busby and Murphy. Stan Crowther, a tough-tackling player who had helped Aston Villa beat United at Wembley the year before, signed just an hour before the kick-off against Wednesday.

Of those who had played against Red Star Belgrade, only Gregg and Foulkes lined up for the game. Taylor and Crowther made their debuts, but the rest of the side had just ninety-one league appearances between them. Ian Greaves, Ron Cope, Freddie Goodwin, Colin Webster and Alex Dawson had all played for the first team before but were more accustomed to the reserve and youth sides. Mark Pearson, at inside-left, was making his debut. So too was the new outside-left, Shay Brennan, a midfield player who had been plucked from the A team.

Poor Sheffield Wednesday did not stand a chance. There were officially 59,848 inside the United ground that night. It was 7,000 below the capacity, but only because many of those with tickets could not get into the ground because of the tens of thousands of mourning supporters who packed the streets all around Old Trafford. The patched-together red side was carried along by the crowd's noise and emotion. Shay Brennan's corner was helped into the goal by the Sheffield goalkeeper, and he scored a second later. Alex Dawson made it three with five minutes left.

Remarkably, after scoring twice on his debut, Shay Brennan got only four more goals in 356 more games for the reds, though most of them were at full-back.

Ian Greaves, replacing Roger Byrne at left-back, recalled later: 'It was an electrifying night but there was no cheering in the dressing room afterwards – we were all sad. I felt in a way that I shouldn't have been there, that I was stepping into someone else's shoes.'

Two days after the Sheffield Wednesday game came the news that Duncan Edwards had died.

Slowly, the survivors of Munich returned to the side – Bobby Charlton, Ray Wood, Albert Scanlon, Ken Morgans and Dennis Viollet – though two players, Jackie Blanchflower and Johnny Berry, were injured so badly that they would never play again. Perhaps not surprisingly, United's league form went to pieces. Of the fourteen league games left to play, Murphy's patched-up side lost eight and won only one. They finally finished ninth. But the stirring Cup performances continued.

In the sixth round United visited West Bromwich and led 2–1 until four minutes from the end, but had to settle for a 2–2 draw and a replay. At Old Trafford the Birmingham side had the better of much of the play, but Colin Webster's goal in the final minute saw United through to the semi-finals. That the Cup competition had drawn that special spirit out of the players was shown by the fact that West Bromwich Albion beat United 4–0 at Old Trafford in the league only three days after the replay.

United were fortunate to draw the easiest of the semi-final qualifiers, second-division Fulham. Once again the fans were treated to two great matches. The first at Villa Park produced a 2–2 draw, while London welcomed United again for what proved to be another historic and high-scoring visit to Highbury, transmitted live on television.

Twice United went ahead and twice Fulham equalised. But in the second half United's superiority was established. Alex Dawson scored a hat-trick and Charlton's goal in the last minute made it 5–3. Incredibly, United were back at Wembley.

Matt Busby, now out of hospital, was able to go to the final as a spectator, hobbling on crutches, though Jimmy Murphy was still in charge of the side – a point acknowledged in typical style by Busby when, just minutes before kick-off, he said to the players: 'Good luck lads. Just go out and follow Jimmy's instructions.' Dennis Viollet had at last recovered from his injuries and was brought into the final team even though he had played only two games since Munich. Two of the youngsters brought in from the reserves, Mark Pearson and Shay Brennan, had lost their places.

Every neutral wanted United to win, of course. But by now the spell over United's remarkable FA Cup run was broken. Their opponents, Bolton Wanderers, were only a middle-ranking first-division side, but they easily overpowered United. Bolton took an early lead through Nat Lofthouse; Bobby Charlton hit a post, but Bolton made it 2–0 when Lofthouse charged Harry Gregg into the goal.

Hundreds of thousands welcomed the losing side back to Manchester, many more than saw the FA Cup taken back to Bolton. At Wembley the United players had worn special badges on their shirts depicting the phoenix, the mythical bird that rose from the ashes. United had indeed risen again, for the third time in thirty years.

That summer the England team suffered in the World Cup in Sweden. Before Munich, with Roger Byrne, Duncan Edwards and Tommy Taylor regularly in the side, England had been unbeaten for three years against foreign opposition and the United trio had contributed seventeen goals in the previous twelve games. The Munich crash destroyed any hopes that England might recover from the humiliations of the early 1950s. It would be another eight years before Alf Ramsay's World Cup side restored national pride. By then Matt Busby had built his third great team and embarked on a further chapter of glory for Manchester United. But from 1958 onwards the Manchester United over which he presided was no longer an ordinary football club.

3 THE MAN WHO BOUGHT UNITED

'The welfare and continued progress and success of Manchester United are now my life ambition.'

Louis Edwards, 1962.

ON THE afternoon of the day after Munich the United board met at the home in Bowdon, Cheshire, of Alan Gibson, son of the late United chairman, James Gibson. It was one of the odd aspects of the Munich disaster that none of the club board had flown with the team to Belgrade. On nearly all United's previous journeys at least one director had gone with the team. This time, however, Harold Hardman had not been well enough to fly, while Alan Gibson himself was recovering from a broken leg.

The brief hand-written minutes from that historic board meeting give only stark details, and fail to reflect the true tragedy of the circumstances in which they met. Indeed, the first item on the agenda was not about Munich at all, but the death five days earlier of the director, George Whittaker, whose funeral Harold Hardman and William Petherbridge had attended that morning. Whittaker had died in a hotel in London on the morning of United's historic 5–4 victory at Arsenal.

The three remaining directors then heard reports on the news from Munich. They extended 'their sympathy and condolences to the families of the deceased and injured', and were told that relatives had been flown out to Germany.

Walter Crickmer, the club secretary, had been among the dead. The directors appointed his assistant, Les Olive, as acting secretary, and authorisation was sent to the bank for him to sign cheques. The board then took a decision that was to have far-reaching effects. 'It was proposed, seconded and carried unanimously,' the minutes record, 'that Mr Louis Charles Edwards of "Caudebec", Alderley Edge, Cheshire, be and is hereby appointed and co-opted as an additional Director of the Company.'

That Louis Edwards should have been elected to the United board the very day after Munich was pure coincidence and nothing to do with the tragedy. According to Louis Edwards' son Martin, the present United chairman, his father had in fact been considered for election a few weeks earlier, but had been vetoed by George Whittaker, though there is no record of this in the club minutes. Now, with Whittaker's death, the opposition to Edwards had been removed. Yet had Whittaker not opposed the appointment initially, Martin Edwards suggests that, as a director, his father would almost certainly have flown to Belgrade with the official party, and might easily have perished in the Munich crash.

It would be several weeks, of course, before Matt Busby, fighting for his life in the Rechts der Isar hospital in Munich, would get to hear of Louis Edwards' election. When the news was finally given to him, he must have been delighted. United's board, in his view, would now be in safe hands for the difficult rebuilding that lay ahead. Busby had long worried that the board members were nearly all getting on in years, and was anxious about what would happen when the present directors passed away. The United manager saw Louis Edwards as a future chairman, and had been pushing him in that direction since first meeting him socially in Manchester a decade earlier.

For a generation after the Second World War the Manchester Opera House in Quay Street was to the city's show-business life what Old Trafford was to football. There Tommy Appleby, one of Britain's top post-war provincial theatre-managers, presided over a different show every week, with a stream of stars from all over the world. On Mondays, after the week's opening night, Appleby would hold a party for his performers, who over the years included names such as Noël Coward, Stewart Grainger and Laurence Olivier. He would invite his own personal guests along to swell the numbers. Usually the party would move on to eat at a restaurant, often Arturo's in Portland Street. Throughout the North-west Tommy Appleby's first-night parties were renowned as great social occasions, to which many of the area's most influential figures would regularly be invited.

From 1947 onwards Matt Busby's wife Jean and his daughter Sheena frequently went to drama and ballet performances at the Opera House. Busby himself did not always share their enthusiasm –

perhaps the weekly drama at United was sufficient. So while the ladies were watching a performance, Busby would often wait and chat in Tommy Appleby's office ready to take them home afterwards. And, of course, as the distinguished manager of the successful local football team, Busby was an obvious guest for Appleby to invite to the Monday-night parties.

Busby found the parties a rare chance to get away from the problems of football, problems which were not always confined to team matters. Busby had sometimes found relations difficult with his first two chairmen, James Gibson and Harold Hardman. The United manager was always insistent that it should be he, not the directors, who ran the club. In the early 1950s it was obvious that Hardman, who was then over seventy, would not be around for ever. Three other directors, George Whittaker, William Petherbridge and Dr McLean were all beyond retirement age. Only Alan Gibson, the biggest shareholder, added any youth to the board. But Gibson had never been well enough to hold a full-time job, was not a forceful character, and admitted he had never been that much of a football fan. There was really no obvious successor as chairman.

Moreover, Busby feared that the club might easily be taken over by certain unsavoury local businessmen, the shady types who hover on the fringes of any top football club. To prevent this, and to ensure that there were more understanding, sympathetic directors in future, the United manager was hoping to influence who joined the board. And Tommy Appleby was able to bring him into contact with more suitable candidates.

Louis Edwards was a local meat trader, co-owner, with his brother Douglas, of Louis C. Edwards and Sons (Manchester) Ltd. He and his wife Muriel, together with Douglas and his wife Emmeline, were keen theatre-goers and often went to the Opera House together. They would frequently rely on Appleby to fix up last-minute tickets. A large, roly-poly, ebullient character, Edwards enjoyed fat cigars, fine food and champagne – in later years he became known as 'Champagne Louis'. But he suffered from a slight stammer, which gave him some insecurity on public occasions. He claimed to have supported Manchester United, the local football team, since his childhood in Salford. Louis Edwards could also boast of a family connection with one of the great historic figures of Manchester United Football Club.

After Matt Busby, it could be argued that the most important figure in the club's history has been Louis Rocca, the man who wrote the letter that brought Busby to Old Trafford. Rocca never played for the club or served as manager, secretary or chairman, but, by all accounts, he enjoyed a leading role in United's affairs throughout the first half of the twentieth century. He had arrived as a tea-boy in the 1890s, during the time when the club was still known as Newton Heath. During the 1920s, '30s and '40s, Rocca served the club as assistant manager and chief scout, and was responsible for finding many of the players whom Busby inherited, including Johnny Carey. He boasted a network of Catholic priests looking for new young talent, and perhaps more than anyone, Louis Rocca's influence gave United the reputation for being a Roman Catholic club. According to Geoffrey Green's history of United, Louis Rocca also claimed credit for suggesting the very name Manchester United, though as he was only nineteen at the time when the change occurred in April 1902, this seems rather surprising.

Like the Edwards family, and like so many Italian immigrants, the Roccas were in the food trade and ran a confectionery business on the Rochdale Road. In 1926 Louis Rocca's younger cousin, Joe, married Beatrice Edwards, Louis Edwards' eldest sister.

In view of the Edwards family connection with Louis Rocca, it is perhaps surprising that Louis Edwards did not meet Matt Busby until Appleby introduced them to each other at one of the Opera House parties. Appleby, who has now retired and lives in Sale, reckons that it must have been around 1950. Until 1988 Appleby had two seats in the United directors' box, where Sir Matt Busby used to pull his leg about that historic introduction, nearly forty years ago. With hindsight Busby probably wishes it had never happened.

After meeting Matt Busby, the meat trader was soon taking a keen interest in the club. Martin Edwards remembers going with his parents to watch his first match at Old Trafford in 1952. Louis and Muriel Edwards were guests of Matt Busby in the directors' box.

Two former United players, Jackie Blanchflower and John Aston Senior, both remember encountering Louis Edwards for the first time on a tour to the United States in the summer of 1952. Aston recalls that, one night on the Queen Mary, the players were invited into the first-class restaurant and treated to champagne by a large man beaming at them from his table on the balcony above. Officially Louis Edwards had gone to America on business, but had arranged his itinerary carefully to be in New York and Chicago when United were playing there, and to ensure that his outward and return sea crossings coincided with the team's sailings. It is also said that when Louis

Edwards discovered that Matt Busby was a strong Roman Catholic, he rediscovered his own Catholic upbringing and background, and began attending dinners of the Catholic Sportsmen's Club.

Another important Manchester businessman whom Busby met through Tommy Appleby was Willie Satinoff, whose family owned a clothing company, Alligator Rainwear. Satinoff was a keen race-goer and owned several racehorses, one of which, Red Alligator, included both his company's title and his allegiance to United in its name. Satinoff would often get Appleby to bring show-business guests along to his private box at Aintree, and after meeting him, Busby sometimes joined them at the races. Occasionally all three men would fly to a racecourse in a private plane. Satinoff was also a keen Manchester United fan and used to go to nearly every away match.

Willie Satinoff was by far the stronger of the two candidates whom Busby might have had in mind for the United board. He had been even more successful in business than Edwards. Unlike the rather hesitant meat-man, he was a good public performer. Satinoff dressed immaculately and was extremely popular with everyone. And in contrast to the 17-stone Louis Edwards, Willie Satinoff was slim; he played five-a-side daily at the Y.M.C.A. and rarely drank. People also say he understood football far better than Louis Edwards and that he was just as close to Busby. 'For many years,' according to the *Manchester Guardian*, 'a deep attachment existed between Satinoff and Busby. Satinoff became almost an honorary member of the Manchester United football team and followed them wherever they went.' Those words, however, were written in his obituary.

The honorary member's fervour for United had cost him his life. Unlike the United directors, Willie Satinoff had gone with the official party to Belgrade in February 1958. He died at Munich.

Many who knew him, including Busby's close friend Paddy McGrath, believe that, had he lived, Willie Satinoff would eventually have been the obvious successor to Harold Hardman as United chairman. They argue that certainly he would have been elected to the club board in due course. There, by all accounts, he would have been a formidable force, and perhaps an obstacle to the ambitions of Busby's other close businessman friend, Louis Edwards. It is unlikely that, had Willie Satinoff lived, whether as a United director or simply as a dedicated supporter, Louis Edwards would have been allowed to get away with the clever plan he was to carry out over the next seven years.

Shortly after Louis Edwards' election to the United board, the club issued ten shares to him in order to comply with rules requiring directors to have a nominal shareholding. They would have cost Edwards just £1 each, the face value, but with more than 4,000 shares at that time in the club, Edwards' ten shares were only a tiny fraction of the equity. To be certain of achieving his next target – the chairmanship – Edwards would require a majority shareholding of more than 2,000 shares.

In the years immediately after his election such considerations were set aside and Louis Edwards quickly immersed himself in the club's affairs. He soon became by far the most active of the four directors. He represented the club at many of the funerals of the Munich victims, and for many at the club it was the first time they had met him. He went to the Football Association memorial service at St Martin-in-the-Fields in London, and in late February attended Duncan Edwards' burial in Dudley.

Louis Edwards became involved in negotiations over the Munich insurance and held consultations with a QC. Discussions over catering at Old Trafford were also left to Louis Edwards at one stage. And, when Matt Busby signed Albert Quixall from Sheffield Wedneday in September 1958 for a record fee of £45,000, Louis Edwards was the only director to accompany him across the Pennines to complete the deal. Three years later Louis Edwards helped Matt Busby in another record signing – Denis Law from Torino for £115,000.

In 1961 the directors set up a three-man sub-committee to deal with financial matters comprising the three youngest directors – Edwards, Alan Gibson and a newly co-opted board member, Bill Young, who was a close friend of Gibson. Harold Hardman had decided not to serve on the finance committee and Louis Edwards was elected its chairman. By 1962 the two directors' signatures on the annual accounts were those of the club chairman Harold Hardman and Louis Edwards.

It was only after more than four years on the United board, however, that Louis Edwards set about acquiring a shareholding to accompany his commitment in terms of activity. At that time Manchester United Football Club Limited was a private company. Most of its 4,132 ordinary £1 shares had been issued before the First World War, though more equity had been issued after James Gibson saved the club in 1932. Many of the original shareholders had, of course, died, and in most cases their equity had passed to their heirs. It was rare that shares were sold by one person to another, since any such transaction had to be approved by the board of directors. A fair proportion of such requests was turned down. As well as the ordinary shares, there were 1,725 preference shares. These had priority when it came to dividend payments, but only a tenth of the voting power of the ordinary shares. Preference shares can therefore largely be ignored when considering questions of voting power.

Sometimes shareholders who wanted to sell would offer their stock to the board and this would then be divided among the directors who paid the face value of £1 for each share. In this way, between 1958 and 1961, Louis Edwards acquired seven ordinary shares to add to his original ten. But overall his holding was still insignificant: less than one per cent of the company's capital.

Of the 142 shareholders at the time of the company's annual return in 1962, none had a majority of the 4,132 ordinary shares in the company. The highest stake was held by the Gibson family. Anne Gibson, wife of the late chairman, James Gibson, held 894, and their son, the United director Alan Gibson, owned 832. So between them Alan Gibson and his mother could command 1,726 shares, 41.8 per cent of the equity. The next biggest shareholder, with 468, was Mabel Whittaker, the wife of George Whittaker, the director who died five days before Munich. Only five other people had more than 100 ordinary shares.

Over the next fifteen months, however, between October 1962 and January 1964, the whole spread of shares in Manchester United Football Club Ltd was transformed in favour of Louis Charles Edwards.

With a copy of the 1962 share register, Edwards drew up a list of those stockholders whom he thought might conceivably be interested in selling their shares. One by one they were approached. To carry out the mundane task of actually knocking on shareholders' doors, Edwards called on the services of a corrupt Manchester Conservative councillor called Frank Farrington. Alderman Farrington had often carried out small chores for Edwards in the past and helped him get meat contracts. In the post-war years Farrington had earned a reputation in Manchester business and political circles as 'the Kingmaker'. As a member of the council since 1927, he had never enjoyed high political office, but held influential positions, such as being on the board of the Manchester Ship Canal Company. The alderman was not very wealthy and lived in a council flat, but through his political and personal connections in Manchester he could 'fix' things.

As a boy, Frank Farrington had helped to clear stones and glass from the pitch in the days before 1910 when Manchester United played on their old ground at Clayton. Now he was being asked to go out and use his contacts to prepare the ground for his friend, Louis Edwards.

On an autumn evening, totally unexpectedly, a shareholder would receive a knock at the door. One such visit was to Norman and Alice Rowbotham at their terraced home in Ilkley Street, which happened to be in Farrington's council ward. Rowbotham had inherited 100 shares from his uncle Albert who had bought them when United were in trouble in the 1930s. Mrs Rowbotham and her two small children were asked to leave the room, and Farrington insisted on secrecy and urgency. It was a matter of 'take it or leave it'. Norman Rowbotham did not earn much from his job at a local ICI factory, and with Christmas on the way they accepted Farrington's offer of £500 – £5 for each share.

Two days later Farrington picked Rowbotham up and took him to New Street, Miles Platting, where Louis Edwards personally handed the money over in the Edwards' company boardroom. Afterwards Farrington demanded £50 from Rowbotham, as his cut of the deal. A few days later Edwards sent the Rowbothams a few chops and ¾lb beef.

Another seller, Nat Rose, had arranged to meet Farrington, whom he already happened to know, for a drink in a hotel off Albert Square. Once a deal was agreed, the councillor took Rose to the meat factory where Edwards handed over the cash in £1 and £5 notes. Rose and his wife used the money to pay for a two-week holiday in Majorca and put the rest in trust for their son when he reached twenty-one. They were sent a turkey for Christmas and a joint of meat.

After Farrington had trudged the streets of Manchester for a while, Edwards decided that it might be simpler to make his approaches by post. He sent out dozens of letters to shareholders in the autumn of 1962 and winter of 1963. Each, it seems, had an almost identical text. 'You will be aware that I am a Director of Manchester United F.C. Ltd.,' Edwards began, 'having been appointed to the Board just after the Munich air crash in February 1958.' Edwards proceeded to claim that United was now his life ambition, and told each recipient how he wanted to bolster his shareholding in the club. Those who received the letters were offered £15 a share – well above the market value, Edwards claimed, but a sign, he said, of his 'unstinted and sincere devotion' to United. 'If you are interested will you please write to me at my office address, a suitably addressed envelope being enclosed for your use. I am sure that the Chairman and my colleagues on the Board would approve the transfer of shares.'

Once shareholders had replied to Edwards' standard letter, much of the day-to-day administration of the operation was then carried out by Thomas McKeown, the secretary of the Edwards' meat company. McKeown sent out subsequent letters to shareholders, stockbrokers, solicitors and to Les Olive, the company secretary at Old Trafford. The work was done from the firm's offices in Miles Platting.

Ironically, among the first shareholders to give a favourable reply, in December 1962, was Mabel Whittaker, widow of George Whittaker, the director who according to Martin Edwards had originally vetoed Edwards in 1958. Mrs Whittaker was offered only £12 for each of her 443 shares – less than other people – but was delighted to accept since she was rather hard up and living on a meagre pension. The transaction meant that Edwards was now the club's third largest shareholder. One can only assume that her late husband would not have been pleased.

Each transaction had to be agreed by the United directors. The first two deals, for 120 shares, were agreed by the board at a meeting on 16 October 1962. Mabel Whittaker's sale went through in early December, and later in the month four more transfers, totalling 300 shares to Louis Edwards, were agreed. The directors had never known so much share activity before. Normally they were asked to approve only a few transfers every year. Now, in the space of just a few weeks, Louis Edwards had become the company's largest shareholder, with a bigger stake than either Alan Gibson or his mother. It must have been obvious what Edwards was doing.

When, at the first meeting in the New Year, the board were asked to approve three more transfers, for 155 shares, they gave their approval but with a condition. In future, it was agreed, no transfers to Anne Gibson, Alan Gibson or Louis Edwards 'would be registered if it would cause any change in the present balance of holdings'. But transfers to outside individuals would be allowed.

The share-buying stopped – at least for a while. Then, rather than try to buy shares himself, which was no longer allowed, Louis Edwards brought in his brother, Douglas, the co-chairman of the meat company, and Denzil Haroun, a Manchester businessman of Syrian ancestry involved in the textile trade who was married to his sister Peggy, a distinguished amateur golfer.

In March 1963 the approaches to shareholders restarted, with Thomas McKeown again responsible for the administration. Copies of the following standard letter were sent out to many different targets:

Dear Mr X

May I introduce myself to you as a regular and ardent supporter of Manchester United. I am in the fortunate position of being a regular guest in the Directors' Box through the invitations of my brother-in-law, Mr Louis Edwards, who, you will be aware, is a Director of Manchester United F.C. Ltd. I also travel to away games whenever possible.

   I would like to extend my interest in the club by becoming a shareholder and I notice from the Annual List that you do hold xx Ordinary shares. I should be very grateful indeed if you would consider selling your shares to me. I am willing to pay £15 (fifteen pounds) for each Ordinary share. This price is far higher than the commercial or economic value of the shares but it represents an earnest desire to support my devotion and interest in the club with a fair sized shareholding. I can give you my personal assurance that if you did transfer your shares to me they would be held very securely in my family and would, therefore, be valued very carefully by persons who had the best interests of the club at heart.

   If you are interested in selling will you please write to me, a suitably addressed envelope to my business address being enclosed for your use.

Yours faithfully,

D. D. Haroun

Virtually the same letter was sent out by Douglas Edwards, with the personal details suitably changed and with variations in the offer price. In May 1963 Haroun secured the largest remaining holding apart from the Gibsons' – 160 shares from Richard Shaw at £15 each. The sale was agreed by the board.

   In July the United board approved eight different transactions to Douglas Edwards, involving 81 shares. It was an extraordinary decision in view of their previous decision on Louis Edwards' share-buying, and they cannot have been unaware who Douglas Edwards was. In October came another nineteen transfers to Douglas Edwards representing 147 shares.

Many shareholders seem to have been delighted by Edwards' approaches. A widow said that her husband had originally bought the shares in 1913 and that selling them was a hard decision. However, she reached it because, as she explained, 'I'm middle-aged and in the course of time [the shares] will go to some relative who maybe is not [as] interested as you are.'

Most had retained their holdings for years without realising what they were worth. One holder of a single ordinary share had acquired it back in 1924 while he was social secretary of the supporters' club in order, he said, to attend shareholders' meetings. Those who sold their shares to Louis Edwards sometimes expected favours in return, such as match tickets or priority in the queue for season tickets. In some cases Edwards obliged. Others found that they had asked too late, after their deal had gone through, and were told that there was nothing the United director could do.

At one point Edwards also expressed some interest in buying shares in Manchester City – for what reason is not entirely clear; perhaps it was to bargain with City supporters who held United shares and were prepared to swap. Occasionally the transactions involved famous names from United's history. Two hundred pounds, for instance, was paid for eight shares from Winifred Meredith. She was the daughter of Billy Meredith, the great Welsh winger who played for United between 1907 and 1921, and had inherited them on her father's death in 1958. Douglas Edwards visited her personally. Another attracted by the Edwards' offer was Clarence Hilditch, a United player from the 1920s, who was also briefly player-manager at one point. He received £500 for his twenty shares.

Over the months the price that the Edwards family were prepared to pay gradually rose – from £5 at the start to £12.50, £15, £20 and then finally to £25. It seems that few people tried to bargain over the price. For many the offer was far greater than what they had thought the shares were worth. 'I have had several requests for this share,' wrote a lady who held just one share, 'but not until I received your letter was anyone prepared to say what they were prepared to pay for it and being financially embarrassed just now I felt it time to take your offer.'

However, it was clear that while deals for small amounts of shares from obscure shareholders might gradually build up Edwards' shareholding, it might never be possible to secure a majority of the equity without acquiring some of the Gibson family's large holding. The deal that effectively clinched control for Louis Edwards came in September 1963, when Alan Gibson agreed to sell 500 of his shares at £25 a share, or £12,500 in all.

At this point the United directors seemed to give in, acknowledging that now Louis Edwards could not be stopped. If the second largest shareholder, Alan Gibson, was willing to sell to Edwards, there seemed little reason to preserve the share balance between Edwards and the Gibson family any longer. On 8 October 1963 Harold Hardman proposed, and Alan Gibson's friend, Bill Young, seconded, that the directors should rescind their previous decision which effectively prevented Louis Edwards buying any more shares, and the deal with Alan Gibson was allowed to go through. At the same meeting it was announced that Denzil Haroun had been nominated to the board for the coming AGM. And when Haroun secured election by the shareholders, the man who nominated him was Douglas Edwards.

Louis Edwards had 1,835 ordinary shares which, together with the 642 preference shares he had bought, gave him 1,899 of the company's votes – or 44 per cent. But the shares which had been acquired that summer by Douglas Edwards and Denzil Haroun meant that he and his relations now had a majority.

An interesting side point is that United's company share register sometimes records the share selling price as £1 per share, when in fact Edwards and his relations had paid far more than that. At that time United had a rule that shares could only be sold at face value – £1 each. Indeed, the board had vetoed several other proposed share transactions because they were at more than face value.

On 14 January 1964, to tidy matters up and to make sure of an absolute majority, Louis Edwards bought 238 shares from his brother Douglas and 150 from his brother-in-law Denzil Haroun. Louis Edwards now owned Manchester United. In December 1964 the meat trader's powerful position on the board was acknowledged when he was proposed by Alan Gibson as vice-chairman of the club and elected. Six months later, in June 1965, Harold Hardman died. He was eighty-three and had served more than fifty years as a director and fourteen years as chairman. Now there was only one possible successor. Louis Edwards was duly elected unopposed.

It had proved a remarkably cheap exercise for the Manchester butcher. Louis Edwards' total bill worked out at somewhere between £31,000 and £41,000, a sum he could easily afford following the flotation of his meat company on the Stock Exchange in 1962. In return for that money he had bought control of one of Britain's wealthiest and most popular football clubs.

Some indication of how inexpensive his purchase had been may partly be gauged by the fact that gate receipts for the 1963-64 season, for instance, were £172,000 - five or six times what Edwards had spent. The year before, United had broken the British transfer record by buying Denis Law from Torino for £115,000. Law's fee was more than three times what it cost Louis Edwards to buy control of the whole club.

It was so simple, and had been carried out with little fuss. No doubt dozens of businessmen, in Manchester and beyond, would have been delighted to pay £35,000 or so at that time to secure the effective ownership of one of Britain's top soccer clubs. Yet, had an outsider tried to do what Edwards did, he would have been stopped by the board who would have refused to authorise the transactions. Even small share transfers were often rejected by the board. In 1965, for instance, David Meek, the *Manchester Evening News* reporter, was stopped from buying a single share.

Edwards only succeeded in his takeover because the United board acquiesced in the process. No director had the wealth or will to stop him. Alan Gibson, the only man with the share-power to stand in Edwards' way, was not strong enough. The chairman, Harold Hardman, dreaded that Edwards would get the chairmanship, but knew it was unavoidable after his death. He even offered to sell his seventy-one shares to a wealthy builder, the father-in-law of the then United goalkeeper, Harry Gregg, if it might prevent the inevitable. Hardman had at one time earmarked as his successor a local Football League referee, Gordon Gibson, who often joined the players' Sunday morning get-togethers. But Gibson had neither the necessary shares nor money. Now that he was in his eighties Hardman was no longer strong enough to stop the new man. And, of course, the real force at Old Trafford, Matt Busby, was not to realise the long term implications. As manager he was happy to support Edwards' plans, which, it must be said, involved ambitious developments for United.

Investing in a football club was even less of a serious financial proposition in the 1960s than it is nowadays. The dividend was limited to five per cent of the face value of the shares - little more than £100 a year for Edwards, even if a dividend was awarded. But the immediate return on Edwards' investment was prestige in Manchester business circles. He was now chairman of one of the most famous and glamorous football clubs in the world. And the potential value of the club – measured largely in terms of the goodwill of the citizens of Manchester to follow United week in, week out – must have been several hundred thousand pounds, even in 1964. However, it would be many years before Louis Edwards and his family realised any great financial return on his shrewd but simple investment.

RIGHT Matt Busby in his playing days with Manchester City. They were not always happy times though, and at one stage Busby talked about packing in and returning home to Scotland. (*Topical Times*)

BELOW Down Memory Lane. A happy re-union for Sir Matt and members of the 1948 FA Cup winning side, Johnny Carey, Jack Rowley and Stan Pearson. (*Manchester United Supporters Club*)

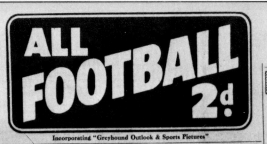

ALL FOOTBALL 2d

Incorporating "Greyhound Outlook & Sports Pictures"

No. 1107 • • • [Registered as a Newspaper] • • • JANUARY 16, 1951

Manchester United manager scotches rumours

'I'M NOT GETTING THE SACK'

by MATT BUSBY

LET me scotch first those rumours which, I am told, go the rounds—I am not resigning, I am not being sacked and there is neither trouble nor panic in our camp.

Those rumours seem to have started because we are not quite the glamour team we used to be. Maybe we are not. You cannot stay on top all the time and we had a longer run than usual.

A set of players hits such a wonderful peak only once in a lifetime. That goes for every sport. Now, I admit, we do not appear to be as good as we were—but we are not so bad, either. We are in the top half of the First Division and there are many worse teams in the land.

Do not forget we had a big shock when Charlie Mitten went off to Bogota. We were not prepared for that. Who was? We were left without an adequate deputy and Mitten's departure had a jolting effect on the club generally.

Some of my critics say I should have gone out and spent "some of that £50,000 profit." Well, you can call me a real canny Scotsman, but I do not believe you can buy success.

I will not spend money for the sake of spending it. If we can buy a player we want at a sensible fee, all right. If not, no deal.

There is no panic

There is nothing to panic about. Before long, you will see Manchester United back on top, beating the best. Look at some of our young players. Don Gibson, just

THE BARRATTS OF COVE

NEXT WEEK

LEFT Even the greatest United manager suffered rumours about getting the sack! This headline followed three successive defeats in the 1950–51 season. Fifteen months later Matt Busby won the first of his five league titles.

BELOW First Division champions 1952. United went to America after winning the title, and so too did Louis Edwards. The trip was the first occasion that a number of players recall seeing the future chairman.

RIGHT Busby was one of the first tracksuit managers. Here he is seen with Duncan Edwards and Roger Byrne, two of his famous 'Babes'. (*Kemsley Newspapers*)

BELOW The 'Babes'. Six months after adding the Charity Shield to their second successive Championship trophy, Busby's hopes for the future were decimated in the Munich air disaster.

Daily Mirror

FRI FEB 7 1958

2ᵈ FORWARD WITH THE PEOPLE
No. 16,843

SOCCER AIR TRAGEDY

Manchester United plane crashes

21 dead

CRUNCHIE makes exciting 4ᵈ biting!

THE END The chartered Elizabethan airliner in which the Manchester United team was travelling home lies shattered in a snowfield near Munich. The pilot, Captain James Thain, escaped through the nose.

AN Elizabethan airliner—on charter to Manchester United football team, the fabulous "Busby Babes," crashed on take-off at Munich Airport, Germany, yesterday, and plunged the world of Soccer into mourning.

Among the twenty-one dead were United stars Roger Byrne (captain), Tommy Taylor (centre forward), Mark Jones (centre half), Eddie Colman (right half), Billy Whelan (inside right), David Pegg (outside left), Geoff Bent (left back).

Also dead was ex-England goalkeeper and sportswriter Frank Swift. While in hospital last night fighting for his life, was manager Matt Busby, who gave his name to the team and made it one of the most famous in football.

Twenty-three of the 44 passengers survived.

THE BEGINNING This picture was taken when the team, accompanied by sportswriters boarded the plane at Manchester on Monday. Left to right, with known sportsmen marked with asterisk: Jackie Blanchflower*, Billy Foulkes*; Walter Crickmer, secretary; Don Davies (Manchester Guardian), Roger Byrne, captain; behind Byrne is Frank Swift, News of the World, Ray Wood*, Denis Viollet*; Ledbrooke, Daily Mirror; Geoff Bent*, Jones and Al Clarke, Kemsley News...

ABOVE The *Daily Mirror*, 7 February 1958, the day after Munich. Eight players died, but it took Busby only five years to rebuild United.

RIGHT Many believed that Willie Satinoff would have eventually become a director. But the United supporter, who was a close friend of Matt Busby, was killed at Munich.

RIGHT Denis Law was Busby's most expensive signing when he fled from Torino to United in a £115,000 move in 1962. (*Daily Express*)

BELOW FA Cup winners 1963. United beat Leicester in the final at Wembley to end the season on a high note after fighting off relegation. The United chairman, Harold Hardman is seated in the centre of the picture.

ABOVE Meat with Royal approval! HRH Prince Philip is shown around the Edwards' meat factory by the two brothers, Douglas (left) and Louis. (*Manchester Evening News*)

RIGHT Alan Gibson, the vice-president and former director, whose decision to sell his shareholding allowed first Louis Edwards to buy the club, and later Martin Edwards to gain a majority. (*Manchester United Supporters Club*)

ABOVE Louis Edwards and Matt Busby travel to Wembley for the 1968 European Cup final. (*London Express News Service*)

RIGHT Tommy Appleby, the man who introduced Louis Edwards to Matt Busby nearly two decades before, at one of his Manchester Opera House parties. (*Manchester Evening News*)

RIGHT Matt Busby with the
European Cup at last, the trophy
that had become his 'obsession'. It
took United much longer to
recover from the 1968 triumph,
than it had from the 1958 Munich
disaster. (*London Express News
Service*)

BELOW The Busby family – Lady
Jean Busby, son Sandy, Sir Matt
and daughter Sheena. Sandy
Busby was meant to become a
United director under an arrange-
ment with Louis Edwards, but he
had to be content with managing
the souvenir shop, until the
Busbys lost the lease in 1987.
(*London Express News Service*)

4 THE SEARCH FOR THE HOLY GRAIL

'Frankly, ever since my wife, Jean, had told me in the Munich hospital that she felt sure the lads who had died would have wanted me to carry on, I had become increasingly obsessed about United winning the European Cup. It was almost as if this glittering trophy were the Holy Grail.'

Matt Busby on the European Cup.

IT TOOK months for Matt Busby to recover from Munich. Indeed, in some ways he was never really the same again. Although Busby was at Wembley for the 1958 FA Cup final, it was not until after a long convalescence that summer at Interlaken that he was really ready to return to Old Trafford.

The United manager had in fact been very close to death. Inside an oxygen tent, he had a collapsed lung, and twice a priest administered the last rites. When Busby began to regain consciousness and learned the terrible news, he blamed himself for what had happened. After all, he had taken the Manchester United team into Europe against the advice of the Football League. 'I will never go back into football,' he vowed.

But his wife Jean persuaded him to reconsider. 'I don't think you are being fair to the people who have lost their loved ones,' Busby recalls her saying. 'And I am sure those who have gone, too, would have wanted you to carry on.'

The spirit which pushed the hastily rebuilt United side through three more rounds of the FA Cup to the 1958 final was not enough, however, to make further progress in the European Cup. To help United, the European Football Association, UEFA, had paired them against the team left in the competition for whom the away leg would provide the easiest journey by boat and rail – AC Milan. United beat the Italian champions 2–1 in the first leg of the semi-final, after being 1–0 down. They did so, moreover, without Bobby Charlton. The FA, in an insensitive decision, had insisted that the United forward should play for England in a friendly match against Portugal the night before. Charlton was also called away by England for the second leg, played a few days after the disappointment of the FA Cup final. The Italian champions overwhelmed United 4–0.

Matt Busby was made a CBE, and the United board increased his salary to £5,000 a year. He knew that any European ambitions would have to be forgotten for the time being. But in the long term the goal was to win the European champions' trophy in memory and in honour of those who died.

The European football authorities at that time had rather more of a human face than their English counterparts. As a gesture of sympathy, UEFA actually invited Manchester United to compete in the European Cup the season after Munich, 1958–59 – in addition, of course, to the new English league champions, Wolves. They were even drawn in the qualifying round against Young Boys Berne, the Swiss champions.

Arguments went on all summer, and only a few days before the first match was due to take place the Football League, after much debate, forced United to withdraw on the grounds that they were not league champions. The Football Association, the superior body, went along with the League's decision, though initially the FA had been quite happy for United to compete. It was a mean, heartless decision by the English authorities, especially since in those early years other sides had competed in the European Cup without being national champions. United played the Young Boys fixtures as friendlies, winning 3–2 on aggregate, and Young Boys went on to the European Cup semi-finals. The reds, had they been allowed to compete, might have done even better. Who knows? Matt Busby's new team did well enough in the league championship the season after Munich to be runners-up to Wolves, who retained their championship, and the reds remained in contention almost until the very end.

The rebuilt side seemed to be carried along by a tide of post-Munich emotion in the 1958–59 season. The average home gate at Old Trafford, 53,258, was the highest in Britain, and the second highest in United's history. Away from Manchester, gates were locked at many grounds as the public paid homage to the team that had risen from the ashes. Crowds of more than 60,000 were recorded at Newcastle, Manchester City, Everton and Arsenal.

Despite prolific scoring by Bobby Charlton, who scored twenty-nine league goals – his best ever season – and a record 103 league goals for the team as a whole, Matt Busby knew that the team were not really good enough. Of the side that had lost to Bolton at Wembley in 1958 only three – Gregg, Foulkes and Charlton – would stay long at Old Trafford. By January 1962 the other eight had all left for new clubs.

The production line of great players from the youth sides seemed to dry up. Of the team that won United's fifth successive Youth Cup in 1957, only David Gaskell enjoyed a long first-team career with United. Three survivors from Munich, Ray Wood, Albert Scanlon and Ken Morgans, never seemed to be the same again, and Jimmy Murphy feels that this was also true of Dennis Viollet, though he carried on scoring regularly. Some of the young reserve replacements may have been called on too early in the emergency situation after Munich. At the same time other clubs, such as Wolves, were copying United's youth programme and getting more of the best young players.

The club had been badly under-insured at Munich, and Busby could not simply buy a new team with the compensation money. A cheque for £112,000 arrived from the insurance company, and it was split equally between the club and the dependants of the dead players. It meant that these relations were badly provided for, living without pensions. This would be a source of some ill-feeling in later years.

Another £10,000 compensation arrived for the two players who were unable to play any more – Jackie Blanchflower and Johnny Berry – and again it was divided 50–50. The airline, BEA, were sued by the club, and after five years of negotiation United finally received £35,000 in January 1963. So, in all, the club itself ended up with around £100,000 to compensate for the loss of ten great players who, even at 1958 prices, would have been worth much more on the transfer market.

Between 1949 and 1958 Busby had bought only five significant players – Ray Wood, Reg Allen, Johnny Berry, Tommy Taylor and Harry Gregg – and three of them were goalkeepers. In his thirteen years at United Busby had a trading surplus on transfers of more than £50,000. Now, in spite of the meagre insurance money, he felt he had no option but to spend as best he could, abandoning his reliance on the youth sides, if United were to remain a leading team. He was only too aware of how Torino had declined after the Superga disaster wiped out their team in 1949. 'I was determined to keep the name of Manchester United on people's lips,' he said later. 'We always had to look as if we were doing something. Having been the greatest, we could not settle for anything else.'

The first new transfer, in September 1958, was the England forward, Albert Quixall, who cost Busby a then English record fee of £45,000 from Sheffield Wednesday. Quixall was never a great success at Old Trafford, however, and failed to win back his England place.

Further transfer activity failed to stop the slide over the coming seasons. Maurice Setters joined from West Bromwich Albion for £30,000 in 1960 as a replacement for Wilf McGuinness who had been forced to retire through injury. Noel Cantwell cost £29,000 from West Ham the same year. In between, a left-back, Tony Dunne, was signed from Shelbourne for just £6,000. Dennis Viollet, who in 1959–60 had created a club record of thirty-two league goals in a season, was replaced by David Herd, who cost £35,000 from Arsenal in 1961.

For five years United did not do well enough to qualify for European competition, though later the runners-up spot achieved in 1959 would have given them a UEFA Cup place. Yet as Busby tried to rebuild his side, buying many more players than he would have liked in normal circumstances, experimenting with different combinations, bringing young players up from the youth teams, the goal of winning the European Cup one day had become all important. In fact it was the only thing Busby really cared about. It became an obsession which permeated the whole club.

Players who went to Old Trafford in the early '60s remember the powerful, overriding importance the European trophy had acquired at United. 'Almost from when I joined,' says David Sadler, who arrived in 1962, 'everything was geared towards winning that cup.' Pat Crerand, who joined a few months later, agrees: 'When I came in 1963 there was this great underlying wish to win the European Cup. I think that was the aim all the time I was here.'

In those years United developed a close relationship with Real Madrid. In 1958 the Spanish champions had offered to pay for the Munich survivors to have free holidays in Spain. At one point Matt Busby was even offered the manager's job at Real Madrid by the club president, Santiago Bernabeu. 'Their actual words were: "We'll make it heaven and earth for you," and I knew they would.' In Spain he could probably have won the European Cup not once but several times. Busby thought about the offer for a week, but decided his heaven and earth were in Manchester. He knew the boys who died at

Munich could be commemorated only by the team they had once played for.

During what was a wilderness period for United after Munich, Busby prepared for the eventual return to European competition with regular friendly games against the very best sides that Europe could offer. In 1959 he flew to Spain to persuade Real Madrid to come to Old Trafford.

> Real Madrid at that time were commanding about £12,000 to visit any club for a match, an enormous sum then. I said the crash had ruined us financially as well as physically and I would be grateful if they would take this into consideration. Mr Bernabeu turned to the business manager and said: 'We must treat Matt and Manchester United generously.' They did, and Real Madrid came at less than half price.

The club that won the European Cup five times between 1956 and 1960 actually visited Manchester three years in succession, 1959, 1960 and 1961, though they were guaranteed a share of gate receipts, worth around £10,000, for the later trips. These friendlies were treated as grand occasions, with big club dinners at hotels and exchanges of gifts. When United went over to Madrid in 1959, Les Olive was allocated £40 to spend on 'fishing tackle' as a present for Santiago Bernabeu.

Equally, the players were expected to treat the games as if they were full competitive matches. Before meeting the Spaniards at Old Trafford in December 1961, the team was sent to the Norbreck Hydro hotel at Blackpool, a treat normally reserved only for big cup games. The sea air perhaps contributed to United's 3–1 victory.

Benfica of Portugal were another team to come to Manchester, in 1962, shortly after winning the European Cup for the second time. Other visitors were First Vienna and Bayern Munich. In turn United played twice at Real Madrid and also visited the Dutch side Feyenoord, Rapid Vienna, Torino, Valencia, Juventus, Roma and Hamburg. They played three times in Munich too. More often than not, United would beat these top Continental teams, but much more important than winning was the experience gained for the time when the assault on Everest – the European Cup – could be mounted again.

Busby's transfer dealings failed initially to build a side good enough even to qualify for one of the three European competitions that now existed. It was not until two Scottish internationals were brought to the club that United really began to click again. In the summer of

1962, after long negotiations, Matt Busby parted with another record sum, £115,000, to Torino for the exciting inside-forward, Denis Law. Law was paid £100 a week on a two-year contract. Before Munich the United manager had once offered Huddersfield £10,000 for the young Law. As Scotland manager he had also awarded him his first cap, again while the player was still only in his teens.

Denis Law's presence, however, was not enough to stop the threat of relegation in the cold winter of 1962–63, and it was not really until a second player arrived, from Glasgow Celtic, that Law began to score with his customary regularity. Busby saw Pat Crerand as the midfield distributor who would deliver the ball to his expensive new marksman in a combination that had already worked successfully for Scotland. Some say that, of all the players Busby ever managed, Crerand was the one who came nearest to the kind of role he himself had once played in the Manchester City side.

While the league campaign of 1962–63 was a fight against the second division which was only resolved successfully in the closing matches, the FA Cup was more encouraging. Three home wins against Huddersfield, Aston Villa and Chelsea, all played within fifteen days because of the winter freeze, followed by victories at Coventry and over Southampton in the semi-final at Hillsborough, put the reds back at Wembley. Leicester City began favourites, but were overwhelmed by the new United side. The Crerand–Law combination produced United's opening goal and two more from David Herd secured the club's first trophy since Munich. United were back.

Busby inherited and remoulded his 1948 side and created his 1958 Munich team. Seven of the 1963 cup winners, in contrast, had been bought – Dunne, Cantwell, Crerand, Setters, Quixall, Herd and Law – and all except Tony Dunne had cost large sums. Only the two Munich survivors, Bill Foulkes and Bobby Charlton, along with David Gaskell and Johnny Giles, were products of United's famous youth programme. That year the United board increased Busby's salary to £6,000 a year and extended his contract to a further seven years.

The 1963 FA Cup victory signalled the beginning of Busby's third burst of success and ultimately the most triumphant team of them all. It was the start of the decade associated with three world stars – Bobby Charlton, Denis Law and the Irish genius who made his debut the following September, George Best. And as confirmation that the club had finally emerged from the dark post-Munich period, in 1964 George Best helped the youth team secure the FA Youth Cup for the first time since 1957.

Winning the FA Cup put United back into Europe for the first time since 1958, if only in the European Cup-Winners Cup. The next five years saw almost non-stop involvement in European competition, as United's attacking team went in search of glory both at home and abroad.

After Munich Matt Busby had adopted a rather different style of management. The United manager continued to suffer back pain from the crash, and he had had trouble with his legs even before Munich. In the winter of 1961 he was in hospital for several weeks for an operation. His poor health meant that he could no longer spend much time in his tracksuit out on the training pitch. Jack Crompton, the former goalkeeper, had come to the club from Luton to look after the training sessions, while John Aston Senior also joined the coaching staff. In recognition of his poor state of health, Busby was given a paid holiday every year by the directors, and £5 a day expenses, to help him recover after each arduous season.

Though the nature of Matt Busby's leadership changed in some respects, he was just the same father-figure, protecting and guiding his United family. Just after the players had made their first air journey since Munich, one of the crash survivors, Bill Foulkes, went to phone his wife to say that he had arrived safely, only to find Busby had called her first. 'He is not only worried about the team winning but that the individual players should do well for themselves,' said Denis Law. 'It is the league side which is his bread and butter, but he will go out of his way to explain to a boy why he has been left out of the sixth team. He knows how hurt that lad could be by failing to find his name listed on the notice-board.'

Busby would rarely raise his voice, and instead remained content simply to puff on his pipe. He would always find time to chat to members of the Old Trafford staff. And he retained his remarkable memory for names and faces. The United manager was not always able to keep the house in order, though. In 1961, while at the Norbreck Hotel in Blackpool, stories that several United players were involved in fixing matches were investigated by newspaper reporters. Lack of concrete evidence meant the story was never published, but it was a matter of great concern at the time.

The board minutes show how Busby was becoming more and more involved in the administrative side of running a large football club. For instance, he drew up the directors' rota for attending Central League matches; he had talks with a QC over the claim against BEA over Munich. Other responsibilities shouldered by Busby included talking to a local brewery over ground advertising and negotiations with the FA over plans to stage World Cup games at Old Trafford.

The year 1964 saw Busby's side finish runners-up in the league, four points behind Bill Shankly's Liverpool. They reached the semi-finals of the FA Cup for the third time in three years only to lose to West Ham, and reached the quarter-finals of the European Cup-Winners Cup competition. The reds won 4–1 in the first leg of the quarter-final against Sporting Lisbon in Manchester and another European semi-final seemed certain, only for the side to fall to pieces in Portugal and lose 5–0. The normally calm Matt Busby felt so angry about the way the team had thrown it away that, totally out of character, he unleashed his rage on to the players. 'What was going to happen to us when we got back to Manchester was nobody's business,' recalls Pat Crerand. 'He told us our performance was an insult to the people of Manchester.'

Yet the Lisbon debacle was typical of United's legendary inconsistency. Bobby Charlton recalls:

> They were remarkable years because we could never guarantee to play well. Brilliant one week, exasperatingly poor the next, and that was part of the fascination. I had a friend who never missed a match, going to quite extraordinary lengths to ensure that he was always there, simply because he didn't want to miss the incomparable performance of which he was convinced we were capable.

In 1965 United won the league for the first time in eight years, though it was a much closer race than Busby's previous successes. Chelsea and Leeds United both led the table for long periods, and in the end success was only achieved on a goal average margin of 0.686 over Don Revie's new Leeds United. The forwards Busby had bought were now piling up the goals – Law got thirty-nine in all competitions, David Herd twenty-eight and John Connelly, the England winger bought from Burnley, nineteen. Busby's home-grown stars Bobby Charlton and George Best contributed eighteen and twelve goals respectively. As his reward Matt Busby got a £4,000 bonus, and the board allotted to him 500 United shares, though it was six years before Busby took them up.

A campaign in the Inter-Cities Fairs Cup that year led them to a narrow defeat by the Hungarian side, Ferencvaros, in a replay in the semi-finals. But the club's latest European setback was compensated by the fact that the championship qualified United for the European

Cup for the first time since the fatal year of 1958. At last they were back at base camp.

It was perhaps fortunate for Matt Busby that, since United's previous appearance in the European Cup, no other English qualifier had won the trophy. Wolves, Burnley, Spurs, Ipswich, Everton and Liverpool had all failed even to get beyond the semi-finals. In view of England's 1966 World Cup win and English clubs' domination of the competition in the late 1970s and early 1980s, it is perhaps surprising that not even the great Spurs double-winners, nor Bill Shankly's Liverpool, reached the European final. At that time the tournament was dominated by the great Mediterranean clubs from Spain, Italy and Portugal. It looked almost as if English clubs had a gentlemen's agreement among themselves that, after Munich, United should be allowed to win the competition first! Spurs and West Ham, however, did achieve success in the Cup-Winners Cup.

United stormed through the European champions' competition in the 1965–66 season, with every forward putting in the goals. The Finnish amateur team HJK Helsingin were beaten 9–2 on aggregate and ASK Vorwaerts of East Germany went out 5–1, but the most remarkable achievement came in the quarter-finals against Benfica, the team that had twice won the European Cup.

The 3–2 scoreline from the first leg at Old Trafford left United in a precarious position for the second leg in Lisbon. The Portuguese champions had played eighteen home matches in Europe since 1960 and won every single one of them, regularly scoring five goals or more. But United fans need not have worried. In front of 75,000 people the reds, and George Best in particular, turned on a magnificent display that established Best's name in world football. Matt Busby said United's 5–1 victory that night was the club's best performance since 1945. In effect, Manchester United had already proved themselves the best team in Europe and worthy successors to Real Madrid and Benfica. But perhaps through the pressure of also going for the FA Cup and league title, the most glittering prize of all would elude them again.

Typically, United threw it away in the semi-final. Partizan Belgrade were seen as a much less worrying proposition than the Portuguese champions had been. But a 2–0 defeat in Belgrade saw United lose George Best with a leg injury, and in the home leg Partizan closed down defensively and the reds managed to win only 1–0. For the third time United had been eliminated from the European Cup at the semi-final stage. The effort of chasing the league title, the FA Cup and the

European Cup all in one season had proved too much and, as so often happens, they had ended up with nothing. Liverpool had become league champions and England's next representatives in the European Cup. After United had beaten Benfica so comprehensively in Portugal, it all seemed so unfair. For Matt Busby the European Cup looked as distant as ever:

> I was at my lowest ebb since the Munich air crash, and it was in my mind to turn my back on football altogether. It seemed the fates had conspired against the club and myself, and I remember telling Paddy Crerand: 'We'll never win the European Cup now.'

Crerand reassured his boss that the team would win the league again the following season and finally clinch the European trophy the year after.

Many believe, though, that the 1960s Manchester United side was at its best in 1965 and 1966. Most of the players – Paddy Crerand, Bobby Charlton, Nobby Stiles, Denis Law and George Best among them – seemed to be in the prime of their career. Real Madrid beat Partizan 2–1 in the 1966 European Cup final, but if United had been given the chance, the odds are they would have beaten the Spanish champions, who were nothing like the Real Madrid of old.

Yet winning the league championship once again, simply to get to base camp, might take years with so many other good teams in contention – Liverpool, Everton, West Ham and the emerging Leeds United and Chelsea sides. Matt Busby, now fifty-seven, seriously considered retirement. But he was again persuaded by his wife Jean that those who died at Munich would have insisted that he try again.

Had Manchester United won the European Cup in 1966, as a prelude to England's World Cup, it might have given Matt Busby the chance to retire then, and a new manager could have rebuilt the side while it was still at its peak. Alternatively Busby could have begun the necessary rebuilding himself. But with another league title needed as soon as possible, and the European Cup still to win after that, it was best not to disrupt what was still a good side. So when Blackburn's centre-half, Mike England, and Blackpool's midfield player, Alan Ball, were available for transfer, Busby allowed them to move to Spurs and Everton respectively. Busby did actually make Blackburn an offer of £85,000 for England in June 1966, but did not want to get into an auction with Spurs, the club England eventually joined for the same sum. Busby preferred his previous method of relying on the club's young players, some of whom, such as John Aston, David Sadler and

Bobby Noble, were already following George Best from the 1964 Youth Cup side. Between buying the two Burnley wingers, John Connelly in April 1964 and Willie Morgan in October 1968, Busby bought only one other player, goalkeeper Alex Stepney, though he proved an excellent buy.

At times Busby came under fire for the way in which his players went about their task. United in the 1960s were frequently criticised for being a rough, dirty side. Critics would point to the number of players who had been sent off. Indeed, more United players were dismissed in the 1960s than in the '70s or '80s when referees have been much more prepared to send players from the field. Often though, especially with Pat Crerand, Denis Law and George Best, it was a case of lost tempers and retaliation.

On the first Saturday in May 1967, Manchester United fans in their thousands flocked to the home of West Ham United at Upton Park in the East End of London. By one o'clock the gates were closed with 38,000 people inside. It was the climax to a season in which United players had devoted everything to giving Matt Busby another go at the ultimate trophy. For once other competitions had taken second place. Fourth position in the league the previous season had not been good enough to qualify for the European Inter-Cities Fairs Cup. Blackpool had knocked United out of the League Cup by a surprise 5–1 score at Bloomfield Road, while in the FA Cup United lost at home to second division Norwich City in the fourth round. Yet the reds marched steadily towards the league title. Since the New Year the formula of winning at home and drawing away had been applied religiously in all sixteen league matches. If United improved on the formula and clinched two points that day in East London, the title was theirs.

Within ten minutes West Ham had conceded three goals. By the end they had let in three more to lose 6–1. As far as the European Cup was concerned, Busby was at base camp for the fourth time. He could not afford to slip up again. Recognising this, the United board decided that no players could be released to play in testimonial or benefit matches over the coming year.

The story of how United progressed up that mountain the following season has been told many times. Hibernians of Malta, Sarajevo from Yugoslavia, and Gornik of Poland were all eliminated before a clash with Real Madrid in the semi-final that, if the United story were a work of fiction, would have been made the final. The reds pulled back from being 3–1 down in the second leg to draw 3–3 and go through to their first European Cup final, 4–3 on aggregate. And, appropriately, a rare goal from Bill Foulkes, one of the two Munich survivors playing, proved to be the winner. The two other Munich survivors, Matt Busby and Bobby Charlton, cried in the dressing room afterwards.

Yet United's famous 1968 victory over Benfica at Wembley could so easily have gone badly wrong. The apparently comfortable 4–1 scoreline was only achieved in extra time, and then after Alex Stepney pulled off a miraculous save from Eusebio in the dying minutes of normal time when the score was 1–1. Had Eusebio not tried to make it a spectacular goal, Benfica might have taken the trophy back to Portugal. Had United failed in that attempt on the European Cup, Matt Busby probably would not have been given a further chance. 'Without being disrespectful to the players involved, the 1968 team was not our best,' Bobby Charlton said recently. 'Manchester City had won the league and we had faded. A lot of us were past our peak. I knew I wasn't going to get another chance and about half the team were in the same boat.'

Perhaps it was that knowledge which made the difference, with extra-time goals from George Best, Brian Kidd and a second goal from Charlton himself. Matt Busby wept again with his players on the Wembley turf that night. The eight players who died at Munich had their memorial at last. 'The moment when Bobby took the Cup,' said Busby many years later, 'it cleansed me. It eased the pain of the guilt of going into Europe. It was my justification.' Young John Aston, son of the 1948 left-back, had a brilliant game on the left wing. Today he remembers the post-match banquet as a rather 'strange' affair. It was not the normal kind of noisy, wild football celebration after a Wembley triumph. There was more of a sense of relief, he says, of a job being completed, particularly for those who had actually been at Munich – Matt Busby, Bill Foulkes and Bobby Charlton. The parents of many of those who had died, and some of the survivors, had also been invited along. Indeed, for one survivor of the crash, Bobby Charlton, the night was so emotional that he could not bring himself to attend the dinner but retired to his hotel room. 'He couldn't take it,' explained his wife Norma, 'with complete strangers coming up and slapping him on the back and telling him what a wonderful night it is. . . . He's remembering the lads who can't be here tonight.'

That summer the Queen knighted the United manager. Manchester had already given him the freedom of the city. For their part the United directors had always rewarded Busby generously over the years. Since February 1967 he had been on £10,000 a year and a ten-year contract, and substantial annual bonuses had been transformed into large pension contributions. In July 1968 Busby's Rover car was replaced by a Mercedes. But rather than grant Busby a testimonial match, as happens with most successful long-serving players and managers, the United directors agreed in September 1968 to what appeared to be a much smaller recognition of the manager's achievements.

A year earlier, in August 1967, Manchester United had opened a small souvenir shop in a hut by the main entrance to the ground to cater for the growing interest in the club. The board had lent the enterprise £1,000 to get going. Now it was agreed that the Red Devils Souvenir Shop would be sold to Matt Busby for £2,000 on a twenty-one-year lease at a rental of £5 per week. At the time the directors had little idea of the true value of the shop, and in later years it would enjoy long queues outside the entrance from 1.30 on Saturday afternoons, as the new generation of football supporters demanded a greater variety of articles bearing the name and colours of their beloved club. In time, also, Busby voluntarily offered to pay more than the initial £5 a week rent.

Eight months after the famous Wembley victory, football reporters were summoned overnight to a 'special press conference' at Old Trafford. What was about to happen had been predicted by some of them in that morning's newspapers. Before the television lights, the stills cameras and reporters with notebooks, Sir Matt Busby, having served as manager of Manchester United for twenty-four years, announced that he would retire from team affairs at the end of the season. But he would not stop working for the club; he would just be taking more of a back-seat, administrative role.

Sir Matt had told the United directors of his decision more than two weeks earlier, just as 1968 was drawing to its close. The board begged him to stay as manager. He turned down their appeals, feeling that the football duties of managing such a major club had become too much on top of his other tasks. 'I could hardly see over the top of the pile of correspondence on my desk every morning,' he said.

After their triumph in the European Cup the previous spring, the 1968–69 season had been an anti-climax. United were sixth from bottom of the league table on the day Busby made his announcement. They had won only one away match so far that season and that was at Queen's Park Rangers who were later relegated with a record low number of points.

United's position that winter was only highlighting the fact that for

Sir Matt there was really nothing else to achieve. United had become the first English team to win the European Cup. No matter what happened now, nobody could ever take that achievement away, and defeat by AC Milan in the 1969 semi-final did not seem that serious. The attempt to go one better and win the unofficial World Cup Championship against the Argentine side Estudiantes had failed. But the violence and acrimony that accompanied both games, with three men sent off, led many to conclude that the contest was not worth playing.

'Manchester United have become rather more than a football club,' Busby had told journalists at the January press conference. 'They are now an institution.' And everybody in the room knew that just one man, almost single-handed, was responsible for making it an institution and creating the United legend – Sir Matt Busby himself.

His team's victory against Benfica at Wembley the previous May had provided such an obvious closing chapter to the Busby story. Winning the European Cup at United's fourth attempt, twelve years after first entering the competition, had partly made up for all the setbacks and nightmares of the previous years. The Holy Grail had been found.

Twenty-three years after arriving at that mediocre club next to Trafford Park, with a bombsite for a ground, Busby had finally built United into one of the greatest football clubs in the world. It was an obvious end to a remarkable career. But as things turned out it was not quite the end.

To many outsiders Sir Matt's successor, Wilf McGuinness, was an unexpected choice. Yet United's policy of keeping things in the family had worked well over the years – the trainer, Jack Crompton, the chief coach, John Aston Senior, and even the secretary, Les Olive, had all once worn United shirts. Even for Wilf McGuinness it was a genuine surprise. 'Someone in the office suggested I ought to come with a tie on the next day,' he remembers. There had been no preparation for the job; McGuinness had barely worked with the first team, though he had coached most of the players at some point in the reserves.

McGuinness would start simply as chief coach under Sir Matt, who would become general manager. 'He has a bit of experience to pick up yet in management,' explained Busby, 'I think it's a question of starting this way. I think he will have enough to bite on without taking on other things which could come later.' The plan was that McGuinness would eventually become team manager.

As a United player, McGuinness' early career had been highly promising, yet sadly short. One of the Busby Babes, he played eighty-three games and won a league championship medal in 1957, but injury ensured that he did not make the fatal flight to Belgrade. He even won two England caps in 1959 before his career was suddenly ended by a broken leg. In the family tradition, United kept McGuinness on the staff – training the youth team and the reserves. He also helped coach the 1966 England World Cup team, and the under-23 side.

His selection in 1969 as chief coach and future manager was popular with the younger players, but the more senior professionals were less enthusiastic. Bill Foulkes, Shay Brennan and Bobby Charlton were all older than McGuinness and had achieved far more in football.

'For one reason or another, whether inexperience or slight immaturity,' Busby says, '[he] did not get the response I had hoped he would get from the players.' Sir Matt feels McGuinness mishandled the older players: 'He was probably too close to them. He had played with most of them and knew their habits and this they resented. Disharmony developed and team discipline waned.'

McGuinness had an atrocious start in August 1969, with home defeats by Everton (0–2) and then Southampton (1–4). Losing to Everton was perhaps forgivable – they became league champions – but the Southampton result was different. Three times Southampton winger John Sydenham beat Shay Brennan to deliver a perfect cross for Ron Davies; three times Davies headed past Bill Foulkes to score.

For United's fourth game, against Everton at Goodison Park, McGuinness went much further than dropping the obvious offenders, and caused a minor sensation by also dropping Bobby Charlton and Denis Law. McGuinness admits now that an away game at Everton was not the time to drop experienced players. United lost 3–0 this time and as a result were second from bottom. Charlton returned for the following game, but Law played only eight more league games that season. Brennan played nine more games but Bill Foulkes never represented United again. The manner of Southampton's 4–1 victory had shown how badly Manchester United needed a new centre-half and a new full-back.

The axings undermined McGuinness from the very beginning. 'Wilf's manner of telling players that they were dropped often rubbed them up the wrong way,' complained Charlton. 'The way he did it meant that he lost their confidence.'

'Not everyone, sadly, would play for Wilf,' said David Sadler later. 'The side as a whole did not give 100 per cent effort for him. It was as simple as that.' One senior player even went to Louis Edwards' home to complain.

Denis Law rejects the accusation that senior players would not play for McGuinness:

> I believe that the real reason he failed was that he tried to introduce an approach to the game which was totally alien to the players who had earned United their years of success. . . . One of the most significant changes brought about by Wilf was his use of blackboard coaching at team talks. Matt Busby had used the blackboard only occasionally. . . . Wilf had it out all the time. . . . Instead of going out to play football, as they had been accustomed to doing, players were going out with their minds stuffed with plans and tactics.

Alex Stepney says McGuinness 'was not strong. He had moments of frightening indecision. He could not stand up and administer the kind of discipline that would gain him respect – adult discipline. Something was missing in his make-up. Perhaps it was simply experience.'

Bobby Charlton and McGuinness had been great pals, but Charlton complained that McGuinness as a superior did not know how to talk to him. A famous incident occurred one morning at The Cliff. Bobby Charlton had finished training early to go to London for an engagement. He returned to the changing room, showered and put on his suit. Then McGuinness demanded that all the players gather on the pitch for a team talk. As it was drizzling and pretty cold, Charlton suggested they meet under the stand by the pitch rather than out in the middle. McGuinness said no. As the rain got heavier Charlton turned up his collar and put his hands in his pockets.

'Right, Bobby Charlton, twenty press-ups,' shouted McGuinness, referring to the traditional penance for anybody caught with his hands in his pockets. Charlton replied that McGuinness had to be joking if he expected him to do twenty press-ups in his suit and shoes out on a muddy pitch. McGuinness insisted he was not joking, and so, in front of everybody, the world-famous star performed his punishment. McGuinness' reputation was the one which suffered, though, not Charlton's.

McGuinness says the incident was misinterpreted, and that it was all in a humorous spirit. When Alex Stepney told the story in his autobiography, McGuinness threatened him with a writ, but several players recall the incident as Stepney does and say that McGuinness was serious. Whatever the spirit in which it happened, the story provided ammunition for those players who felt that McGuinness was not up to the job.

The squad which McGuinness took charge of included several ageing stars, but there was young blood too: it was not quite as decrepit as some have since made out. Alex Stepney, aged twenty-four, had not even reached his peak, and kept United's goal for another nine years. Tony Dunne, twenty-seven, would play first-division football for another decade. George Best, twenty-three, Brian Kidd, twenty, John Aston, twenty-one, and David Sadler, twenty-three, were still young, and the latest signing, Willie Morgan, was only twenty-four. Nobby Stiles was twenty-seven, Pat Crerand thirty, and even Bobby Charlton, at thirty-one, would play in the 1970 World Cup. Denis Law, twenty-nine, would play for Scotland in the World Cup five years on. Only Bill Foulkes, thirty-seven, and Shay Brennan, thirty-two, were past their best in 1969. It would be four years before United replaced either player adequately.

After the dismal start in 1969 United bought Arsenal's Scottish centre-half, Ian Ure, for £80,000. He was in fact Busby's choice, selected in spite of unfavourable reports from scouts, and McGuinness was only too pleased to accept the deal. At nearly thirty-one, Ure was only a temporary stop-gap, but he made an immediate impact and United went unbeaten for ten games. McGuinness wanted to buy other players, but says he was not allowed to. Among those he would have liked were Colin Todd, the Sunderland defender, Malcolm Macdonald, the Luton centre-forward, and Mick Mills of Ipswich. Another target, particularly after the problems he had caused United, was Ron Davies, but the board decided in April 1970 that Southampton's £200,000 price was too high.

The rest of the 1969–70 season went fairly well. In the league the team finished only eighth, but Cup campaigns were more successful, with semi-final places in both domestic competitions. But United's position was made worse by the sudden burst of success at Maine Road. After the league in 1968 and the FA Cup in 1969, City won two trophies in 1970 – the European Cup-Winners Cup and the League Cup. Yet United could so easily have taken the latter trophy. In the semi-final United lost 4–3 on aggregate after Alex Stepney had instinctively parried the ball as it sailed into the net from a City indirect free kick.

Similarly United might have contested the FA Cup final rather than Leeds United. The semi-final went to a third game after goalless draws at Hillsborough and at Villa Park, where United might have won. Denis Law missed a good chance, while George Best seemed to have his mind on other things. Heading for goal, Best trod on the ball and fell flat in the mud. He had spent the afternoon trying to evade McGuinness to make love to a woman he had met at the team hotel.

Best was a major problem for McGuinness. Some of the team resented the way the Irishman got away with such behaviour before an important game, and criticised McGuinness for apparently being powerless to stop him. 'If I had been manager of Manchester United, George would not have played that match,' says Alex Stepney.

However, Best's brilliance often let the rest of the team off the hook. The United star was still in his early twenties, and these were still his best years. Yet the decline of the team around him is partly, Best thinks, why he went off the rails and resorted to drink:

> My goals became all-important because others weren't scoring them so frequently. Instead of revolving around me, the team now depended on me and I lacked the maturity to handle it. I began to drink more heavily, and on the field my list of bookings grew longer as my temper grew shorter.

In the summer of 1970 McGuinness was promoted to team manager, though he still did not enjoy the status of every other post-war manager in being invited to board meetings. The first part of the following campaign ensured his dismissal. By Christmas United were fifth from bottom, having won only five games. The sole consolation was another League Cup run, and with third-division Aston Villa in the semi-final this time, Wembley seemed assured.

Over the twelve days before Christmas things went badly wrong. In three successive home games United lost 4–1 to City, scrambled a 1–1 draw in the first leg against Villa, and lost 3–1 to Arsenal. Then United went out of the League Cup 2–1 at Villa Park.

On Tuesday, 29 December 1970, after eighteen months as chief coach and team manager, Wilf McGuinness was dismissed with half of his contract to go. Busby originally suggested that to avoid humiliation, McGuinness should ask to return to his old job of reserve trainer. McGuinness accepted at first, but later said that the board would have to sack him. So they did.

Sir Matt agreed to take over again to allow time for a new manager to be chosen. 'I feel very sorry for Wilf,' Busby said. 'He might have been a wee bit raw.' Privately he had seen early on that McGuinness was not going to work, but compassion prevented him from doing anything. McGuinness seemed so happy. He was assuming that he would be manager for good. Private schooling had been fixed up for his children.

McGuinness had been put in charge of several players nearing the ends of their careers who had managerial ambitions of their own. It was easy for them to mutter how they could have done things better. The close contact that some kept with Sir Matt – Denis Law, Pat Crerand and Willie Morgan, for instance – on the golf course or in restaurants on Saturday nights maintained a channel for discontent, perhaps more imagined than real. 'I didn't mind other players going behind my back,' McGuinness said recently. 'What I did mind was that he accepted their side of the story rather than mine.'

Pat Crerand believes that McGuinness would have succeeded as manager had he been given the job several years later, 'when Bobby, Denis and I had retired'. He shares the view that Sir Matt Busby's decision to appoint a manager from within the 'family' was correct in principle, only that McGuinness was too inexperienced, unable to stop the joking and laughing and become a figure of authority. Yet the failure probably turned United against further inside appointments when that may have been just what was needed to ensure long-term continuity in the Busby way of running the club.

Wilf McGuinness was shocked by his sacking and went around almost in a daze. He harboured mixed feelings, partly wanting to get his own back and yet not wanting to harm the club he loved. He had expected to have longer to prove himself. United believed in loyalty, didn't they? They were not a club to sack loyal employees.

Sir Matt brought back several players dropped by McGuinness – Alex Stepney, Pat Crerand, Willie Morgan and Alan Gowling – and form improved quickly. Busby had only done what he had always done: motivate players, the prime requirement of a successful manager. He might have exercised better discipline than McGuinness, but underneath the tensions between United's fading stars remained and would trouble his successor.

Wilf McGuinness spent two months with the reserves, then left to run Aris Salonika in Greece. He later managed York City, with little success, and is now physiotherapist at Bury. It is downhill after Old Trafford, as so many have found.

'He came as a boy and left as an old man,' says Tony Dunne. In Greece, McGuinness' hair started falling out. Then it grew back, but white and wispy, before disappearing again. The doctors said it may have been delayed shock. Today he is totally bald, and looks almost unrecognisable from his United days. He is in popular demand as an after-dinner speaker and often involved in get-togethers of former United players. And he has regained his jovial outlook on life, cultivating a new 'Kojak' image.

'When you look like I do,' he says, 'you have to laugh at things.'

5 DECLINE AND SCANDAL

'We cheat, we tell lies, we con people. Any manager who says we don't do that isn't being honest. That's the only way to survive. It's the law of the land.'

Tommy Docherty on football managers, 1979.

THE TWO men met secretly late one Wednesday night in April 1971. They had chosen a petrol station near Haydock, at the point where the East Lancs Road crosses junction 23 of the M6. Both men had just been to see Leeds United record a historic 1–0 victory over Liverpool in the Inter-Cities Fairs Cup semi-final at Anfield. But what they wanted to discuss was too delicate a matter for the Liverpool directors' box.

The younger of the two Scots, who was driving with his son back to Glasgow, was the first to arrive. A few minutes later the older man turned up. His journey was much shorter – just 40 miles back to Chorlton-cum-Hardy in Manchester. For about three-quarters of an hour the manager of Celtic, Jock Stein, sat in Sir Matt Busby's Mercedes and discussed the possibility of his coming to Manchester United. They parted with a hand-shake, and it looked as though there was a deal.

After the failure of his own first choice for United manager, Wilf McGuinness, Sir Matt felt relieved that his club would now be in capable hands. The two men came from very similar backgrounds in the Lanarkshire coalfield. Both had a similar approach to football – allowing freedom of expression, attacking play and building up a family atmosphere within their clubs. Stein had proved himself a good manager with more than one team. He had transformed little Dunfermline Athletic to the extent that they won the Scottish Cup in 1961. Now Jock Stein's Glasgow Celtic were unchallenged in Scottish football and just about to win their sixth successive league champion-ship. Moreover, in 1967, Stein had actually gone one better than

Busby himself when Celtic became the first British club to win the European Cup.

For Sir Matt it had been a risky, secretive process luring the new man in, and extremely difficult to avoid publicity. The first approach had been made by one of the United players Busby was close to, Pat Crerand. This had been after another European game – the second leg of Celtic's European Cup quarter-final against Ajax in Glasgow a few weeks earlier. Crerand had once played for Stein at Celtic, and during a small party at the manager's home after the match Crerand took him upstairs and told him that Busby wanted to know if he was interested in United. He certainly was. A meeting with Busby and Louis Edwards in the Manchester area followed, and then that late-night secret encounter at the petrol station.

A few days later, though, Jock Stein rang Busby to say he had changed his mind. He would not be coming to Old Trafford after all.

The Celtic manager said later that his family had persuaded him to say no: his son George was due to go to Manchester as a student anyway, but Stein's wife Jean did not like the idea of leaving all her friends. Stein also felt a sense of loyalty to Celtic. Some believe, however, that he had simply used the United offer to get a bigger pay rise out of Celtic.

There was also another reason to turn Manchester United down. His son George explained in the recent biography by Ken Gallacher:

He had always insisted in every job he had that he was in complete control of the playing side. He would not take a job under any other circumstances. Basically he wondered if he would be allowed to be his own man. He was insisting that he wanted to bring in his own backroom staff so that he had his own people round about him. But Sir Matt had his own loyalties, and he wanted this one kept on and the next one kept on, and he was suggesting that maybe this bit of business should be handled in this way, and so on. The conversation in that car at the petrol station went through all of this. Dad did want Sir Matt to be there. He knew that he would need to have him around the place when he needed advice about the club – but he wanted to be his own man and he agonised over whether that would be possible or not.

Ironically, in wanting to be his own man, Jock Stein was taking exactly the same attitude that Sir Matt himself had taken on arriving at Old Trafford a generation earlier.

In later years Stein regretted his decision not to take on United. In spite of his continued success with Celtic, the Glasgow club treated him badly and eventually pushed him aside. Stein's only period in English football was forty-four days with Leeds United in 1978 before he became manager of Scotland. But Manchester United probably suffered from Jock Stein's decision even more than he did. Had the Celtic manager taken over in 1971, United might well have avoided the years of decline and scandal that were to follow in the 1970s.

The Chelsea manager, Dave Sexton, also turned the United job down after seeing Busby in Manchester when the London side played Manchester City in the European Cup-Winners Cup semi-final. Eventually, in June 1971, six months after Wilf McGuinness had been sacked, another secret motorway rendezvous, just off the M1 near Coalville, led to Frank O'Farrell, the Leicester City manager, taking the job.

Busby explained to O'Farrell that he himself would have nothing more to do with team matters. O'Farrell said a few days later:

> I didn't have to ask about full control. He had made it all very clear, and to have pressed it further would have been insulting. I don't think enough people have realised what this must have cost him. This is his club, these are his players. Cutting himself adrift like that must be almost like walking out on a family. He must believe it's the best thing, but I still think it was the action of a great man.

Sir Matt had originally intended to carry on as United's general manager, in charge of administrative affairs, but he gave the job up after a few months. He was appointed to the United board and took up the 500 shares which had been allotted to him six years before.

Once the new league season started, United hit top form. Frank O'Farrell was only using the players left to him by Busby, but the crucial difference was how he deployed them. Because Pat Crerand was suspended for the opening two matches, O'Farrell played Alan Gowling in midfield instead, and Willie Morgan was brought back from the forward line to play alongside Gowling and Bobby Charlton in a 4–3–3 formation. Crerand never played again. By mid-December United had built up a five-point lead – the equivalent of seven points today. The star forwards were scoring regularly once more – by Christmas Best had seventeen goals and Denis Law eleven.

The bookmakers made United odds-on favourites for the championship. Closer observers were more sceptical, arguing that United had been lucky, that the team's defence was weak and that the side depended too much on George Best. Results in the New Year showed just how justified such scepticism was. United lost seven league matches in a row and slipped from the top spot.

The frailty of United's early-season dominance was most cruelly exposed at Elland Road in February 1972 when, with no score at half-time, Leeds United scored five times in the second half to win 5–1. Towards the end of the game Leeds players were simply passing the ball from player to player, taunting United to come and get it, egged on by a home crowd who cheered every pass and each failed tackle with increasing intensity. Some observers see that afternoon at Leeds as marking the real end of United's post-war period of greatness. It was the day when exciting red gave way to clinical dull white, when Leeds United's hard, methodical game began to dominate British football. And the board were quickly losing faith in the new Manchester United manager.

So long as the men he had inherited from Sir Matt were doing well, O'Farrell saw little point in buying new talent. When the slide began, however, O'Farrell was slow to react. Perhaps O'Farrell's biggest missed opportunity was not buying the England World Cup midfield player Alan Ball from Everton. In Christmas week 1971 Ball joined Arsenal instead for a record £220,000. Yet Ball might have been ideal for United. He lived in Bolton, was friendly with many of the players, often watching United games and sometimes wore a United scarf. 'I made it quite common knowledge,' Ball says, 'that if I'd had the chance to join United I would have jumped at it.' His father, Alan Ball Senior, was a frequent visitor to Old Trafford and kept begging United officials to sign his son. On the morning it was announced that Ball was about to sign for Arsenal, O'Farrell and Malcolm Musgrove made frantic efforts to contact him. They tried to work out what train he was on, and left messages for Ball to contact Old Trafford, but they had left it too late.

In the meantime O'Farrell also faced increasing difficulties with George Best. After his brilliant form in the autumn, Best's play had slumped dramatically, especially after a threat to his life before a game at Newcastle in October. Observers say that to avoid any gunmen in the crowd, Best never stopped moving that day at St James's Park. With his Irish background, the threats had to be taken seriously. A police guard was put on his home and he withdrew from an international in Belfast. The anxiety only increased when Best's sister was shot in the leg after leaving a Belfast dance hall.

The troubles in Ireland also caused Best to worry about his parents. He was seeing them less often than before, and at one point he seriously discussed the idea of United arranging to move his parents over to Manchester for safety and so that he could be close to them.

The Irishman's business interests were also worrying him. At that time the rag trade was going through a bad spell and Best's Manchester clothes boutiques were proving not to be the money-spinners that people believed they were.

The first week in January 1972 Best failed to turn up for training on every single day. The other players insisted that he should not be included in the team, but because Best had played such an important role in United's early-season success, O'Farrell desperately needed him. When United had been through this before, in January 1971, Busby had suspended Best, but O'Farrell argued that doing so this time was not in the best interests of the club. Instead, he fined Best two weeks' salary, ordered him to do extra training and told him to leave his modern £30,000 house and return to his former landlady, Mrs Fullaway, until the end of the season. However, the second requirement was largely ignored and in reality there was nothing O'Farrell could do to stop Best's life of late-night drinking, gambling and seemingly non-stop sex, as described so graphically in the book he wrote later with Michael Parkinson.

It was probably too late to stop the sad demise of one of football's greatest players, a decline coinciding almost exactly with the decline of one of its greatest clubs. George Best argues that both were closely linked:

> When the bad times started I couldn't bear the thought of going out on the pitch. I used to drink, so I didn't have to think about it. Which came first? The bad times then the drinking or the drinking then the bad times? I'm still sure it was the thought of playing in a bad team, of not winning anything, of not having a chance to play in Europe that drove me to it. All right, you could say that if I'd trained and lived properly, United might have stood a better chance of doing well. That's true, but I just couldn't see myself doing it single-handed.

With Denis Law and Bobby Charlton approaching the end of their careers and Pat Crerand already retired, Best was a last relic of the club's greatness. United felt a need to cling on to him – at no matter what cost, it seemed. He was still only twenty-six, yet no one realised that by 1972 he was beyond reform, that the great days of George Best would never return.

Frank O'Farrell did not spend much time with the players. He might give a friendly team talk at the start of training on Monday, praising the good points from Saturday and drawing attention to weak spots, but it was rare to see him in a tracksuit on the training pitch, and indeed on some days he might not meet the players once. His coach, Malcolm Musgrove handled the day-to-day running of the team.

Yet it was not until late February 1972 that O'Farrell forked out any money to improve the side. Martin Buchan, Aberdeen's young defender, cost £125,000, while the Nottingham Forest winger Ian Storey-Moore was bought for £180,000 after an embarrassing public tussle with Brian Clough at Derby. Despite these two deals, United had bought only four new players in the four years since winning the European Cup.

Then came George Best's sudden announcement that summer, from a beach in Spain, that he was retiring from football. Nobody really believed it, and after several weeks Best returned to Manchester and agreed to play on. O'Farrell demanded that he go and live at Pat Crerand's house in the hope that Crerand would be able to keep him from the bottle. In fact Best spent no more than a week with the Crerands. He was even sent to a psychiatrist.

In the 1972–73 season United's goal-scoring skills almost totally deserted the star-studded midfield and forward line-up of Morgan, Best, Kidd, Charlton, Law and Storey-Moore. By late September, nine months after holding top spot, they were bottom, having lost five games and drawn four. As results got worse so did relations between the players. Malcolm Musgrove drew lots to decide which of them would share rooms at a hotel in an effort to break up the old alliances. 'The big three, Denis Law, Bobby Charlton and George Best, were at loggerheads,' according to Stepney. 'There were long days when they simply did not speak to each other.'

Charlton felt that 'there was no feeling of fun in the club any more'. At one point he was so annoyed about Best's behaviour, and O'Farrell's failure to deal with it, that he thought of leaving the club. Charlton had long ago been annoyed by what he felt was Best's selfishness on the pitch. (George Best would never take up golf, it was joked, because he hated parting with the ball.) Now, as club captain, Charlton felt it was his job to pass on the players' complaints about Best's behaviour to Sir Matt. 'It seemed at times that Best was the club. The atmosphere was terrible.'

George Best himself felt that Charlton should have retired. Their rift was most public when Best declined to play in Charlton's testimonial match. The Irishman said that to do so would be hypocritical. He spent the night drinking instead.

Some of the players resented what they felt was Charlton's superior attitude. Charlton's low opinion of some of his famous colleagues at that time is exemplified by a comment made in 1973, just before he retired. 'I may be thought odd, but when I think of United,' he told the *Sunday Telegraph*, 'I think of Roger Byrne, Duncan Edwards and Eddie Colman before the [Munich] crash, and Harry Gregg, Bill Foulkes and Nobby Stiles afterwards. Those like Best, Law and Crerand, they were replaceable somehow, they weren't the heart of the team.'

When O'Farrell acted to strengthen his squad, he went for goal-scorers. First he paid £60,000 for Wyn Davies from Manchester City, then parted with another £200,000 for Bournemouth's prolific goal-scorer, Ted MacDougall. Yet O'Farrell failed to find any good defenders. Peter Shilton could not be persuaded to leave Leicester, while a good opportunity was missed when Don Revie briefly put right-back Paul Reaney on the transfer list at Leeds. O'Farrell went for another Leicester player, David Nish, but would not match Derby's £225,000 offer, which he thought was too much for a left-back.

Impressive victories over Derby and Liverpool were outnumbered early in the 1972–73 season by poor defeats, often by mediocre sides, and third-division Bristol Rovers knocked United out of the League Cup at Old Trafford. Tottenham visited Manchester in late October after nine successive league defeats at United's ground. Their 4–1 victory, in which Martin Peters scored all four goals, summed up United's demoralisation.

It was soon clear that Frank O'Farrell had lost the confidence of the United directors, particularly after an extraordinary incident involving the *Manchester Evening News* reporter, David Meek. On the Monday after the Spurs defeat, Meek wrote an article calling for more support for the United manager, who had received a mauling in the national press. Under the headline 'Be Fair to Frank', Meek argued that responsibility for the club's troubles should be shared with O'Farrell by the players and directors. 'I would like to see dynamic leadership from the board to counter hypothetical questions about O'Farrell's future at Old Trafford,' he wrote. The United manager privately thanked Meek for writing it.

Others at Manchester United, however, were not so happy about the article and three days later the *Evening News* sports editor received a letter from United saying that Meek was 'no longer welcome' to travel on team coaches and trains to away matches, as he had been doing for the previous fourteen years. The ban quickly became known, and most journalists and supporters realised that Meek had touched on a sensitive subject – the directors now had serious doubts about O'Farrell.

The atmosphere among the players grew progressively worse. George Best admitted publicly that there was a possibility that United might be relegated. 'If that happens I will ask for a transfer. If United said no, then I would quit.' Ted MacDougall, meanwhile, found the other players hostile to him. 'I was regarded as nothing more than a third-division upstart,' he said afterwards. Of Bobby Charlton, MacDougall said later, 'I once asked him the best way to United's training ground and I'm still waiting for an answer. If he didn't feel like it, Bobby just wouldn't bother to reply.'

The George Best situation grew worse. In November he began to miss training again. The player made it clear that he wanted to talk to the directors, not the manager, and in despair O'Farrell asked the board to see him. So the United directors stepped in, suspended Best and put him on the transfer list.

Perhaps embarrassed by the lack of interest, Louis Edwards and Sir Matt Busby met George Best again a week later and tried to persuade him back into the fold. O'Farrell was not even consulted about this meeting. Best agreed to resume training and, when questioned, Louis Edwards admitted that Best was now off the transfer list.

O'Farrell was furious at the way in which Busby and the directors had taken over responsibility for Best behind his back, though it had been his original decision to let Best meet them. What little authority he still had with the players was being publicly chipped away, while George Best was being allowed to behave as he wanted. Had this state of affairs continued much longer, O'Farrell might have resigned. But results overtook him.

O'Farrell's career at United effectively came to an end two Saturdays before Christmas 1972, in front of 39,897 spectators at Selhurst Park, Crystal Palace's ground in South London. The 5–0 defeat was perhaps United's worst performance in post-war football. Palace were one of the worst teams in the first division, in bottom place when the match began. They were relegated to division two at the end of the season, and to division three a year afterwards.

Two evenings later, at Bobby Charlton's testimonial dinner, the United manager was denied a place at the top table. First the Meek

84

business, then the Best matter, now the dinner placings – the public signals about Frank O'Farrell's reduced standing were as clear as Politburo positions on the Kremlin balcony.

The following day, Tuesday, 19 December 1972, was mild for the time of year. That afternoon Frank O'Farrell, Malcolm Musgrove and the chief scout, John Aston Senior, were summoned before the board at Old Trafford. 'A nice day for an execution,' O'Farrell remarked as Aston arrived to give him a lift to the ground.

There they were officially dismissed. On the same day the United board announced, by mutual agreement, the end of George Best's career at United.

Frank O'Farrell believed his overriding problem, as it had partly been for Wilf McGuinness, was Sir Matt Busby's continued presence and status within the club. Relations had gone badly almost from the very first day when Busby had shown O'Farrell round Old Trafford. O'Farrell was taken to what Sir Matt intended should be the new man's office, which was being fitted out down the corridor from Busby's bigger room. O'Farrell insisted that, as the man in charge of team affairs, he should have the main office and that Busby should move.

That was the kind of small thing that irritated O'Farrell but which others might hardly notice. As a director Sir Matt also had the right to draw whatever expenses he wanted without being held accountable for them, whereas O'Farrell was allowed to claim only £40 a month without saying what the money was for. O'Farrell resented this too.

A short way into the 1971–72 season, when United had been doing well, Busby was quoted as saying that he regarded O'Farrell as his 'last great signing, possibly the greatest of the lot'. To most people that would be a compliment, but not to O'Farrell. He felt Busby was trying to steal his glory, and was so angry about the comment that he has kept the newspaper cutting ever since.

Moreover, Busby's personal relations with the players were still a problem. They referred to Sir Matt as 'big boss' and O'Farrell as 'little boss', while in team talks the older members of the team would mention how they liked to do it 'Matt's way'. O'Farrell particularly disliked the fact that Busby would socialise with the older players, though it probably did not happen as often as he feared.

Frank O'Farrell found his dismissal hard to accept. He was unemployed for the first time in his career. At the last minute, he and his wife had to buy their own Christmas turkey – the one promised by Louis Edwards never arrived!

Initially, the United directors promised to honour O'Farrell's five-year contract in full, but he took legal action to recover other income he felt he had lost. Eventually a £45,000 payment was negotiated, but only in return for O'Farrell's agreement not to talk publicly about his time at the club. O'Farrell felt that the agreement had been nullified by the comments in Busby's book, *Soccer at the Top*, published in 1973, and some years later he wrote his own book with James Lawton of the *Daily Express* entitled *Nice Day for an Execution*. Extracts were due to be serialised in the *Sunday Mirror*, but then, only a few days before publication, O'Farrell withdrew them on legal advice.

Sitting in the directors' box that dismal December afternoon at Crystal Palace was the Scotland manager Tommy Docherty. As the players left the pitch after the final whistle, Docherty remarked to Sir Matt Busby that the 5–0 scoreline could easily have been 10–0. 'If anything happens over the weekend,' Busby asked, 'are you interested in coming to Old Trafford?'

The following Wednesday Sir Matt Busby was playing golf with Willie Morgan at Mere golf club in Cheshire. Despite the conversation with Tommy Docherty at Selhurst Park the previous Saturday, the United director did not have Docherty's home telephone number, and he asked Morgan if he could give it to him. Morgan said that Docherty would be an ideal manager for United and added that he had been most impressed with him while playing for Scotland during the 'mini-World Cup' tournament in Brazil the previous summer. Another Scotland player, Denis Law, expressed the same view when asked by Busby. The tempestuous, loud-mouthed Tommy Docherty of old was now a reformed character, they argued. Docherty had restored the international career of both players, but Law and Morgan would later bitterly regret those testimonials.

Louis Edwards and Tommy Docherty shook hands in Edwards' silver Rolls-Royce on its way from Manchester airport. And so, three days before Christmas 1972, there was installed in the manager's office at Old Trafford one of the most complex and interesting characters to appear in this long and twisted tale.

The more one talks to people who know him, the more one is forced to conclude that Thomas Henderson Docherty is two characters, not one. Every individual has good and bad characteristics; Tommy Docherty has them in extremes. The attractive Tommy Docherty is immensely generous, friendly, down-to-earth and a great motivator of players – qualities which have helped bring him success. The unpleasant Tommy Docherty can be totally unreliable, cruel and callous – traits which led to his undoing at United and at many of the other clubs with which he has been involved.

Once settled at Old Trafford, Docherty plunged into the transfer market as he had so often done before. His first target was George Graham, who cost £120,000 from Arsenal. Scotland full-back Alex Forsyth arrived from Partick Thistle the following day for £100,000. Three weeks later Lou Macari was bought from Celtic for £190,000. No fewer than six of the players who had represented Scotland in the Brazil 'mini-World Cup' were now at Old Trafford – Forsyth, Buchan, Morgan, Graham, Law and Macari.

A much less well-known (and uncapped) Scottish player, Jim Holton, was signed from third-division Shrewsbury Town. Docherty himself had never seen Holton play, but the rugged, young centre-half probably made the most immediate impact of all Docherty's signings at that time. Harry Gregg, the former Shrewsbury manager, had originally recommended him to Docherty when he was manager of Scotland. Within just a couple of weeks of Docherty taking over at United, Jimmy Murphy and Docherty's assistant, Pat Crerand, watched Holton and backed Gregg's tip.

Yet Docherty believed he had been brought to Old Trafford to perform the unpleasant task Busby, McGuinness and O'Farrell had all failed to do: get rid of players – the 'dead wood', as he called them. 'I sussed it out very quickly. I knew I'd been called in to do the dirty work,' he wrote some years later. 'I would have suffered . . . if I hadn't gone "Chop, chop, chop . . ." and been ruthless and firm.' It was a policy he followed at many clubs he managed.

The first man to find himself out of favour, and almost straight away, was Ted MacDougall. Docherty felt that MacDougall did not have any technical ability. He dropped him almost immediately. By the end of February MacDougall was transferred to West Ham for £170,000 – £30,000 less than United had paid Bournemouth for him five months before. (The transfer later led to a court case. Bournemouth successfully argued that they were entitled to an extra £25,000 which United had promised to pay when MacDougall scored twenty goals, since he never had the chance to score that number.)

Some argue that O'Farrell's other striker, Wyn Davies, was also discarded prematurely. He played only four matches under Docherty before moving on to Blackpool in the summer.

In just three months Docherty bought seven players, as many as Busby, McGuinness and O'Farrell had brought to Old Trafford in the previous six and a half years. A revolution was under way at United. 'A club riddled with cancer,' is the dramatic way in which Docherty has described the United he found in those early, hectic months: 'Old players, skivers, players who were more concerned with getting rid of the next manager, whoever he may be. . . . Not all the players had a bad attitude, I hasten to add. Just a section. They had virtually taken over. It was like a canker.'

In Docherty's first season United gathered enough points to remain in the first division without really playing well. The young Jim Holton at centre-half made a tremendous difference, and United fans immediately took to a player who clearly gave his best in every game. 'Six foot two, eyes of blue, big Jim Holton's after you,' chanted the Stretford End, though Holton's eyes were in fact brown! To many observers Holton was the hard kind of central defender United had lacked since Bill Foulkes retired in 1969. He missed little in the air, tackled well and frightened opposition forwards.

After George Best's second retirement at Christmas 1972, the summer of 1973 saw the departure of the two other United superstars – Bobby Charlton and Denis Law. Docherty admits that Charlton's decision to give up made things much easier. There was still, however, the question of what to do about Denis Law. Docherty clearly saw Law as part of the 'dead wood'. He persuaded the United board that Law should be given a free transfer, though Busby disagreed with the decision. And, much against his own wishes, Law left United to join his old club, Manchester City, but the move came only after an extremely unpleasant dispute with Docherty.

Law had confidently expected to stay at United. He says that Docherty had told him at least twice 'that when I had finished playing there would be a job for life for me at Old Trafford'. According to Law, the manager then forgot these promises and offered him a free transfer instead. Law did not like the idea at all. So, to save the player any embarrassment, Law says the two men agreed that, rather than move to another club, it would be more dignified for him to announce his retirement from football altogether after his testimonial game, due early the next season.

Then, while watching television the following lunchtime in Aberdeen, where he had gone to collect his children, Law heard a report that he had in fact been given a free transfer. In the light of what had been discussed with Docherty twenty-four hours earlier Law was astonished. He was also very embarrassed when his friends and family wanted to know why he had not told them. On returning to Manchester he complained to Sir Matt Busby, who said that Docherty had been forced into the announcement under pressure from the media.

Denis Law was only the first important United figure that Docherty seriously upset. In time he was to have bitter disputes with three others – Pat Crerand, Willie Morgan and Alex Stepney.

Another attempt was made, however, to restore George Best. While the Irishman was in hospital recovering from thrombosis of the leg, Sir Matt Busby walked in carrying some fruit. ' 'Bout time you were back playing, isn't it?' Best recalls Busby saying as he left.

The Irishman worked hard to lose weight and get himself back to full fitness, doing extra training sessions during afternoons and on Sundays. He played a dozen first-team games that autumn and scored twice, but often his performances were indifferent. A particularly ineffective contribution at Queen's Park Rangers on New Year's Day 1974 turned out to be Best's last appearance for Manchester United. The Irishman missed training for two days trying to recover from the New Year celebrations and so was dropped the following Saturday. The humiliation of not being able to hold his place, even in a struggling side, was just too much. In the years ahead he played for virtually any second-rate club that would have him in Britain, Ireland and America, but the old Best magic flickered only occasionally.

Docherty played George Best in midfield, but his presence did little to help what was now United's main problem – the team's failure to score regularly. In thirty-six competitive games that season, up to the end of March 1974, United had suffered the most barren run in terms of goals in club history. There had been twenty-six goals shared between thirteen different players and in half those matches United had failed to score. With Martin Buchan and Jim Holton in the centre of the defence, the forty-eight goals conceded was the best defensive record since the team won the championship in 1967. But because of the lack of scoring power United were now in bottom spot and relegation looked certain. Perhaps it was the apparent certainty of going down to the second division that produced the sudden change in United's style in the spring of 1974.

Things started going well on the last Saturday in March at Stamford Bridge. Steve James went off injured and Brian Greenhoff was moved back to the centre of the defence. Suddenly United found a new fluency. Willie Morgan opened the scoring with a thunderbolt from the edge of the penalty area and second-half goals from Gerry Daly and Sammy McIlroy made it 3–1. United began playing simple possession football with short passes. Instead of kicking the ball upfield, Alex Stepney would now throw it to the nearest defender and build up a new attack. Several of United's younger players were beginning to perform well together, including Gerry Daly, Sammy McIlroy and Brian Greenhoff. Two new recruits, Stewart Houston and Jim McCalliog, also improved the side.

United scored thirteen goals in a six-game spell and gained ten points out of a possible twelve. If it was not quite enough to save them from the second division, it was at least the necessary boost for the following season, when United's defensive, aggressive style would be dropped in favour of more adventurous play, which would eventually lead to the adoption of two wingers. 'We tried to play tight, to play defensively,' said Docherty, 'and we were relegated. From now on we attack.'

'Busbyites' such as Pat Crerand claim that Sir Matt himself, not Docherty, deserves the credit for the sudden transformation in United's style. 'When do I get the sack?' Docherty is said to have asked Busby after another defeat at Old Trafford late in the season. Busby replied that Docherty would not be sacked, that he would take the side down into the second division and rebuild it from there. It is claimed, by Busby's friends, that the former United manager then suggested that Docherty ought to return to playing 4–2–4, the formation Busby had helped pioneer in the 1950s, and indeed to which he himself had returned during the brief post-McGuinness era.

Whether such a conversation actually occurred is difficult to ascertain. Pat Crerand, Docherty's assistant, claims he was there when it took place. Sir Matt Busby himself told the *Sunday Times* in 1976 that he had said to Docherty towards the end of the relegation season: 'Let's go out with dignity, Tommy,' and suggested that now United's fate was known, the team ought to go back to its more attacking style. Whether it was actually that advice from Busby which caused the dramatic change may never be certain. The Busbyites conviction that Sir Matt was totally responsible also illustrates the strength of feeling they now have against Docherty. Their contempt is so great that they could never accept that he himself was responsible for anything good at Old Trafford.

In spite of the new approach, a 1–0 defeat at Goodison Park made United's position desperate again. That Saturday, 27 April, United faced Manchester City at Old Trafford, the last home game of the season. In the City side was Denis Law, playing out the end of the season in preparation for the World Cup finals in Germany. Law's return to Maine Road had proved surprisingly successful, with twelve goals and a League Cup finalists' medal. He did not want to play that day at Old Trafford. United needed to beat City, and Stoke the following Monday, even to have a chance of survival.

By 4.35 p.m. there was still no score, and eight minutes left for United to do something. When the ball came across into the United penalty area, Denis Law, with his back to the goal, backheeled it instinctively towards the net. The result made him feel sick. That goal was Law's last touch in club football. In fact, other results were such that, even without conceding that goal, United were doomed.

Denis Law always felt bad about scoring that day, in spite of the way he had had to leave United a year before. Yet, if Tommy Docherty had kept the promise Law says he made, the Scottish forward might not have been playing for City at all. The Scot could have joined the United coaching staff or retired altogether. How typical of United that such a disastrous season should have ended with such a dramatic twist! 'Whether that is poetic justice, I don't know,' an Old Bailey judge would remark seven years later.

Throughout United's single season in division two there was never any great doubt that the reds would win promotion at the first attempt. The sixty points with which they took the second division championship was a comfortable total, but not outstanding. Docherty's youthful United team had an average age of twenty-three, like the 1956 Busby Babes, and had an equally refreshing, confident pattern. Stuart Pearson, bought from Hull City, added new goal-power up front. The crude aspects of United's game had now disappeared. It was a highly enjoyable season for the fans, who were visiting many new grounds, and for most, but not all, of the players.

By the time the team emerged from the second division in 1975 there was some internal discontent within the camp which, remarkably, did not seem to affect team performances. The seeds of Docherty's eventual downfall were already being sown. One by one Tommy Docherty added to his enemies with players he tried to get rid of. In most cases it was not the axing itself that hurt – that was to be expected in football – but the way in which the United manager carried it out. Probably the player Docherty most angered was Willie Morgan, the other Scotland player who had originally recommended Docherty to Busby. Eventually Morgan and Docherty were to become embroiled in a libel action that would cost the former United manager more than £50,000 and which he would describe as the 'biggest mistake of my life'.

Publicly, the growing tensions between the two men did not show themselves until early on during the 1974–75 season, United's year in the second division. During a dour match at Portsmouth one October night, Docherty brought Morgan off and sent on a young substitute, David McCreery. Morgan was furious and made it clear as he left the pitch. Eleven days later the United captain was substituted again, at home against Southampton. This time Morgan was so angry that he left the ground before the final whistle. By the end of that season Morgan was in and out of the team, being challenged for his place by a young winger Docherty had bought from Tranmere Rovers, called Steve Coppell.

Morgan says that he was determined to stay and fight for his place. In the summer of 1975, however, the players were due to go on a six-week tour of Iran, the Far East and Australia, but Docherty suggested that after a hard season Morgan might like to rest at home. Morgan happily agreed, only to see it reported in the press that he had refused to go on tour. By now relations with Docherty had become impossible and Morgan agreed to go back to his former club, Burnley, for £35,000, widely regarded as less than his true value. Morgan was still playing first-division soccer – for Bolton Wanderers – five years later.

Docherty's version of events is simple. Morgan, he says, was never the same player after an eye injury suffered while playing tennis in the summer of 1974. This required an operation. Docherty actually cut short a holiday to visit him in hospital, an indication perhaps that the manager felt Morgan still had a place at Old Trafford.

Eighteen months after leaving, on a local Granada television programme, Morgan described Docherty as 'about the worst manager there has ever been'. That comment led to Docherty's unsuccessful libel action against Morgan and Granada, and his subsequent prosecution and acquittal on perjury charges. Morgan spent two years preparing his defence and drew up twenty-nine allegations against Docherty to support his claim, many of which were never mentioned in court. Morgan even went so far as to subpoena the minutes of United board meetings during the 1974–75 season, his last year at the club. These showed that Docherty had reported to the directors that Morgan wanted a transfer. Docherty recommended that the requests be rejected and the board quite naturally agreed.

Yet Morgan denies he ever asked to leave, and says Docherty's reports to the board were completely false. He interprets Docherty's action as an attempt to present him, Morgan, in a bad light, so that it would be much easier to get rid of him when the time came.

Pat Crerand, who served as Docherty's assistant manager, was another who eventually left after, he claims, he had frequently been humiliated by the Doc and made to feel unwanted. On one occasion, for instance, before a game at Manchester City, Docherty even asked Crerand to leave the dressing room.

According to both Willie Morgan and Alex Stepney, Docherty also tried to get rid of his coach, Tommy Cavanagh. The two men say Docherty wanted them, as the club's senior professionals, to state that they were unhappy with Cavanagh because of his bad language and his treatment of younger players. Docherty also made efforts to transfer Morgan's successor as team captain, Martin Buchan, to Arsenal.

It was Docherty's quite extraordinary way of handling players that caused so much resentment. So long as you were in his favour he was all sweetness and light. But once he no longer saw a need for a man in his team, he could be totally unreliable, cruel and callous. There were reports of how Docherty would rubbish some of his players to supporters he happened to meet casually around Manchester. On the training field he would criticise players with precise references to the amount of money they were earning. Invariably it was the more experienced players Docherty fell out with, while the younger members of the squad, men he had brought into the side, remained full of admiration for him. Some people argue that it was simply a matter of the older, more experienced players rumbling Docherty. Once they had got the full measure of the man, they claim, he could not afford to have the older players around any longer.

Not only did Docherty succeed in discarding all except Stepney of Busby's senior players – McIlroy and Greenhoff had been signed as youngsters by Busby but never played in his first teams – but there is a belief among the Busbyites that Docherty also tried to get rid of Busby himself. The theory is that he deliberately struck up a close relationship with Louis Edwards to do this. There is no doubt that Docherty and Edwards did get on extremely well and often socialised together at a time when, as we shall see later, Edwards and Busby were themselves moving apart.

In contrast, many of the younger players benefited from the other side of their manager. Steve Coppell was particularly impressed with the way in which Docherty insisted that he should continue with his studies at university, and then flew back from a holiday in Malta to attend his graduation ceremony in Liverpool. Coppell also remembers how some months earlier he had been feeling depressed about his form and his university work. Docherty came up to him, took a piece of paper out of his pocket with the address of a hotel in the Lake District written on it and told Coppell and his girlfriend to go and spend the weekend there at his expense. Brian Greenhoff tells of a similar experience. His wife, who was expecting their first child, had not been feeling well, and Greenhoff asked if he could take the next few days off training so that they could both go away to Anglesey for a short break. After a match at Coventry, Docherty handed Greenhoff a bag with playing gear so that he could train on his own while he was away. He told Greenhoff he did not want to see him back until the following Thursday.

Coppell, now pursuing his own managerial career, still admires 'the Doc' as a manager for understanding the real spirit of Manchester United. 'He was smashing. He identified with everybody, especially the spectators. He would go around the country visiting each supporters' club. He was manager in the eyes of the spectators and helped create a better club.' On one occasion Docherty even asked each of the players after a match if they were going to a supporters' club dance that night. If they said no, Docherty wanted to know why not.

On the other hand Docherty would not miss a chance to make money for himself, and sometimes upset others by doing so. Steve Coppell will not forget the time Gillette asked him to make a TV commercial:

> As it was the first commercial deal I had been involved with, I thought I had better obtain permission and advice from my manager. I took the letter with me to show him, and he told me to leave it with him and he would look into it. A week later he had sorted it all out, but it was no longer just me, but now Gordon Hill, Tommy Docherty and me. Doc, inevitably, was the star of the show and it was his car boot which was full of razors and blades rather than mine.

Relations between Docherty and some players were never the same again following the particularly acrimonious tour to Iran, the Far East and Australia in the summer of 1975, after United had won promotion. The players suddenly noticed in Australia that United were being advertised in the local papers as taking part in a head-tennis competition, yet most of them knew nothing about it. The United head-tennis team, it soon emerged, consisted of three relatively junior players, Brian Greenhoff, Sammy McIlroy and Steve

Coppell, as well as Tommy Cavanagh and Tommy Docherty himself. It also became known that they were getting a large sum of money – around £1,000 between them – just for playing in the first round of the contest, and that further rewards would follow if they progressed beyond that. This arrangement ran completely against the spirit of the players' pool, whereby all such payments were shared equally amongst the first-team squad. The players quickly made their anger known.

The dispute came to a head in an extraordinary scene more appropriate to gangland than to Britain's most prestigious football club. Late one evening in Sydney, before a match the following day, Docherty gathered the players together in the team's hotel. Realising that what was likely to follow would be unpleasant, he even excluded Arthur Albiston on the grounds that, at seventeen, he was too young for such things. Docherty sat on his own at a table at the front of the room, with the players sitting in chairs around him in a horseshoe. Topping up his glass regularly from a full bottle, the United manager called on each player to express his grievances. He next admitted to arranging the head-tennis tournament with an agent in Manchester long before the party set off. Then, addressing each player one by one, progressing around the room, he criticised them in detail in front of all the others, saying just what he thought about them as players and, in particular, their shortcomings. The confrontation lasted about an hour. By the end, says Alex Stepney, the bottle was empty.

This was clearly not the way a football manager should act. In particular, it was not the kind of behaviour associated with Manchester United. And the directors came to hear about such things. The experiences of Willie Morgan, Pat Crerand and Alex Stepney quickly created an unflattering image of the United manager in the eyes of the United board-members.

None the less, the reds charged to the top of the first division with delightful attacking football which attracted the second highest average home crowds in the club's history. What made a particular difference was that a third of the way into the season Docherty brought back the idea of playing two wingers – Steve Coppell on the right and Gordon Hill, just signed for £70,000 from Millwall, on the left. The enthusiasm and confidence which had carried United to the second division championship bubbled through the first division too. It was a remarkably young team, none of whom had great reputations in English football like the Best, Law and Charlton team of only three years before.

United's exciting form carried over into the FA Cup, where they reached the quarter-finals with a series of comfortable wins. But Wolves looked to have upset the run when they came to Old Trafford and went 1–0 up. Gerry Daly equalised, but then at Molineux the following Tuesday all looked lost again when Wolves went 1–0 up in the nineteenth minute, scored a second only two minutes later and then, worse still, Lou Macari was taken off injured. The match might have seemed over, but only to those who did not know United. Brian Greenhoff moved to Macari's position while the young Jimmy Nicholl replaced Greenhoff in defence and had a super game. That night at Molineux was to exemplify the spirit of a United side for whom opposition goals were only an incitement to play even better.

'We weren't really bothered about being 2–0 down,' says Steve Coppell. 'We knew we were better than them.' Before half-time, Stuart Pearson had pulled one back. Sixteen minutes from the end Brian Greenhoff struck the equaliser after Parkes had saved a shot from Coppell. Sammy McIlroy's goal in extra time took United into the semi-final. For United fans it stirred memories of the glory days of the 1960s. Two goals from Gordon Hill against Derby County in the semi-final took United to a Wembley final to play second-division Southampton.

In the league, meanwhile, United were only a point behind the leaders, Queen's Park Rangers, at the start of April, and had a game in hand. Like so many teams in recent years who have had a chance of winning two or more trophies, United ended up with nothing. Injuries to Steve Coppell and Stuart Pearson were followed by the kind of pathetic result that United have so often suffered late in the season, losing 1–0 at home to Stoke City. The title went to Liverpool again, with Queen's Park Rangers second. United were third, four points behind Liverpool.

Wembley overwhelmed Docherty's young players in the final against second-division Southampton. United started well but began playing badly after a header from Sammy McIlroy hit the woodwork. Bobby Stokes' goal for Southampton eight minutes from the end was perhaps offside, but it won the match. Again the drama was twisted further by the fact that Stokes had had the ball touched into his path by another of the Scottish players whom Tommy Docherty had discarded at United and sold to Southampton – Jim McCalliog.

When United returned to Manchester for a civic reception, Docherty made the usual FA Cup losers' promise about returning and winning next year. Few believed it.

In the 1977 FA Cup competition, Walsall, Queen's Park Rangers and Aston Villa were all eliminated at home at the first attempt, while revenge was taken on Southampton with a 2–1 win at Old Trafford in the fifth round, after a replay. For the third time in thirteen years United were drawn against Leeds United in the semi-final at Hillsborough. This time goals from Steve Coppell and Jimmy Greenhoff saw the red shirts triumph for the first time in the series.

At Wembley in 1977 United were the underdogs. Their opponents, Liverpool, had already won the league championship, and they hoped a European Cup final appearance four days after the Wembley final would mean the first treble in English football history. But Docherty told the squad that he would pay them £5,000 in cash to share among themselves if they won.

Liverpool were superior over the first half, but the nearest they came to a goal was when Alan Kennedy hit the foot of the United post. Five minutes into the second half Jimmy Greenhoff headed the ball on for Stuart Pearson to open the scoring, only for Jimmy Case to equalise just three minutes later. But within two minutes United were ahead again with Lou Macari's shot accidentally glancing off Jimmy Greenhoff's chest, past Ray Clemence. It was the winning goal. Liverpool had to settle for the league championship, and the European Cup – becoming only the second English side, after United, to win the trophy.

Martin Buchan collected the players' £5,000 cash from Docherty a few days later. But with so many of the squad now away on holiday, Buchan had second thoughts about keeping that amount of money. He asked Docherty to hold on to it until the new season. Events ensured that Buchan never saw the money again.

A month after United's victory over Liverpool, reporters were summoned to an unusual press conference at a house in Mottram, a village 10 miles east of Manchester on the edge of the Peak District. Crowded into the small room the reporters and photographers were faced by the United manager, Tommy Docherty, hand in hand with Mary Brown, the wife of the club's physiotherapist, Laurie Brown. Docherty announced that three weeks earlier he had left Agnes, his wife of twenty-seven years, to live with Mrs Brown, with whom he had been having a secret affair for three years.

At first it did not look as if the announcement would affect Docherty's job. He had after all just won the FA Cup, and produced the most exhilarating football at United for a decade. Initially Louis Edwards seemed unconcerned. When Docherty telephoned the

Edwards' home to notify his chairman, it was his son Martin who answered. His father was not available, and when Docherty explained the situation, Martin said that he did not think it would matter. Louis Edwards later told Docherty not to worry and said that it would blow over within forty-eight hours. It was a personal affair and would not affect his job as manager. Edwards even opened a bottle of champagne and toasted Docherty's future at United. And the United chairman also stopped an approach from Derby County who had been trying to get Docherty as their manager. Edwards assured the Derby chairman that Docherty would be staying at United and publicly described reports that Docherty would be sacked as 'nonsense'. That position prevailed until a full board meeting could be assembled.

Ten days after the initial revelation, while Docherty was staying in the Lake District, the club secretary, Les Olive, summoned him to see the United board at Edwards' home in Alderley Edge. There the five directors told Docherty to resign. When Docherty refused, he was suspended on full pay. To the press afterwards, however, both Docherty and the club secretary, Les Olive, denied that he had been suspended.

On Monday, 4 July, the United board met twice at Louis Edwards' house. First, at 9 a.m., they spoke to Laurie Brown. He explained to them how Docherty had used his position as manager to pursue his affair. The two lovers had been seeing each other at times when Docherty had told Brown to come in and treat United players, and the manager had arranged for other members of staff to keep Brown busy. But Brown did not just give details of Docherty's affair. He told of several other actions by Docherty, and in particular explained how the United manager had used journalists to publicise his request for a new contract.

The board was now resolute that Tommy Docherty had to go. On top of everything else they feared that if Laurie Brown left the club he would sell his story to a newspaper, and they knew he had already been offered a large sum to do so.

At 4 p.m. the board held its second meeting. This time Docherty was simply sacked. A statement said that it was for a 'breach of the terms of his contract'.

Had Tommy Docherty simply been having an extra-marital affair, he might have survived. But it was much more complicated than that. Firstly, it was an affair with the wife of a club employee who was actually under Docherty's control. The board now knew how Docherty had been exploiting his superior position as manager.

Secondly, there was the extraordinary way in which Docherty had handled the news and the bad publicity it had brought the club. The manager had sold the story to the *Sunday People* for an estimated £5,000, then held a press conference to announce further details, just as if he had signed a new player. Doing so was just inviting the press to probe further. Moreover, Docherty was reported to be charging £100 for interviews. He could not have arranged for more coverage if he had employed a PR company. It was on the front pages of all the tabloids.

Thirdly, there was also the question of what to do about Laurie Brown. It would be totally unfair to compound the misfortune of losing his wife and two daughters by forcing him to resign. At first the physiotherapist had insisted to Louis Edwards and Sir Matt Busby that there was no way he could stay at Old Trafford, even if Docherty left the club. He argued that United should compensate him for the loss of his wife and family and help him make a new start. Eventually Brown did agree to stay and was given a big pay rise.

Finally, once news of the affair broke, the directors came under tremendous pressure – from players, club staff and ordinary supporters. There were personal approaches, telephone calls and letters containing numerous other allegations about Docherty's activities, most of them totally unrelated to Mary Brown. The United manager had made many enemies in Manchester and it was inevitable that they would seek their revenge.

Tommy Docherty claims that it was the ladies who got rid of him – wives like Muriel Edwards and Jean Busby. Others say that Denzil Haroun was among those most vociferous in arguing that he had to go. Sir Matt Busby had created a club with high standards of public conduct. If only a few of the allegations were true, keeping Docherty would fly right in the face of United's traditions. There was even talk of a surveillance report floating around, supposedly written by a private investigator in Stockport called Steve Hayes. It was claimed that for two years Hayes had followed Docherty everywhere and had built up a complete dossier of his movements. In truth, although the suggestion of having Docherty followed was mooted after he fell out with Jim Holton, there is no evidence that it ever happened.

The board had also seen at first hand how Docherty had lost the support of leading players. A year earlier, at the club banquet, held at the Midland Hotel in Manchester after the 1976 FA Cup Final defeat, Martin Buchan had been called on to say a few words in praise of the team's success but, much to everyone's embarrassment, he simply walked up to the top table, had a word with Les Olive and sat down again. It seems that he did not want his remarks to be construed in any way as praise of the United manager.

This explains why it had taken weeks that spring for Docherty to secure a new four-year contract worth £100,000 with United. The board was only forced to agree when Derby County offered Docherty a job, though the contract remained unsigned at the time of his sacking. The United manager might well have been sacked anyway had the team lost to Leeds in the FA Cup semi-final. The relatively disappointing league form during the 1976–77 season – the reds finished sixth – would have been sufficient excuse.

Many of the accounts of Docherty's behaviour that reached the directors' ears were to become public during Docherty's unsuccessful libel action against Willie Morgan a year later. Perhaps the most damning claim made in court was that Docherty had demanded a personal payment of £1,000 to allow George Best to play for Dunstable Town in August 1974 and to arrange for United reserves to play a match there. The Dunstable manager at the time, Barry Fry, a former United player, stated that he was satisfied that the money was for Docherty's personal use. Pat Crerand alleged that he had actually seen Docherty being given the wadge of £5 notes while he was sitting naked in his bath. Morgan also intended to produce dramatic corroboration from Keith Cheeseman, the Dunstable chairman, who had supplied the cash. Cheeseman was by then in Albany prison on the Isle of Wight, serving six years for fraud. Morgan had received special permission from the Home Office for Cheeseman to be brought to court to give evidence.

It was also alleged that Docherty had been selling Cup final tickets on the black market. In 1974, it was said, Docherty sold two £10 tickets for £100 each. In 1977 the United manager had sold 200 tickets for £7,000 and, counsel alleged, he had even invited the ticket tout Stan Flashman into United's executive suite to carry out the deal. Tommy Docherty himself said on radio in 1988 that Martin Edwards told him that selling tickets was another reason why he was sacked; this was contrary to his contract which stated that he must uphold FA rules. Docherty says his reply was that he had been selling Cup final tickets since 1959.

The profits from Docherty's ticket-dealing may have provided the £5,000 he had promised the players if they won the FA Cup. After his dismissal, some United players were furious with Docherty for never paying them the money. So when Morgan was assembling evidence to defend his allegations against Docherty, there were members of the existing team only too happy to assist.

The two organisers of the United players' pool, Alex Stepney and Lou Macari, were lined up as witnesses by Morgan. Morgan's other witnesses included several of Docherty's enemies from his United days – Laurie Brown, Ted MacDougall, Pat Crerand and Denis Law. The Busbyites in particular saw the libel case as another opportunity to put matters straight. Morgan even hoped to persuade Busby himself to take the witness stand. But Sir Matt, who was probably closer to Morgan than to any other former player, and played golf with him regularly, would not have involved himself to that extent.

In the end none of Morgan's star witnesses had to testify. The case collapsed before the prosecution had even finished its arguments. Docherty accepted under fierce questioning that not telling Denis Law about his free transfer 'was very wrong'. During cross-examination about discrepancies in his evidence, Morgan's barrister put it to Docherty that he had told 'a pack of lies'. The former United manager admitted that he had.

Docherty was ordered to pay Morgan's and Granada's costs, estimated at £30,000. His own lawyers and further action arising from the libel case cost him another £20,000–30,000. In 1981 a jury at the Old Bailey cleared Tommy Docherty of two charges of perjury arising from the Morgan court hearing, having decided that his lies were not deliberate.

In the years since 1977 United fans have occasionally chanted Tommy Docherty's name at moments of crisis. To those on the Stretford End the street-fighter Docherty was one of the lads. Ticket-dealing and running off with a colleague's wife were something they might do themselves. It is his exciting young team they remember, a team which had attracted home crowds as great as those who followed the Busby Babes and the 1968 side.

6 THE EDWARDS FAMILY BUSINESS

'United have begun to think that "class" is something that comes with big office suites and fast motor cars.'

Harry Gregg, United goalkeeper 1958–67.

LOUIS CHARLES Edwards was born on 15 June 1914, two months before the outbreak of the First World War. His parents, Louis and Catherine, had married twelve years before, and although they already had two young daughters, Beatrice and Kathleen, this was their first son. The baby Louis, named after his father, came into the world at the family home in Liverpool Street, Pendleton, Salford. It was about 1½ miles from the impressive new football ground that had opened at Old Trafford four years earlier.

The Edwards family had a long history in the food and grocery trade. Louis' father, Louis Charles Panizza Edwards, is described on his son's birth certificate as a 'preserve manufacturer'. Their family had originally lived in Pimlico in London, then moved to Liverpool before settling in Salford. The 'Panizza' that Louis Edwards Senior carried in his name was that of his mother's Italian family, silversmiths who had emigrated to London from Florence.

In 1919, Louis Edwards Senior set up on his own in the meat trade in Salford, as a manufacturer and wholesaler of sausages. In 1921 he opened the first of several shops in the Manchester area, and in time both his sons, Louis and Douglas, born in 1916, helped out when they were not at school. Louis went to the local Roman Catholic grammar school, De La Salle College, but he left at fourteen to work full-time in the family firm. Later, during the Second World War, Louis served in the Hussars in India, Africa and the Middle East.

Just before war broke out in 1939, the family business became a limited company, Louis C. Edwards & Sons (Manchester) Ltd. When the founding father died in February 1943, it passed to his two sons,

Louis and Douglas, who ran the business together. But their father's will specified that Louis should inherit seventy-seven shares, and Douglas only seventy-five. Louis, of course, enjoyed the extra prestige of carrying the same name as the business. At that stage the company had a turnover of around £25,000 a year from a few butchers' shops in the Manchester area and a sausage and cooked meats factory. Within two decades the Edwards sons would turn this small operation into one of the largest meat suppliers in the kingdom.

During their early years of working together, Louis and Douglas Edwards found that the trade inevitably suffered from wartime and post-war meat rationing which did not end until July 1954. They were nevertheless determined to expand. As well as increasing the number of high-street shops, they made an important advance in the mid-1950s by winning the franchise for meat counters in dozens of Woolworths stores and in shops owned by Littlewoods. Another line was tendering for contracts with local authorities. Councils in Lancashire, Manchester and Salford were obliged by law to provide hundreds of thousands of school meals every day, and it proved a very lucrative business.

By 1962 the Edwards company had more than eighty retail outlets, including forty with Woolworths and Littlewoods, and it enjoyed an annual turnover of £5 million – 200 times the 1945 level. That year the company went public, and shares were floated on the stock exchange. The move made both brothers wealthy men and provided Louis Edwards with the extra funds to buy his control of Manchester United.

Yet the business was not the ideal model of success. The Edwards meat firm thrived throughout the post-war years by providing low-quality meat, and through methods which were often corrupt. In 1978 and 1979 researchers for Granada Television's *World in Action* gathered considerable evidence about the company's dishonest business practices. Only a small portion was ever used in the programme finally broadcast in January 1980.

One of the firm's most important customers was the Education Committee of Lancashire County Council. Across the county, children were eating more than 300,000 school meals a day at one point, and by 1961 the authority's meat contracts were worth £393,000 a year. That year Louis C. Edwards and Sons (Manchester) Ltd received £203,000 of the trade, and although the amount varied annually, the firm would nearly always get between a half and two thirds of Lancashire's meat supplies. By 1974 meat provided for Lancashire school meals was worth £1.5 million a year. Because of the size of the operation, and the extensive transport required, there were few firms in the North-west able to fulfil such contracts. The Edwards brothers' main rival, primarily in the north-eastern divisions of the county, was F. Lord & Son Ltd, the company owned by Bob Lord, the chairman of Burnley.

But the Lancashire contracts were acquired only at a price. Every few weeks a van would leave the Edwards' factory in New Street off the Oldham Road in Miles Platting. From there it would head north up the A6 to deliver a large consignment of meat to a house in a small village called Elswick, situated half-way between Preston and Blackpool. The address, 'White Gables', was the home of Sidney Hilton Whittaker, an assistant chief education officer of Lancashire Council and the man with overall responsibility for the county's school meals.

A former Edwards company sales manager, Thomas O'Hora, told *World in Action* about one occasion on which he himself had delivered Sidney Whittaker's gift:

> It would be in weight roughly about 100 lb. I think it was about seven or eight parcels. It would appear as if Mr Whittaker was expecting me, and a lady, whom I've reason to believe was Mrs Whittaker, met me and showed me to an annexe where there was a very large deep freeze and I put the meat into it.

According to another former Edwards' employee, a typical order for Whittaker would include 'six sirloin steaks, six lamb chops, a leg of lamb, a leg of pork, a number of pounds of sausages and a number of pounds of best stewing steak'.

Similar gifts were regularly sent to officials and councillors concerned with school meals contracts for Manchester and Salford City Councils. Put bluntly, the Edwards company was bribing many of the people who recommended whether or not the firm should be given the councils' meat contracts. A list of the beneficiaries was kept in a slim, brown, hardback book at the New Street offices. Next to each name was written 'N.C.', which stood for 'no charge'. This was the kind of corruption that was common in local government in the Poulson days. Making gifts to chefs, catering managers and other people responsible for ordering meat is still a fairly common practice in the meat trade – 'danglers', such gifts in kind are called.

Between fifteen and twenty clients of the Edwards company would also get 'sweeteners', or cash bribes, delivered every month in plain brown envelopes. So common did these payments become that the extra expense of 'sweeteners' was automatically built into the figures whenever the cost of a contract was calculated. 'In some instances,' according to O'Hora, 'we renegotiated contracts within a couple of months of starting them. In this way, the cost of the backhander could be covered by the firm or council involved and the person who received the payment in the first place would invariably sanction the increase.' And O'Hora insists that both Louis and Douglas Edwards were fully aware of what was going on. Yet they were quick to sack employees caught pilfering the tiniest amount of scrap meat.

Executives and directors of Woolworths, including a former chairman, Fred Chaplin, also received 'danglers', in recognition of the Edwards' valuable franchise in many of the company's stores. A van which left New Street on Thursdays for the weekly tour of Woolworth employees' homes in London and the home counties became known inside the Edwards' company as 'the Oxfam run'.

At Christmas, Edwards' contacts would get an additional large package delivered by the firm's drivers, usually a tea-chest full of best-quality meat and bottles of spirits. Other Edwards beneficiaries, according to Granada's extensive research and affidavits, were ICI executives, managers of several Butlin's and Pontin's holiday camps and even Sir Billy Butlin himself.

Yet few of the firm's ordinary customers received such good meat. Throughout the catering trade the Edwards company became well known for the poor quality of its products. A report by Manchester Council in 1966 complained of the bad supplies they were getting, and said that the firm delivered the worst meat to the poorest parts of the city. More than ten years later, in 1978, the company was fined on several occasions under the Food and Drugs Act for poor quality and excess fat in the meat supplied for Cheshire County Council's schools. Shropshire and Staffordshire Councils were also unhappy with the company's supplies.

By the '70s, the public were also beginning to understand what they were getting in Edwards' shops – 'second-class meat at first-class prices', in the words of one former senior executive.

Louis Edwards would often treat Manchester United Football Club simply as an extension of his meat business. United's affairs were sometimes transacted at the meat company offices in Miles Platting, most notably the sacking of Frank O'Farrell as United manager in 1972. Similarly, people from the meat business were sometimes drawn into football matters. Thomas O'Hora regularly spent evenings arranging the distribution of more than a hundred United tickets for

Edwards. Drivers would deliver them to a wide range of contacts – councillors, local government officials, health officers, senior police-men – though in the vast majority of cases the tickets were paid for. In another instance, in 1974, the meat company's property controller, Norman Redfern, attended a United board meeting to advise on plans for the club's proposed Executive Suite. When the suite was opened, who should supply the meat but a firm called Louis C. Edwards & Sons (Manchester) Ltd. They had already been supplying the canteen at The Cliff training ground for several years.

Officials at Old Trafford, and others in the football world, were also sent regular free meat, though these parcels were simply gifts not bribes. The home of Alan Hardaker, the Football League Secretary, next door to the League headquarters in Lytham St Annes, was another delivery point. To avoid embarrassment on such visits, the Edwards' drivers would be told to keep their vans parked away from the house, preferably round a corner, and they were advised not to wear their company overalls.

By the mid-1970s, however, Edwards' meat business, like his football club, was in difficulty. In 1973 the company made a profit of £360,000 on a £20 million turnover, but it was the last year the company's shareholders were to receive a dividend under Edwards' regime. The company planned to expand by buying more retail outlets all over the country and opening new stores selling a wide range of fresh food, but things did not work out. In 1975 they had to announce redundancies at Miles Platting, and though the accounts returned to profit in 1976, by 1978 there was again a loss, of £340,000.

Part of the problem may have been that both Louis and Douglas had become more distant from the company's affairs and drawn into more glamorous activities. 'Mr Louis', as employees called him, was more interested in running Manchester United, and in the Football League Management Committee, to which he was elected in 1968. His brother, 'Mr Douglas', was heavily involved in local Conservative politics. He had been a Manchester city councillor since 1951, and later became an alderman and city lord mayor. He also served as high sheriff of the new county of Greater Manchester. The men assigned to manage the company in the brothers' place lacked the Edwards brothers' determination and business style.

Alan Simmons, who was appointed chief executive in 1974, says that the business was being run in a 'fairly relaxed atmosphere with not much pressure being exerted to produce results'. Plans to expand by buying more retail outlets were abandoned. Other former Edwards employees argue that a major problem for the firm was Britain's entry into the Common Market in 1973. European meat regulations were much stricter than the rules that had applied until then in the UK. The Edwards company could no longer import carcasses from abroad which had been slaughtered inhumanely, for instance. And local government officials were also getting more fussy about the meat they were prepared to accept. In 1975 the firm lost the Lancashire Council contract.

The family's demoralisation would be compounded by the collapse in the late '70s of the building firm John Lee and Sons – Louis Edwards' daughter Catherine had married David Lee. Coincidentally the collapse came only a few months after the firm had built the United Executive Suite that Norman Redfern was consulted about.

In 1973, while his football club was recovering under the managership of Tommy Docherty, Edwards had called on Roland Smith, Professor of Marketing at the University of Manchester Institute of Science and Technology (UMIST). Smith is a fascinating character, a part-time businessman and part-time academic, who as chairman of British Aerospace was largely responsible for the dramatic takeover of the Rover Group in 1988. He also hit the headlines in the early 1980s with Lonrho's attempted takeover of Harrods. During his brief period as chairman of Harrod's parent company, House of Fraser, Professor Smith made a name for himself by telling Tiny Rowland to get his 'tanks off my lawn'.

In the early '70s Roland Smith was largely unknown outside the North-west of England. Yet already, when not teaching students at UMIST, the professor specialised in being a business consultant to companies in trouble, and was becoming known as 'the man of a thousand boardrooms'. The Edwards brothers made Smith a non-executive director and vice-chairman of their meat company. He gave them advice on how to reorganise their operations and suggested the appointment of Alan Simmons from outside as chief executive. While giving advice to Louis Edwards about his meat business, it was only natural that Professor Smith should turn his attention to Edwards' other concern, Manchester United Football Club. Roland Smith was himself a local boy and had been educated at Manchester Grammar School. Moreover, he claimed to be a life-long supporter of Manchester United.

Roland Smith saw great financial potential in United. He suggested to Edwards that it would be possible to devise a shares scheme which would not only raise a considerable amount of extra money for the football club, but which would also help Edwards realise some of his own investment in it. Louis Edwards found Smith's ideas attractive, not just because they might bring in cash to buy new United players, but also because he hoped they would make money for him at a time when the meat company was in deep financial difficulty. Moreover, Smith's plans would enable the family to retain control of the club.

In September 1976, a few months after United's defeat by Southampton in the FA Cup Final, Louis Edwards and Roland Smith were accompanied by United directors Alan Gibson and Sir Matt Busby on a visit to the merchant bankers Kleinwort Benson in London. Among the possibilities the four men discussed with the bankers was a rights issue – selling off new shares to the existing shareholders in Manchester United Football Club Limited.

It was the start of a plan which would change radically the whole nature of Manchester United, effectively transforming it from a football club into a business. The scheme would eventually cement the Edwards family's control over Manchester United, and yet also cause a battle that would irreparably rupture relations between Sir Matt Busby and his former protégé, Louis Edwards.

The city bankers came up with several different schemes that would raise money both for Edwards and the club. Yet at one point Louis Edwards briefly considered a free issue of shares, whereby each existing shareholder would be entitled to a certain number of new shares in direct proportion to the number of shares already held. Somebody with one share might get ten new, free shares for instance, while someone with a hundred would get a thousand more. The idea was dropped when shown to be against FA rules. It is highly significant, however, because the effect would simply have been to increase the total number of Manchester United shares, without raising any new capital. Why Edwards should have wanted to do this may not seem clear initially, but a clue may be provided by a comment Edwards made to a colleague in the meat business shortly before the 1977 FA Cup final. 'How much,' Edwards reportedly asked, 'would the fan in the street pay to have a Manchester United share certificate on his wall?'

It seems that Louis Edwards partly planned to use his greatly increased shareholding simply to sell off his spare shares to supporters who would want them for sentimental reasons and pay well above the commercial value. The idea of a free issue without any new capital, however, was rejected by the Football Association.

Kleinwort Benson and Roland Smith eventually worked out a

proposal for Edwards that involved a rights issue which would not only increase the total number of United shares, but would also mean £1 million in new capital. That money would then, it was argued, be used to buy new players. Rather than issue shares to the general public and anybody who wanted to buy them, they would be issued only to existing shareholders. For every Manchester United share already held, shareholders were allowed to buy 208 new shares at £1 each.

While details of the scheme were still being negotiated in private between United directors, Roland Smith and the merchant bankers – and before the plans had been made public in any way – the Edwards family had already embarked on a second round of frantic share buying to rival that of 1962 and 1963.

Since Louis Edwards had succeeded Harold Hardman as chairman in 1965, neither the United board nor the share register had changed significantly. Apart from Sir Matt Busby's election as a director in 1971, the only other change was the election of Louis Edwards' elder son, Martin, in 1970.

Alan Gibson, who had sold most of his existing shares to Louis Edwards in 1963, had his portfolio greatly replenished when he inherited 894 shares from his mother in 1971. Apart from that, the only other major share change had been the promised allocation of 500 new shares to Sir Matt Busby in 1971, but these were being held in trust for Busby by his solicitor. Because this increased the overall number of shares to 4,644, Louis Edwards' own holding had in fact been diluted below the 50 per cent mark, to around 47 per cent. But the United chairman had little need to fear a takeover bid since a rule change in 1973 had restricted the price at which shares could be bought. In addition Edwards had placed 1,500 of his own shares into a trust for tax reasons so that they could be passed on to his sons in due course.

Another rule change, at the 1977 Annual General Meeting, was the prelude to the second round of Edwards' share buying. The shareholders agreed to the board's recommendation to remove the 1973 limit on the price of shares. Now the Edwards family were again free to start offering people prices they could not refuse, in an operation which over six months radically increased their holding from 47 to 74 per cent of the club. Their targets were the three largest remaining shareholders apart from Sir Matt Busby, all of whom were the descendants of important figures in the club's history.

The first to sell, in November 1977, only a few weeks after the

AGM, was Beryl Norman. She had fifty-one shares which she had inherited from her father, the former club secretary, Walter Crickmer, who had died at Munich. One evening she received a telephone call from Jim Smart, the sales manager at the meat company. Smart was acting as Edwards' fixer, in much the same way Frank Farrington and Thomas McKeown had in 1962 and 1963. Smart asked if she would be willing to sell for £200 a share. Smart told Beryl Norman that Louis Edwards needed the shares to retain control, having handed over some of his holding to his sons. 'To tell you the truth,' she remembered later, 'the offer he made us was absolutely gorgeous. I'd always wondered what the shares were worth but as I'd have to offer them to the United Board I didn't think they were worth anything.'

Smart went to Beryl Norman's house in Timperley with a cheque for £7,650. A further £2,550 was paid in cash – in used £5 notes taken from Smart's briefcase – to avoid capital gains tax. But the United minute-book and the share register simply recorded the transaction as having cost only £7,650 – £150 a share, £50 less than the actual price.

Then, in December 1977, Jim Smart went to see Elizabeth Hardman, the daughter of the former chairman, Harold Hardman, and arranged for her seventy-one shares to be sold to Louis Edwards' wife, Muriel. These shares also cost £200 each – £14,200 altogether.

Just as in 1963, the last and most important decision to sell to the Edwards family was taken by the long-serving club director, Alan Gibson. In February 1978 he agreed to sell 1,138 shares to Martin Edwards at £172.70 each. The deal cost the United director £196,545 in all, for which he had to take out a £200,000 overdraft. Martin Edwards' bank manager was told that the money would easily be recouped later by selling off a small part of his stock. Edwards intended to sell up to 10 per cent of the total holding in two separate batches of 5 per cent and make around £125,000 for each batch. In other words Martin Edwards was hoping to make more than £1,420 each from shares that Alan Gibson had sold to him for only £172.70.

Between them Louis Edwards and his two sons, Martin and Roger, now owned nearly 74 per cent of United's ordinary share capital. The first two transactions – with Beryl Norman and Elizabeth Hardman – were carried out before the holders could possibly have known about the intended rights issue – an issue which would have considerably increased the value of their holding. Alan Gibson, however, had been on the trip to Kleinworts, and his decision to sell to Martin Edwards can only be described as financially unwise.

What the Edwards had done was insider trading, since the family was taking advantage of their own private knowledge that the shares were likely to increase in value. At that time, such transactions were regarded as unethical, but not illegal. Nowadays they are against the law. The Edwards knew that the more shares the family accumulated, the easier it would be to retain 50 per cent control and sell off the surplus at a large profit.

The deals also breached United's articles of association, which stipulated that shares had to be offered to the board of directors first – a rule passed in 1973 to prevent a threatened takeover bid. Yet even had the board been offered the Norman, Hardman and Gibson shares, it seems unlikely that any director apart from Louis or Martin Edwards could have afforded them at the prices they sold for.

When the rights issue formally came before the board in September 1978, Louis Edwards easily won approval for it, though not all the directors were keen on the idea. Alan Gibson said that he had reservations about whether it was necessary to raise money in this way, but that he would vote in favour if the meeting felt it was in the best interests of the club. Bill Young said that he agreed with Alan Gibson and asked whether the club needed the money. Yet he would vote for the plans if the money was free of tax. Louis Edwards' brother-in-law Denzil Haroun and his son Martin, spoke and voted in favour. Martin Edwards argued that the club might need £350,000 to buy a new goalkeeper since Alex Stepney was nearing the end of his career.

Only Sir Matt Busby spoke out strongly against the scheme. He argued that the club did not need to raise money in this way, since there were more than 50,000 regular spectators, £425,000 in the Development Association accounts, and the club had no financial troubles. He was, he said, completely against the principle of a rights issue and, moreover, insisted that his opposition be registered in the minutes. By five votes to one, however, the board gave its approval. Yet of the six directors, only the three members of the Edwards family, Louis and Martin Edwards and Denzil Haroun, were enthusiastic. Strangely, both Alan Gibson and Bill Young voted with them in spite of voicing strong reservations.

When the rights issue was made public, many people, including highly experienced local businessmen, argued that it was not the best way to raise capital for United. Instead they suggested that it would be better to raise a bank loan or to make a public share issue. Even the Stock Exchange described the scheme as unusual. Louis Edwards replied that bank loans would involve heavy interest payments and debts, while a public issue might mean his family lost control of the club. The Edwards family said that, simply to keep that control, they were willing to spend £740,000 on the new shares they would be entitled to under the rights issue. Moreover, they also promised to buy any entitlement to shares which other shareholders did not want to take up.

There were few observers who did not see the scheme as a money-making exercise for Edwards. He could expect to sell his new shares for much more than the £1 he would have to pay for each of them, possibly for as much as £4 apiece or even more. In addition the greatly increased capital within the company would mean much greater scope for annual dividend payments – up to a total of £150,000 under the then Football Association limits. Previously the maximum amount the company could pay out in dividends had been about £600 a year.

Ted Croker, the secretary of the Football Association, was also extremely concerned about the plans. Sir Matt Busby was so worried that he went to visit Croker in London to see if the scheme could be stopped. Busby even considered resigning from the board, but friends persuaded him not to. The former United manager felt almost as hurt by Edwards' plans, according to one friend, as he had been after Munich, although obviously in a different way. It was particularly upsetting since Sir Matt had himself brought Louis Edwards to United in the first place. This dispute came on top of the Docherty scandal, in which Busby must have felt Edwards had let Tommy Docherty get away with far too much for far too long.

Even though Edwards had given up his place on the League Management Committee to Busby in 1972, other tensions had developed between the two United men. At one time Sir Matt had an understanding with Edwards that he would be the next chairman of Manchester United. Indeed, Jack Crompton remembers Edwards saying so publicly, and at one point Edwards had even agreed to hand over straight away, but Busby had insisted that he remain in place. This gentlemen's agreement was less important, however, than the understanding between the two men that both their eldest sons, Martin Edwards and Sandy Busby, would eventually be elected to the board. The young Edwards had been duly elected as long ago as 1970, before Sir Matt himself. But Busby's son was having to wait.

Sandy Busby had never managed to emulate his father's success in football. After having his son-in-law Don Gibson – Sheena's husband – at Old Trafford in the early '50s, Matt Busby decided it would be best for his own boy to play elsewhere. Sandy went to Bury and Oldham, and then played under Johnny Carey at Blackburn, without ever getting into first-team competitive football. He also played for the Surrey side, Kingstonian, in the FA Amateur Cup. Later Sandy Busby set up a bookmaking business, but this in itself delayed his election to the United board, since Football League rules prohibited football directors from owning betting shops. But by 1978 Sandy Busby's betting business had long been sold.

Busby first became worried during an informal directors' meeting on a summer tour to Majorca. When Louis Edwards suggested the election to the board of his youngest son, Roger, Busby had expressed his opinion that his own son should have priority. When Sir Matt formally proposed the election of his son in August 1977, the matter was deferred to the next meeting, whereupon it was put off again. Sir Matt Busby gave up. It was becoming clear to the former United manager that the Edwards boy was now being groomed as the future chairman, and his own son was not even going to be elected a director.

Once it was obvious that the Edwards rights issue could not be stopped, Sir Matt Busby gave up his public opposition in the long-term benefit of United. 'I decided that it is in the best interests of Manchester United Football Club that I should drop this matter,' he declared. 'I do not think that to carry on with it would be good for the club's image, and that matters to me more than anything.'

Privately Busby felt betrayed. Friends say that directors of other first-division teams came to offer him well-paid positions with their clubs. One chairman even turned up at Sir Matt's home in his Rolls-Royce. Again, though, the overwhelming loyalty to the club he had built forced Busby to turn such offers down.

But Sir Matt was not the only long-serving United insider to have great reservations about the rights issue. The club secretary, Les Olive, wrote to Edwards on 9 October 1978 advising him to prepare for the probable criticism when the issue was announced. Olive warned of 'personal attacks on the directors who might be thought to benefit most from the issue', and pointed out that legally it would be necessary to disclose details of the Edwards' meat supplies to the club, and of Sir Matt Busby's ownership of the souvenir shop. Moreover, Olive argued, the expanded share capital might mean dividends of up to £75,000 a year as well as £7,000 for a registrar to run the share ownership scheme.

Ten days later Olive sent Louis Edwards an even stronger letter, asking him to 'reconsider' the rights issue. 'I am convinced that in the long term it will cause many problems,' the United secretary cautioned, 'if not for yourself then certainly for some future chairman.' In his carefully reasoned appeal Olive set out in detail several strong reservations he had about the scheme. First, he argued, it could not be 'justified for financial reasons' – not only did United have good reserves, but there was also a healthy income from the Development Association. Then, in his role as company secretary, Olive warned again that the scheme might mean dividends of nearly £75,000 a year, or possibly double that amount if FA rules were interpreted in a certain way. 'This can be paid EVERY year,' Olive added prophetically. 'You may argue that a dividend is only paid at the discretion of the club but it is quite possible at some future date that the private financial position of your family (or of anyone else holding control) could be such as to influence the payment of a dividend even when it was against the interests of the club.' And Olive expressed particular concern about what might happen if control passed out of the hands of the Edwards family 'in 40, 50 or even a hundred years' time'. Mentioning the Football Association's disquiet, and the likely press criticism and comment – particularly if there was a split among the directors, Olive appealed to Louis and Martin Edwards to explore other possibilities. 'Is there any reason why you cannot sell some of your existing shares for a substantial price without losing the balance of power? I am sure this would avoid a major upset for the club and would still be beneficial to yourselves and in the long-term interests of the Club I beg you to take this alternative.'

It was a courageous letter for Les Olive to write to the man who was effectively his employer. And his carefully thought-out arguments were remarkably prophetic, especially on the question of dividend payments. But Olive's warnings had absolutely no effect.

Publicly, the strongest opposition to the scheme came from John Fletcher, a United supporter for more than forty years and the millionaire owner of Trumann's Steel in Walkden, a firm which often advertised in the United programme. He argued that under Louis Edwards' plan the shares were being sold too cheaply, and that the sale was benefiting the Edwards family. There was enormous goodwill among United supporters, he claimed, which would enable a much larger public rights issue instead. Fletcher formed the Manchester United Action Group '78 and put advertisements in the press. He organised a petition against the Edwards' plan and attracted 6,000 signatures.

John Fletcher offered to underwrite his own proposed alternative share issue which would raise twice as much capital for the club – £2 million. A million shares would simply be offered to the general public at a price of £2 each. Fletcher even went so far as to deposit £2 million of his own money with his solicitor as surety, and as a sign of his sincerity.

The United board refused to see Fletcher, and argued that the club did not need as much as £2 million. So Fletcher went to the High Court to try to stop the Edwards' scheme going ahead. The judge ruled against him on the grounds that it was unreasonable to expect the Edwards family to support a scheme which would dilute their control of the club and make them vulnerable to a takeover.

Meanwhile, Martin Edwards was preparing to finance the purchase of his share of the issue. He was the largest individual shareholder with nearly 400,000 shares, and so would have to pay almost £400,000. According to Granada TV's research, various local business-men were approached, including Archie Thornhill, a Manchester bookmaker, John Lawlor, a building contractor, and John Tabner, the owner of a taxi firm named Mantax. Martin Edwards suggested that if they were prepared to help finance his share buying, they would get a cut of any profits when some of the shares were sold later. It seems that none of those he approached was able to go along with the idea, and in the end he had to go to the bank.

Martin Edwards could have calculated that after the £200,000 he paid Alan Gibson, and the £400,000 spent on the new rights issue, each of the 400,000 shares he now owned had cost him about £1.50. How many shares he would need to sell to recoup his outlay would obviously depend on the amount at which they were valued after the issue. He approached friends to ask if they would promise to buy some of his shares later.

With Fletcher defeated, Busby silent and Olive ignored, the rights issue sailed through United's Extraordinary General Meeting on 18 December 1978 in less than half an hour. By thirty-seven votes to three the allotment process went into operation.

Martin Edwards' new bankers, National Westminster, had made it a condition of granting him the necessary overdraft that afterwards shares should be traded freely on the open market. Indeed, he would need this to have any hope of selling shares at a profit later. Board approval must no longer be necessary to make share transfers, they insisted, and there should be no restriction on the share price. Ever since then, whenever United shares have been sold, the price has been given in the following Saturday's *Financial Times*. The change also meant that the total number of shareholders eventually shot up from ninety to almost 2,000. United's Annual General Meetings became large gatherings of two or three hundred people, who were often prepared to voice strong criticisms of the board and management.

In the early days of trading, however, in February 1979, Manchester United shares did not reach anything like the £8 apiece that Martin Edwards had hoped for. A few changed hands at around £4.50 or £5, but then the price fell to between £1.50 and £2.75.

At first, Martin Edwards sold around 60,000 of his allocation to relatives and friends. Many of them went to people who bought only small blocks of a few hundred. One block of 15,400 shares, however, was sold to a Manchester fur trader, Mike Edelson, for £125,000 – just over £8 a share. The agreement, referred to in the accounts of one of his fur companies, gave Edelson the option of selling the shares back to Edwards at the same price at a later date. This condition was probably incorporated to ensure that Edwards carried out a promise to get Edelson elected as a United director in due course. It would also explain why Edelson paid twice as much as other people, and never insisted on selling the shares back. It would take him nearly four years, though, to get into the boardroom.

Although Martin Edwards made £320,000 on immediate sales of United shares, he retained most of his £600,000 overdraft. Today, ten years later, he still claims to be burdened with much of that debt. The reality is, however, that he could have paid it off years ago by selling off his substantial shareholdings in other companies. Edwards has obviously calculated that the rate of interest payable on the overdraft is less than he could earn on investments elsewhere. Meanwhile, his bank has demanded that so long as his overdraft persists his United shares should remain in the hands of a company run by the bank, Control Nominees Ltd. This gives Edwards the voting power to which his shares entitle him, but also gives the bank security.

Just four days before the United shareholders approved the rights issue, Louis and Douglas Edwards agreed to hand over the family's control of the meat business to the second dynamic businessman to become embroiled in the affairs of Manchester United. Like Professor Roland Smith, James Gulliver has achieved considerable national fame in the years since then.

Gulliver, a Scot, had been negotiating with the Edwards to purchase their business for nearly two years. It was a natural target after his career in the food industry with Fine Fare supermarkets and Oriel Foods. Gulliver believed that the Edwards company would provide him with something he had long wanted, a stock-exchange-listed company which would be a vehicle for rapid expansion into the food-processing industry.

The deal struck with Louis and Douglas Edwards in December 1979 involved Gulliver buying 500,000 of the family's shares at 5p each, and then the company issuing Gulliver with a further 1.5 million shares, also at 5p each. The whole deal cost the Scotsman just £100,000. In addition, Gulliver was granted an option to buy a further million shares from the family over the next forty months at a much higher price. The family also agreed to wield 2.4 million of its votes in favour of whatever Gulliver proposed at any company meeting. Together with his own shares, this provision gave him 44 per cent of the company's votes.

James Gulliver was also given an important management role in the firm. Both Louis and Douglas Edwards retired from the board, and from their positions as joint chairmen and managing directors. In return they both received golden handshakes, pensions, consultancy contracts and company cars. Martin Edwards, though, carried on working for the new owner as a director.

It was a sign of how close the Edwards' firm was to bankruptcy that James Gulliver's effective takeover of the business in 1978 cost him so little. 'I'll make it one of the largest food and drinks groups in Britain,' he is reported to have promised at the time. 'Just wait and see.'

And he did. Louis C. Edwards and Sons (Manchester) Ltd was valued at around £½ million by the terms of Gulliver's takeover, though at £2.3 million by the quoted share price at the time. Twenty months later the firm's name was changed to Argyll Foods, after the part of Scotland where Gulliver grew up. Within less than ten years Argyll had become one of Europe's largest food firms. What happened to the Edwards company in James Gulliver's hands is one of the most extraordinary recent growth stories in British business.

Once in charge, the new owner launched a rapid series of successful takeover bids for bigger and bigger targets, including Yorkshire Biscuits, Cordon Bleu, Dalgety Frozen Foods, Oriel Foods, Allied Suppliers, and later Safeway supermarkets. Argyll's swift expansion was interrupted in 1986 only by the unsuccessful and notorious battle with Guinness to acquire the drinks company, Distillers. Even so, by 1988, thanks largely to Gulliver's hard work and clever dealing, the Argyll Group was worth an astonishing £1.7 billion, in other words 34,000 times what the Edwards company had initially cost him ten years before.

Gulliver took up his options to buy a million more shares early in 1981. One by one the Edwards family sold most of the rest of their remaining 43 per cent stake in the firm. Between them they received an estimated £8 million, eighty times more than the price Gulliver paid for his initial purchase. Sir Matt Busby was less fortunate with the Edwards shares he owned, and failed to realise several thousand pounds, having already sold near the bottom. Had Gulliver not come along, the meat company would probably have gone into liquidation. On the other hand, if the Edwards family had held on to their remaining stake in the firm, between them they might be worth hundreds of millions today.

Just six months after James Gulliver rescued the Edwards' ailing meat firm, the Scot was to strengthen his business links with the family still further. At the dramatic FA Cup final in 1979 when United lost 3–2 to Arsenal, James Gulliver was Manchester United's guest in the Wembley royal box. Soon afterwards Gulliver bought 100,682 of Louis Edwards' United shares for around £¼ million. He had spent almost three times as much investing in the football club as he had initially in the firm that was to become the Argyll Group.

Gulliver promised that he would get involved in making the club more profitable and help to develop United's marketing potential, and that he would also try to organise a better market for United shares. He arranged for the accountants Arthur Andersen to carry out an inspection of the club's finances, partly to ensure that he was making a worthwhile investment. And there was one further condition that Gulliver insisted the Edwards agree to before buying his United shares. Accordingly, on 26 July 1979, the board co-opted James Gerald Gulliver as a director of Manchester United. Sir Matt Busby, however, abstained from the vote, saying that he did not know who Gulliver was.

Meanwhile, what had happened to the £1 million that the rights issue had supposedly raised for new players? Contrary to Martin Edwards' suggestion, it was not spent on a new goalkeeper. Agreement was originally reached to buy Jim Blyth from Coventry, but he failed a medical test. Then, a month before the rights issue was approved, United gave a debut to young Gary Bailey, who wore United's number 1 shirt for seven years before injury forced him to retire in 1987. Bailey cost no more than a £5,000 donation to the football club at De Witts University in South Africa where he had come from.

Most of the rights issue money was spent when United signed the

England midfield player Ray Wilkins for £700,000 in August 1979. But the United board seemed to take the attitude that it was a deal they could barely afford and forced the price down to well below the £825,000 figure that was publicly stated. It was as if the rights issue had never happened. They also insisted that Dave Sexton, the team manager at the time, should balance the books by selling other players. So Stuart Pearson went to West Ham for £200,000, David McCreery to QPR for £170,000 and Brian Greenhoff was transferred to Leeds for £350,000. The directors' instructions to Sexton looked even stranger after their arguments against John Fletcher less than a year before – that the club did not need £2 million and that £1 million would be sufficient.

After his retirement from the meat firm, Louis Edwards was able to devote himself almost entirely to Manchester United – apart from his four-days-a-month consultancy for Gulliver, of course! He would now come into Old Trafford most mornings. Here was the opportunity to concentrate on achieving his ambition of building up an income from United's commercial activities that would at least match the club's turnstile receipts. Louis Edwards wanted to step up the process of turning the Manchester United magic into money, profit and dividends.

But during the course of 1979, Louis Charles Edwards' past quickly caught up with him. On 28 January 1980, Granada Television's *World in Action* broadcast a programme called *The Man Who Bought United*. It was the result of sixteen months' meticulous investigation by a research team which included Paul Greengrass, the journalist who was recently the ghost-writer of Peter Wright's controversial book, *Spycatcher*.

Granada's half-hour report explained how Louis Edwards had quietly acquired his majority shareholding in United in the early '60s, and then bolstered his family's holding in the late '70s in preparation for the rights issue. The broadcast included a secret recording of a telephone conversation in which Louis Edwards told Beryl Norman's son that she committed only a 'technical offence' by not paying capital gains tax on the profit on her shares.

The programme also provided details of how, over many years, Edwards had used bribes to secure and maintain his company's meat contracts. Thomas O'Hora gave details on camera of the corruption that had been carried out, while Granada had evidence from numerous other Edwards employees to back the claims. *World in Action* also showed how, over many years, Manchester United had used similar inducements to parents to get their teenage sons to sign for the club. A cash reserve had been built up for such payments in a secret 'No. 2 account'. Brian Greenhoff was one of the players the account had been used to acquire.

For well over a year both Louis Edwards and Manchester United had been fully aware of what Granada were investigating. The club consulted a solicitor, John Gorna, who contacted Granada about the planned broadcast. Later United went to see George Carman, the clever Manchester QC who had helped get Jeremy Thorpe acquitted of attempted murder only a few months earlier.

Once the programme was broadcast, Louis Edwards' solicitors advised against suing Granada. The United chairman should let the wind blow over it, they argued. And no legal action was ever taken. Granada's evidence was rock solid and had been examined by one of the most formidable firms of solicitors in the land, Goodman, Derrick and Co. – Lord Goodman's practice.

The Inland Revenue began asking questions about United's hidden 'No. 2 account'. The Manchester police started investigations too. Both enquiries lasted no more than a few weeks.

While having a bath at his home in Alderley Edge, Louis Edwards had a fatal heart attack. It was almost exactly four weeks to the hour since the *World In Action* broadcast.

'Let's not kid ourselves,' said Martin Edwards at the news. 'This is what brought about his premature death. What Granada did was a complete character assassination. I have never seen anyone deteriorate so quickly.'

Louis' brother, Douglas Edwards, said he was less certain that the programme was the reason. Louis Edwards had a history of cardiac disease and had been badly overweight. Indeed, members of the United staff could tell of embarrassing situations in which he had collapsed.

ABOVE Sir Matt Busby announces his retirement in January 1969. It was three months before his successor, Wilf McGuinness, was named. (*Manchester Evening News*)

BELOW Wilf McGuinness (third from right) meets the players for their first training session under his command, but Busby remained in the background as general manager. (*Syndication International Ltd.*)

ABOVE Wilf McGuinness, Ian Ure, Jimmy Murphy and Sir Matt Busby, after Ure had been signed from Arsenal for £80,000 in 1969. It was Busby's initiative to sign the Arsenal centre-half, one of only two players bought by United between 1967 and 1972. (*London Express News Service*)

BELOW Sir Matt Busby introduces Frank O'Farrell and his wife, Ann, to Old Trafford. It was on this occasion that the men first clashed – over who should occupy which office. (*Syndication International Ltd.*)

RIGHT This photograph from the official club Christmas card of 1969 showed George Best, European Footballer of the Year, receiving his award from Sir Matt Busby C.B.E. and former holders of the award, Bobby Charlton and Denis Law. (*Manchester Evening News*)

ABOVE George Best scores at Newcastle United in October 1971. Before the game the IRA had threatened to kill him, and his brilliant form for United that season was rarely the same thereafter. (*Syndication International Ltd.*)

RIGHT No, he hadn't. Best made two comebacks for United, and several more with a stream of other clubs. (*Syndication International Ltd.*)

ABOVE Steve Coppell and Gordon Hill have Tommy Docherty firmly in their sights. A number of other United players would have jumped at the opportunity. (*County Press*)

BELOW Denis Law (second from right) scores the goal for Manchester City in April 1974 that confirmed United's relegation to division two (*Manchester Evening News*)

RIGHT Exactly a year later United paraded with the second division championship trophy, though judging by their expressions it looked as if they had been relegated again! Lou Macari (fourth from left) felt the celebration, for a club of United's standing, was a big embarrassment. (*Manchester Evening News*)

LEFT Lou Macari celebrates after his shot hit Jimmy Greenhoff and led to the winning goal against Liverpool in the 1977 FA Cup final. (*Manchester Evening News*)

RIGHT Tommy Docherty and his team run round Wembley after beating Liverpool 2–1 in the 1977 FA Cup final. The players never got the £5,000 Docherty had promised them for winning the trophy. (*Syndication International Ltd.*)

LEFT Three weeks later Docherty announced he was setting up home with Mary Brown, wife of the United physiotherapist, Laurie Brown. This gave the United board a good reason to sack Docherty. (*Syndication International Ltd.*)

BELOW Barry Fry, Willie Morgan and Pat Crerand celebrate outside the Law Courts after the collapse of Tommy Docherty's libel action against Morgan in November 1978. Fry and Crerand would have testified in support of Morgan's allegation that Docherty received £1,000 after allowing George Best to play for Dunstable. (*Mail Newspapers p.l.c.*)

ABOVE Some of the estimated 300,000 who welcomed United back to Manchester *without* the FA Cup, after the dramatic 1979 FA Cup final. (*Manchester Evening News*)

RIGHT Ray Wilkins joined Dave Sexton at United in August 1979 – his £700,000 fee accounted for most of the £1 million raised by the 1978 rights issue. (*Syndication International Ltd.*)

LEFT Dave Sexton signs Garry Birtles for £1,250,000 in October 1980. It took Birtles thirty games and eleven months to score his first league goal. After two years he returned to Nottingham Forest for £275,000, just one of several strikers who have failed after moving to Old Trafford. (*Syndication International Ltd.*)

BELOW Bryan Robson became Britain's costliest player when Ron Atkinson bought him for £1.5 million in 1981. Despite regular absences through injury he has probably been the most successful of all Atkinson's signings. (*Manchester Evening News*)

7 WE'LL SUPPORT YOU EVERMORE

' "Manchester United" stands for something more than any person, any player, any supporter. It is the "soul" of a sporting organisation which goes on season after season, making history all the time.'

United Review, August 1937.

THE CONCOURSE of Euston station is remarkably busy around ten o'clock on winter Saturday mornings. The crowds are swelled by hundreds of London football supporters following their teams around the country. Spurs may be playing in Liverpool. Charlton might be at Coventry and second-division Chelsea travelling to Stoke. But often the biggest contingent, meeting friends, selling lottery tickets to each other, stocking up with sandwiches, waiting for the 10.20 departure, are the Cockney reds embarking on their fortnightly pilgrimage to Manchester. The journey has become routine by now. The same transport police travel with them to avoid clashes with any rival supporters, and if the trains run on time, the Cockney reds should be back in town by 8.40 that evening. Indeed, until the early '80s so many London United supporters used to go to Old Trafford by train that British Rail arranged special services. Not many London clubs need special trains when they play in Manchester.

By the time the 10.20 is whistling through Bletchley, a coach has already set off from Holyhead with a party of fifty or so Irish supporters who sailed across the previous evening by ferry from Dun Laoghaire. The trip costs each of the Irish reds 49 Irish punts (about £40), and includes bed and breakfast in Holyhead. These are just some of the dozens, sometimes hundreds, of Irish United fans who go to matches at Old Trafford. Some spend £31 on a ticket for the longer ten-hour overnight ferry from Dublin to Liverpool; others begin as far away as Cork or Limerick.

A party from Belfast often takes the 8.10 a.m. British Airways flight to Manchester, stays in a hotel in West Didsbury and does not return home until Sunday or Monday. Other Irish fans travel north to Larne for the short crossing to Stranraer and stop off for breakfast in the Lake District on the way. Yet more come on trips organised by agencies such as Tara Travel, run by the former Manchester City player Dave Bacuzzi in Dublin, or by International Sports Travel in Manchester, a firm jointly owned by Norman Whiteside and Pat Crerand.

Meanwhile, on the motorways leading to Manchester – the M1, M5, M6, M56, M61, M62 and M63 – coaches are bringing yet more fanatical supporters from all points of the compass. Parties set off at 7.00 a.m. from Torbay in Devon and from Colchester in Essex, others at 8.00 a.m. from Glyncorrwg in South Wales and from Epsom in Surrey. More supporters leave at 8.15 a.m. from Witney in Oxfordshire, at 9.00 a.m. from Carlisle and at 10.00 a.m. from Leamington Spa and Birmingham. Some will not get back until after midnight. And throughout the morning planes landing at Manchester Airport bring small groups of fans from all over Europe – Scandinavia, Holland, Malta and Austria.

No other club in Britain can boast such consistent and world-wide support as Manchester United. When Celtic and Rangers play in England they bring tens of thousands of supporters south of the border, yet often in the past these same supporters might not bother to attend the next home game in Glasgow against, say, St Mirren. When Sunderland or Newcastle get to the Cup final, tens of thousands of Wearsiders and Geordies may rediscover their red and white or black and white scarves, and the words of 'Ha'way the Lads' or 'Blaydon Races'. Anfield and Goodison may overflow when Liverpool and Everton battle with each other, or against United or a top European side, but no club in Britain can boast a following that has been as consistent, as faithful and as widely based, through good times and through bad, home and away, week in and week out, year after year.

During the season of 1967–68, in which Manchester United won the European Cup, more than three million people watched the reds at home and away. The average home attendance figure was a remarkable 57,759 – a record in English football history. At thirteen home games that season – nine in the league – more than 60,000 were packed inside the ground. Only once did a home game attract fewer than 50,000. It is a record that Manchester United are likely to retain for many years, if not forever: no club ground in England now has the capacity to house 57,000. Even Old Trafford is restricted to 56,339 these days.

It seems strange, therefore, that the present Manchester United Supporters' Club was not formed until after United won the European Cup in 1968. The explanation lies in the troubled history of relations between the club and fans who have tried to organise into a representative body over many years. The first recorded supporters' club was formed around the mid-1920s, with a local taxi owner called Greenhough as the main driving force. It was an era when even top football clubs depended on supporters to help with refreshment huts, ground maintenance and, in some cases, money, raised from supporters' social events and raffles.

Greenhough's attempted boycott of Old Trafford after the atrocious string of results in 1930 contributed to the suspicion which has often existed between football clubs and their supporters' organisations. The delicate state of the relationship at clubs in general eventually led to the FA rule: 'It must be realised that there is no official link between a Supporters' Club and a Football Club – they are two distinct clubs.'

By the time of Matt Busby's arrival at Manchester United in 1945, the club founded by Greenhough had collapsed through inactivity and there seemed little interest in forming a new one. And until the Busby Babes era in the mid-1950s, Manchester United were no better supported than many other big city clubs. Indeed, in the decade after the war when football as a whole was booming, United's average home crowds were often lower than today. The season 1947–48, the year United won the FA Cup, was exceptional, with an average home gate of 54,890, but in subsequent seasons attendances dropped rapidly.

In the early 1950s crowds of 40,000 or more were not unusual at most first-division grounds. Several clubs could regularly boast more support than United – Sunderland and Newcastle in the North-east; the two Merseyside clubs; Wolverhampton Wanderers in the Midlands; Arsenal, Chelsea and Spurs in London. Even Cardiff City, West Bromwich Albion and Sheffield Wednesday attracted better crowds than United in one or two years during that period. In the 1953–54 season United's average home gate of 33,637 was actually below the first-division average, and in 1954–55 even Manchester City were better supported at home than United. Throughout most of Busby's first decade, from 1946 to 1956, the crowds United attracted to away grounds were barely better than clubs welcomed for most visiting teams.

The transformation came after the Busby Babes' first league championship in 1956. Everywhere fans flocked to see United in unusual numbers. At Old Trafford gates were roughly 50 per cent higher than the rest of the first division, while at away venues United increased normal attendances by 30 or 40 per cent – an extra 10,000– 15,000 spectators at each game.

The greater enthusiasm led naturally to the formation of a new supporters' club. Its headquarters were in Collyhurst, not far from United's roots in Newton Heath. But the club did not receive much encouragement from Old Trafford in the two years before Munich. The Manchester United secretary, Walter Crickmer, had witnessed the rebellion in the 1930s of the Greenhough organisation and kept the new group at arm's length. It was only after Crickmer's death at Munich that more encouragement was shown. At Christmas in 1958 Bobby Charlton, Dennis Viollet, Wilf McGuinness and Gordon Clayton acted as judges when the supporters' club held a Miss Manchester United contest at Chorlton Palais.

By 1963, the supporters' club needed new premises because of redevelopment in Collyhurst. There were also rumblings within some local branches that United should recognise the club as an official body. The dissidents were actually expelled for making these protests, to the long-term detriment of the supporters' club. New headquarters were found in the basement of Ralli Buildings, off Deansgate in the city centre, and a social centre was established with a loan from a local brewery. But it was too far from Old Trafford and not enough fans used it. In 1966 the organisation folded, with outstanding debts of about £5,000.

It seems odd that the club should collapse in the mid-1960s, the halcyon days of Manchester United, when support for the team had never been greater. Never had one English football club boasted three such entertaining world-class players as George Best, Denis Law and Bobby Charlton. This exciting line-up, and the new silverware that the side were collecting, brought crowds back after attendances had fallen in the immediate post-Munich era to around 33,000 again. People would go out of their way to see any one of the trio of Best, Law and Charlton. In 287 competitive games between 1963 and 1973 United presented all three for the price of one. Analysis of attendance figures for away matches during the decade the three world stars played together shows United's remarkable drawing power (see

Appendix A, page 227). The team would add between a third and a half to normal gates, and the official figures would have been higher still if many thousands had not regularly been locked out.

It was often said that George Best alone put several thousand on the gate, and figures up to 12,000 were cited. In fact, the Best factor was probably overemphasised. When the Irishman was suspended in 1970, 41,000 still flocked to watch United at West Ham and 60,000 saw the reds at home to both Derby and Leeds. Again, when Best was dropped in 1971, Chelsea still attracted 53,000 for United's visit.

During this period Manchester United could also guarantee to score eighty or ninety league goals a season at a time when scoring seemed a dying art. Denis Law, David Herd, George Best and Bobby Charlton enjoyed regular hat-tricks, and spectacular goals. Yet United were also extremely unpredictable. While locals might expect a magnificent display from the visiting reds, they might also see the local home team humble the mighty Manchester United. Such uncertainty only added to the aura that surrounded the club. United's pulling-power at away grounds has rarely been the same since 1973, when Best, Law and Charlton all left within eight months of each other.

Outside Manchester, it was in London that the public's love affair with United was most passionate. In the late '50s, '60s and '70s there seemed almost as much support for United in the capital as for the top London sides. From the days of the Busby Babes, Manchester United have given many of their best performances on London grounds. In 1954, 56,000 at Stamford Bridge watched the emerging Babes side, with Roger Byrne, Tommy Taylor and Duncan Edwards, beat that season's champions, Chelsea, by the extraordinary score of 6–5. A crowd of 63,000 at Highbury on 1 February 1958 saw Arsenal beaten 5–4 by the Babes in their historic last appearance in Britain, five days before Munich. The post-Munich reds won 6–3 at Chelsea in 1959. Other big London victories were 5–1 at Charlton in 1957, 5–3 over Fulham in the 1958 Cup semi-final replay at Highbury, 5–0 at Fulham in 1960, and 5–3 at Crystal Palace in 1971.

In 1967 London was the stage when United clinched the league title with the famous 6–1 victory at Upton Park; and the 1968 European Cup triumph, of course, was at Wembley. On other occasions United might produce more normal scorelines, but fabulous matches. No wonder that Arsenal, Spurs, Chelsea and West Ham would often secure their biggest crowds of the season for visits by 'Man U', as Londoners called the team, rather than for London derby matches. Geoffrey Green points out that in 1959–60, for instance, the league's biggest crowd, 66,579, was recorded for United's 6–3 win at Chelsea. The second biggest league crowd anywhere that season, 62,602, saw United at Spurs. Even in the dismal 1972–73 season, when United were almost relegated, seats for the final game of the season, at Chelsea, were sold out four months earlier, just before Christmas.

In the mid-1960s London boasted one of the biggest United supporters' club branches, with more than 3,000 members. When the Manchester headquarters folded in 1966, the London and district affiliate quite understandably dissociated themselves from what had happened. Old Trafford officials encouraged the London club to continue on their own, and for a year or two London became the unofficial headquarters of the Manchester United supporters' movement. There arose the extraordinary state of affairs whereby applications to Old Trafford for details of how to join the supporters' club were referred to an address 180 miles away.

After the fall of the main Manchester body in 1966, two small groups – the Association of Manchester United Supporters that met at the Manchester Arms Hotel in Millgate by the side of Victoria station, and the Manchester United Social Club based at the Bay Horse, a pub on Thomas Street a few hundred yards away – continued to organise sports, social events and travel to matches. The minutes of a meeting of the Association in September 1968 report, for example, details of a trip to Sunderland costing £1 per person and with a return time of midnight so that members could be entertained by Sunderland supporters in the Black Cat social club at Roker Park. It was obvious that by combining forces the two pub groups could form the nucleus of a new supporters' club in Manchester. Agreement to merge came in October 1968.

On 18 November 1968, six months after the European Cup win, the inaugural meeting of the new club took place at the Seven Oaks Hotel in Nicholas Street, Manchester. The new organisation had to call itself the Manchester United Supporters Association (MUSA) – the word 'club' was avoided so as not to become liable for the debts of the defunct organisation. The force behind the amalgamation, and the club's first chairman, was Roy Priestley, a fan who had moved to Manchester from Suffolk. The new committee, comprising members of both bodies, included Anne Gilliland, Michael Goldstone and David Smith – each of whom remained involved until Martin Edwards announced twenty years later that the organisation was 'surplus to requirements'.

It was another three years before MUSA made much progress,

however. Developing good relations with United officials proved difficult, largely because of previous misfortunes, and in particular the financial embarrassment from the winding up of the recent Ralli Buildings group. It did not help that one of MUSA's aims was 'to provide supporters of Manchester United with the one facility they are lacking – a social club', for this was the very problem that had caused the previous organisation to fold. Negotiations were already under way with Vaux Breweries about sponsoring the facilities.

Manchester United were quite happy to continue dealing with the London and District club and the half-dozen or so other local bodies then in existence. The London organisation was keen to remain the 'recognised' headquarters and their secretary even wrote to United objecting to the formation of the new Manchester club. During the 1970–71 season, however, the new supporters' association established itself as a serious organisation, and relations with the football club slowly improved. In September 1971 Les Olive wrote to Anne Smith (*née* Gilliland) to say that he needed more marshals at the ground on match days and asked her to 'recommend a dozen of your members who may be interested in coming along and assisting in this way'. It was a small but significant request – a sign that Old Trafford was impressed at the way the new club was run.

Six months before, the supporters' club had sent a petition to the FA about the annual problem of Cup final tickets. The petition was strengthened by the fact that United had already been knocked out of the FA Cup that year: the request for more tickets for supporters of the finalists could not be seen as self-interest. MUSA also had new premises for match days – the 'Red Room' at the Dog and Partridge Hotel on Chester Road, a few minutes' walk from Old Trafford. This became the focal point of the club's growing activities. As well as weekly social events in their new headquarters, two dances were arranged every year at Belle Vue. The Miss Manchester United contest was resurrected and a Player of the Year award began. Denis Law agreed to be club president.

Club newsletters, published almost from the start of the new organisation, developed from duplicated sheets to a more professional quality. August 1972 saw the first *Manchester United Supporters' Yearbook*. By now the organisation felt legally able to call itself the Manchester United Supporters' Club.

The new club had emerged while United fans were gaining a reputation for being among the most violent in Britain. Against AC Milan in the 1969 European Cup semi-final, a piece of brick was thrown from the Stretford End. It knocked out the Italian goalkeeper, held play up for five minutes and possibly put United out of their stride when they seemed to be getting on top. In 1971 a knife was thrown on to the pitch in a home game against Newcastle. As punishment United had to play their first two home games the following season at neutral grounds, and part of the Stretford End was closed.

In the mid-1960s gangs of United fans had often attacked programme sellers at away grounds – the programme covers were accepted for applications for Cup tickets. Soon the violence and vandalism became widespread. Train seats were carved up and windows of shops and houses smashed as United followers went on the rampage at away matches. Cars would be overturned, shops looted and battles fought in the streets with opposing fans. The police could not cope, and the violence was often so extensive that serious incidents outside grounds, away from the press, sometimes went unreported.

The supporters' club, therefore, might have appeared rather unwise in starting its own excursions to away matches. But the move helped the club show its organisational skills and greatly increased membership. The trips began on a small scale when, for United's final match of the 1972–73 season at Chelsea, Anne Smith hired a carriage from British Rail on an ordinary train to London and thirty-one members bought tickets. That summer, BR asked if the club would be interested in organising the notorious 'football specials' they already ran for United fans. It was a daunting prospect: in two seasons £50,000 of damage had been done to railway property by United followers. The challenge was accepted. The club hired its own trains and insisted on complete control over tickets, stewarding and refreshments.

The first supporters' club 'special' left Piccadilly station at 8.30 a.m. on Saturday, 8 September 1973, bound for Ipswich. David Smith recalls it as a 'hairy occasion, a journey into the unknown'. Long-standing club members were appointed stewards, and Smith spent £150 on two bouncers who normally worked at a Manchester nightclub.

The 'special' completed its 500-mile round trip without trouble. Smith insisted that only members could use the trains, and as a result the club gained thousands of recruits and large profits. And there was little hooliganism on the trips. British Rail agreed to overlook minor incidents, such as stolen light bulbs, and the damage bill over two years was just £70. Meanwhile, the travel arrangements got so hectic that David Smith, who was by now club chairman, gave up his job as a milkman to work full-time. Smith received no regular salary, just the profits from the travel, which in 1974–75 were £4,509.

The supporters' organisation was now on excellent terms with Old Trafford. In 1974, after Smith had lobbied both Sir Matt Busby and Louis Edwards, he was given an office at Old Trafford free of charge at the back of K stand in order to sell rail and coach tickets. The club also got a free half-page in every match programme. United players and directors became regular visitors at supporters' gatherings.

Tommy Docherty's period at Old Trafford saw the second great surge in United support, even though the club no longer boasted stars of the Best-Law-Charlton calibre. Regular crowds of more than 50,000 at Old Trafford appeared at a most unexpected time – after United's drop to division two. The average home gate of 48,388 was more than any first-division side enjoyed, while a United visit doubled most clubs' normal crowds.

If anything, though, the fans' violence grew worse in division two. Many towns were not ready for the great United invasions. In the first match at Orient, Sir Matt Busby had to appeal to the fighting fans over the loud-speakers, while glass was thrown into the Orient goalmouth. Tommy Docherty even banned his eighteen-year-old son from away games because of the danger.

In 1975 the supporters' club abandoned its highly successful rail travel. The problem was that railway stations became the focus for opposing fans preparing an ambush, and the streets between the station and the ground were often a chance for further trouble. The 3-mile walk to the grounds at Liverpool, Everton and Leeds always caused problems, while the route along the river at Norwich saw cars pushed into the water. Instead the club organised coaches for away matches. They could drop United fans much closer to each ground and so avoid most opposition supporters.

Club membership rose to a peak of 22,500 during Tommy Docherty's time, and there was a profit of £9,912 in 1976, but it was difficult to know how to spend it. An offer to donate the surplus to United was turned down. So too were plans to pay for a clock inside the ground, and a platform for wheelchair fans. The fear seemed to be that it might place United under an obligation to the supporters' club, although that was not the intention. Instead the money went towards better club publications, and membership fees remained unaltered despite high inflation.

Even with supervised travel, however, the violence at grounds and in surrounding streets continued, and a match at Norwich in April 1977 led to action by the Government. United fans attacked the home crowd and destroyed part of the stand, and it was recorded by television cameras. The sports minister Dennis Howell decided that the only option was to prohibit United fans from attending away games.

Court reports showed that much of the trouble was caused by United followers from outside Manchester. To tackle this David Smith had been developing supporters' branches nationwide. Well-organised cheap coach travel from around the country, he thought, would reduce the numbers who travelled independently. These followers often arrived at venues early and spent the time before matches in local pubs. In the mid-1970s drink was a major cause of football hooliganism, though nowadays football violence is more organised and it seems that many hooligans regard drink as an impairment to fighting.

David Smith would often denounce the trouble-makers in the press and on radio and television. He was regularly consulted by sports minister Dennis Howell, and when Howell imposed his all-ticket restriction, Smith refused to organise coach trips to away matches even though it drastically affected his personal income. He also insisted that club branches should not organise travel either. Individual supporters still travelled to away matches in the hope of gaining admission, but the numbers were greatly reduced, making it far easier for police to control them.

Further violence during a European Cup-Winners Cup tie at St Etienne in France in 1977 initially saw United expelled from the contest. David Smith helped them appeal against the decision by collating a detailed report of the travel arrangements and first-hand accounts from United fans. UEFA's reprieve involved United playing the home leg well away from Manchester, in Plymouth.

After fierce fighting at Valencia in Spain during a UEFA Cup game in 1982, the supporters' club imposed its own ban on overseas travel. David Smith took the decision on the way back from Valencia's stadium to the airport. The previously promised police escort was refused and the United coaches were attacked by Spanish fans. Windows were smashed on every coach, supporters were cut by flying glass and two ended up in hospital. It was a difficult decision for Smith since it meant a further loss of income. He felt the possibility of having to tell parents that their sons or daughters had been seriously injured far outweighed any personal financial loss.

By the early 1980s, Smith was increasingly involved in other activities at Old Trafford. He supplied nearly all the photos for the *United Review*; he collated the programme's statistical records and proof-read all copy. This work, along with producing the supporters' club's own publications, demanded long hours. He often worked until midnight seven days a week.

The supporters' club finally found a way of contributing towards the football club by buying the photographic equipment and materials Smith needed for his work for the United programme, and paid for a darkroom extension to the club office. At one stage United even considered bringing the club in house. The idea, which might have meant Smith's becoming a United employee, was even discussed by the board. However, Denzil Haroun, a director who took a friendly interest in supporters' club affairs, advised against this idea. He argued that such a move would deprive United of invaluable political support from an independent body. Moreover, Haroun told Smith privately that the supporters' club was not seen as a viable commercial enterprise by the board, which had been one of the main reasons the idea was considered at all.

Through his involvement with the National Federation of Football Supporters' Clubs, Smith found many fans complaining that their organisations were being eroded by a new breed of football club employee – the commercial manager. Not having experienced this problem himself, and having had only cooperation from Bill Burke at Old Trafford, Smith argued vehemently that supporters' clubs should work closely with the commercial departments of the football teams they supported. In the years ahead, however, he was to discover at Old Trafford that the fears of federation members had been fully justified. The first sign came on the day United played Liverpool in the 1983 Milk Cup final. The Wembley programme contained a full-page advertisement encouraging people to join an 'Official Manchester United Fan Club'. This new body had been set up by a company named Scanlite. Scanlite had already started a similar fan club for Liverpool and had reached an agreement with United officials to do the same at Old Trafford. United were promised large royalty payments.

Remarkably, the Milk Cup programme was the first Smith knew of the fan club. Smith challenged the new United commercial manager, John Lillie, about it the following week. Although sympathetic, Lillie explained that Scanlite had made an offer United could not refuse and suggested that Smith contact the firm to see if the supporters' club could be linked with it in some way. Smith was furious at how the deal had been agreed by United behind his back – especially in view of the board's previous refusal to accept money from his own organisation. It was a sign of the new commercial spirit that was prevailing at the club. And there was little doubt that his own club's membership would be hit by the new group. Meeting the Scanlite organisers only increased Smith's fears. It was also obvious that the fan club's membership fee of £2.99 could not cover its costs. The supporters' club had to decide whether to boycott the venture or become involved.

A boycott would have put Smith in conflict with the football club. He decided that the only option was a degree of cooperation between the supporters' club and Scanlite's fan club, partly to ensure some control, and in the hope that fans would not be cheated. It was agreed the supporters' club would contribute articles and photos for fan club magazines, and process membership applications. Smith wrote to United explaining that the subscription fee for his own organisation would be cut, and in future his members would receive only an annual yearbook. But supporters' club members could join the new fan club at a special reduced rate of £2. Smith also told United that because of the financial effect of the new body, the supporters' club could no longer afford to pay the costs of providing photos for the *United Review*. United therefore agreed to pay all film and processing charges in future.

The supporters' club restructured its work to fit in with the commercial fan club operation. But it was not long before problems arose. The printers of the first fan club magazine had not been paid and the work was swiftly switched to another company. Fan club membership cards were proving difficult. A computer system embossed names on to cards that were similar to credit cards. In theory the idea was good; in practice it was disastrous. A backlog of applications built up and the computer regularly broke down. Many applications were made by parents for their children, but the names embossed on the fan club cards were taken from the cheques with the result that hundreds of cards were incorrectly labelled and had to be altered.

By the time the fourth fan club magazine came out in January 1984, the creditors were already at Scanlite's door. The Post Office, the printers, the computer company and other suppliers were all owed large sums of money. United too claimed that they had not received royalty payments. The only people not to have lost money were the supporters' club. Because of his suspicions David Smith had deducted the sums his club was owed for contributions to the fan club magazine from money received with membership applications at the office.

Meanwhile, problems were arising over David Smith's photography for United and John Lillie was questioning the costs. At one point United's lawyers even drew up a draft agreement which would have resolved the matter by making Smith the official club photographer. It was never offered to him. The problems were soon reconciled, but because of the uncertain future of the supporters' club, Smith would undoubtedly have signed the contract.

In January 1984 the fan club finally folded when Scanlite went into liquidation with estimated debts of £1 million. In spite of its poor administration, the fan club's basic strategy had been reasonably sound. Thousands of United fans had applied to join and the publications were good. Smith decided that thereafter the supporters' club would provide equally attractive colour magazines and subscriptions were increased to cover costs. Although his membership was now down to roughly 11,000, the new plan proved reasonably successful.

But relations between David Smith, his supporters' club and United never really recovered from the Scanlite affair. They grew worse in 1986 when Smith tried to defend a friend, Tony Woodward, who was wrongly accused of fraud in the United Development Association. There are those still employed at Old Trafford who are convinced that Smith's involvement in the Woodward affair, and his knowledge of irregular practices within the Development Association, had a bearing on Martin Edwards' eventual decision to tell him in March 1987 that, with the introduction of United's in-house membership scheme, he and his club were no longer wanted.

David Smith felt that his supporters' club was being sacrificed purely so that United could make money from their fans. He had expected that United followers would be charged only a small administrative fee for their ID cards, or perhaps nothing at all. The supporters' chairman was not in principle opposed to an identity card scheme, but the £5 charge, and the fact that internal club documents showed that United expected to make a profit on each member, persuaded him against it. He felt it would be wrong, and indeed a betrayal of United supporters, to provide United with either the goodwill or the membership lists that Martin Edwards was asking for.

Edwards denied at a press conference that the new membership scheme was a money-making exercise. The United chairman referred to the fact that, in the fight against hooliganism, the Government and the football authorities were asking all clubs to introduce membership schemes for specific areas of their grounds by the beginning of the 1987–88 season. Edwards admitted that up to eighty of the ninety-two league clubs might not comply with the recommendations, but he felt it was in football's interests that Manchester United be seen to support the plans. This was despite the fact that Old Trafford had long been one of the safest grounds in the country. Only two months earlier, United had been distributing a pre-printed condemnation of identity-card systems to supporters who asked about the club's position on the matter.

Rejecting Martin Edwards' offer of £15,000 compensation, David Smith decided that he would continue running his Manchester United Supporters' Club even if it meant that the club no longer enjoyed any assistance from Old Trafford. Enrollment, of course, was bound to suffer from the existence of United's own membership operation. But he was determined to continue publishing club newsletters and a yearbook, and to carry on running coaches to away matches, the activities that had built such a successful supporters' organisation in the 1970s.

Thanks in some part to the supporters' club's work over the previous twenty years, the burden United once carried of the most violent supporters in football had by the mid-1980s passed to other clubs. Leeds United, Millwall, Chelsea and West Ham are much more likely to be involved in violence, though there are still occasional outbreaks of trouble when United play away. There have been few problems at Old Trafford for more than a decade, mainly because of the segregation of opposing fans and advanced policing methods. Old Trafford saw the Manchester police using high powered binoculars to watch the crowd nearly twenty years ago. If there is any ground where a membership scheme is least needed, it must be Old Trafford. During the early months of the 1987-88 season it was publicly acknowledged by United that the new scheme had lost them around £80,000 in reduced attendances. And David Smith is not alone in believing that the £5 United scheme is only the most blatant example of the way in which the present administration at Old Trafford is gradually trying to turn United's fanatical support into hard cash – to convert the red magic into money.

In generating United's fanatical support, and casting the club's magic spell, the winning of trophies seems to have been less important over the decades than the nature of the teams that have worn the red and white shirts. Three FA Cup triumphs since 1968, coupled with relegation in 1974, cannot account for the sustained levels of fanaticism enjoyed over the last twenty years. Relative to football as a whole, United's support in the mid-1980s was higher than ever (see the graph on page 227). In the 1986-87 season there were twenty-two first-division grounds, but one in nine spectators who went to a first-division match that season went to Old Trafford.

The great surges in United support have occurred when the club has boasted attacking skilful teams – the Busby Babes; the 1960s team of Best, Law and Charlton; Docherty's two-winger side of the mid-1970s; and Ron Atkinson's cup-winners of the mid-1980s. While the last two teams never won the league title, they often led the first division or were in a challenging position for much of each season.

Not even United's reputation for entertaining football over the years can provide the whole answer. Tommy Docherty's 1972-74 relegation side played very unattractive, physically aggressive football in which goals and victories were rare. Sexton's team in the year before he left was extremely dull, yet during both periods United boasted the strongest following in the league. To some extent fans may still have been going out of habit, in expectation of seeing the United that had once been. In Docherty's case the fight against relegation itself seemed to generate interest, and it is interesting that the most popular player of that era was a tough defender, Jim Holton. Yet part of the explanation has to be less tangible – the aura, the charisma, the magic and the tradition of the club.

The magic casts its spell too over those who have worn United's red shirts. For many players United was just one club in a long football career, and after leaving Old Trafford they went to clubs in other parts of the country. But in retirement many ex-players find themselves attracted back to the North-west and make the area their home. Glasgow-born Pat Crerand became landlord of a pub, The Park, in Altrincham. Tony Dunne, who came to Manchester from Ireland, runs a golf driving range in the same town. David Sadler still lives in Hale and until December 1988 was managing a building society branch in Liverpool. Another Scot, Denis Law, lives in Bowdon and combines his job as a sales representative at a local printing company with regular football commentary work for the BBC. Martin Buchan works for Puma sportswear in Manchester and lives in Wilmslow. Even Tommy Docherty, the manager sacked in disgrace in 1977, cannot get away from Manchester and acknowledges his time at United as the peak of his stormy career. He finally married Mary Brown in May 1988 and they live with their children in Charlesworth on the edge of Derbyshire.

In 1985 several ex-United players got together to form the Association of Former Manchester United Players, the only known organisation of its kind with the exception of the Ex-Clarets at Burnley. They meet together regularly for social occasions and to raise money for charity. Though few former players go regularly to matches, they still consider themselves United fans. It is hard for anyone to escape the Manchester United magic.

8   THE BUTCHER'S BOY

'All the money is ploughed back into the football club.'

Martin Edwards, 1988.

THE QUESTION of who would succeed Louis Edwards as chairman after his death in 1980 looked simple to outsiders – it was a choice between Sir Matt Busby, the man who had effectively built Manchester United, and Martin Edwards, whose family had bought it.

In fact, there was no contest. Those close to Sir Matt, like Pat Crerand and the former nightclub owner Paddy McGrath, urged him to go for it. But Busby was now highly disillusioned. His rebuffed attempts to get Sandy Busby on to the board, the rights issue and the election of James Gulliver had shown that the Edwards family now intended to run Manchester United as their new family business. The former United manager had spoken at Louis Edwards' funeral service, but relations between the two families were now extremely strained. Even if Busby still harboured any ambitions to be the United chairman, he knew it was beyond his reach anyway. He might have had the fans and the sentiment on his side, but if it came to the crunch Martin Edwards had the shares behind him.

The directors met to make their choice on the morning of Saturday, 22 March 1980, before United's home league match against Manchester City. It was an unusual time for a board meeting, but the best way of ensuring that James Gulliver could pull himself away from his other hectic business affairs. When they reached the election of a new chairman, Sir Matt informed his fellow directors that he did not wish to be considered. The vice-chairman, Alan Gibson, said the same thing. Gibson then proposed that Martin Edwards be elected chairman. There were no other nominations. Bill Young then suggested that Sir Matt Busby be elected to the position of club president and remain a member of the board. The directors readily agreed, though the position had been vacant since the death of James Gibson in 1951.

137

At thirty-four, Charles Martin Edwards was, after Elton John at Watford, the second youngest chairman in the Football League. So young, in fact, that on 24 July 1945, the day he was born, at Adlington near Macclesfield in Cheshire, five months had already passed since Matt Busby had accepted the manager's job at Old Trafford. Today Martin Edwards proudly takes out of the bookcase in his office the programme for a match against Wolves in March 1952, six weeks before Busby won his first league championship. Edwards was just six years old at the time and it was the first occasion on which his father and mother had brought him to Old Trafford. In those days Louis and Muriel Edwards would sometimes watch from the directors' box as guests of their friend, Matt Busby.

Such visits were largely confined to the holidays when the following year Martin was sent to Terra Nova, a preparatory school near the Jodrell Bank telescope at Holmes Chapel in Cheshire. The Edwards' eldest child was not an outstanding pupil according to some of his teachers. The general view was that he was a diligent lad who showed plenty of effort, but he needed time to take in his work. At thirteen Edwards failed to achieve a good enough mark in the Common Entrance – the entrance exam for public schools – to get into his parents' first choice, Stowe in Buckinghamshire, one of Britain's most prestigious independent schools. Instead he had to settle for Cokethorpe, a far-from-distinguished private school of about 200 boys which had just opened in 46 acres of parkland near Witney in Oxfordshire. His former English teacher, Ron Lyle, remembers Edwards as 'an ordinary boy who was very keen on sport'. The young Edwards enjoyed playing rugby in the first XV, was captain of his house cricket team and played basketball. But for a man who would one day have to juggle with millions of pounds as chairman of Manchester United, he was slow at maths.

By the time he was eighteen and a half, Edwards had collected six 'O' levels – in British History, English Literature, Bible Knowledge, Economic and Public Affairs, Economics and English Language – though only after several unsuccessful sittings. He was not good enough to take 'A' levels or to go on to further or higher education. The nearest Martin Edwards got to university was a summer marketing course held at Emmanuel College, Cambridge, many years later.

He had no need to worry, however. A job awaited him back home in the family meat firm. Both Louis and Douglas Edwards had followed their father into the business he had founded, and in due course all their four sons were to follow them into the firm. The company house journal later reported how Martin Edwards began as a trainee in the summer of 1964, working initially as an assistant in Edwards shops and on meat counters around the North-west. Then he moved to head office in Miles Platting to work for the quality control and sales departments of the manufacturing division. After that he was in the sales office of the catering division.

Martin Edwards was then promoted to the post of assistant to the managing director, Arthur Peacock. In the summer of 1967, Peacock arranged for the twenty-one-year-old Edwards to act as a relief manager in various Edwards shops, including the store in King Street, Stretford, near Old Trafford, in order to understand meat finances on a small scale. This job was followed by appointments overseeing retail stores and working in the property division. In 1973, as part of the firm's reorganisation, Edwards achieved the position of retail/whole-sale controller.

After his return to Manchester, Martin Edwards had also begun playing rugby for Wilmslow, as a centre three-quarter. This regular commitment every Saturday meant that Manchester United had to come second. Trips with his mother and father to matches were now generally limited to midweek fixtures. Many United fans would give the world to sit regularly in the Old Trafford directors' box. Yet even after Louis Edwards had his son elected to the United board in March 1970, at the age of only twenty-four, Saturdays for Martin Edwards were still devoted to Wilmslow and his 'first love', rugby. According to Martin Edwards, his father had in fact suggested his election to the board in the hope that it would make him give up rugby. He had just suffered a serious concussion which required a lumbar puncture. When he was concussed a second time, in 1971, Wilmslow did indeed make way for Manchester United, though he still maintained a great affection for rugby.

Martin Edwards was not a very frequent attender of board meetings in his ten years as an ordinary United director. Business commitments and regular holidays caused him to miss more meetings than any other board member. He had no special responsibilities, nor, it seems, did he say much. He was less than half the age of any other director and it appears that he was mostly prepared to listen and watch. Martin Edwards' only notable contribution recorded in the minutes throughout most of the seventies came after United had just met Norwich City over two legs in the 1975 League Cup semi-final. He thought it was unfair that the gate receipts should have been divided equally between the two clubs when the attendance for the game at Old Trafford was almost twice as high as for the second leg at Carrow Road. The other directors said that the League would be unlikely to change their minds on the matter, but it was a sign of Edwards' thinking in years to come.

The junior United director clearly found that his position in the Old Trafford boardroom provided useful business contacts. In 1974 he explained to the Edwards company's house magazine how football had helped the firm win meat counter franchises in five Cee-N-Cee supermarkets in Manchester. 'As a director of Manchester United I have many friends in the world of football, including Mr Alex Humphreys, the managing director of Cee-N-Cee and a director of Stoke City,' he stated. Humphreys confirms the story. Again, it was indicative of the way Martin Edwards would operate in future.

In his new job of retail/wholesale controller in the family firm, Edwards helped close many of the firm's high-street stores in the mid-1970s as the business tried to turn itself round. On the other hand he developed what the company regarded as 'an entirely new concept in shopping' – fresh food markets, where people could buy not only meat but also dairy products, ground coffee, fruit and vegetables. But there is evidence that Martin Edwards did not entirely have his heart in the job as the company battled for survival. One colleague recalls him saying, round about 1976, how he would be quite happy to sell up, move to the south of France and do nothing. Another remembers that Louis Edwards was fairly contemptuous of both his sons' abilities.

Edwards still found an outlet in sport, though, and not just in watching it. Readers of his local newspaper, *Wilmslow World*, learnt how in 1976 and 1977 the United director triumphed in the Alderley Edge Cricket Club fun-day. Edwards achieved the highest combined score in nine events – the shot-putt, standing jumps, press-ups, squat thrusts, interval running, the 100 metres, shooting, throwing a medicine ball and welly chucking! On the first occasion, when he was only joint winner, Edwards had the honour of receiving his trophy from the former Manchester City winger Mike Summerbee. Edwards swam regularly too and played cricket, tennis and squash.

After the takeover of the family meat company by James Gulliver in 1978, Martin Edwards was kept on by the new owner and, unlike his father and uncle, retained his position on the board. But he resigned from his full-time job in April 1980 within a few weeks of his election as United chairman and received a golden handshake of £12,500. Gulliver also kept Edwards as a non-executive director, and paid him a consultancy fee of £5,000 a year. Edwards remained on the board of what shortly afterwards became Argyll Foods for three and a half years though now nearly all his time was spent on United.

So the new United chairman had no full-time income, though his consultancy money from Argyll was nevertheless far more than some clerical staff at Old Trafford earned. He was preparing for a proposed change in FA rules which would allow each soccer club to have one paid director – a reform designed to bring football into the modern business world. Edwards cast United's vote in favour of the reform at a special FA meeting in November 1981. Within two months, in January 1982, the United board had appointed him as one of the first full-time chief executives of a British football club. His appointment took effect from December 1981.

The United accounts for the 1981–82 financial year show that Edwards was paid £15,000 in that year and press reports at the time gave the impression that this was his *annual* salary. Edwards himself remarked at the time that he would be 'very surprised if my salary was among the top ten at Old Trafford'. In fact his annual rate of salary was £30,000, and it was only because he had held office for six months that half the figure was paid. As for not being among the top ten earners at Old Trafford, his full annual salary was exceeded only by that of eight other employees. Within a matter of months he had progressed even higher up the wages table, and there were also many perks associated with the job. In 1982 the directors authorised several thousand pounds to be spent on a new bathroom and toilet facilities next to Edwards' office, which at that time was situated in the new executive suite complex.

In August 1982, Edwards' salary was increased to £40,000 a year – only four United players, according to the 1982 accounts, had earned more than that amount over the previous year. Denzil Haroun explained that it was in recognition of more than £500,000 the new chief executive had brought into the club since he had begun his full-time job. It is true that several commercial deals had been secured during Edwards' first few months of full-time employment by United. But these were arranged in conjunction with Bill Burke's successor as commercial manager, John Lillie, who had previously worked for Makro, the Dutch wholesalers, and also at the Edwards meat company, before opening his own business in Birmingham. A contract worth £500,000 had been signed with the Japanese firm Sharp Electronics, under which United players would carry the Sharp name on their shirts. Sharp were introduced to United by Harrington

Kilbride & Partners Ltd, an agency who then negotiated the contract. (For further information see Chapter 13.) Yet football clubs everywhere were arranging such deals at that time. Indeed, Everton and Liverpool had carried shirt advertising since 1979. The Sharp contract was hailed at the time as the biggest football sponsorship arrangement ever, yet anybody could have secured a lucrative sponsor for United, Britain's most watched club both on television and in the flesh.

There were two other projects by which Martin Edwards justified his large salary increase – a joint prize competition planned with Glasgow Rangers and a scheme to hold Sunday markets in the club car-park. Both schemes failed. Another idea Edwards came up with – pop concerts at the ground – also fell through. Plans for a performance by the group Queen were delayed after protests to Trafford Council from local residents, and the group went to Leeds United instead.

Martin Edwards was determined to run Manchester United in a more businesslike manner. When he took over at Old Trafford there was, he says, 'no such thing as a club budget. . . . We worked out cash-flow on the back of an envelope.' Edwards' comments may not be entirely fair: there had long been a directors' finance committee, which kept an eye on weekly expenditure. He might also have recalled that his father was once its chairman.

Gradually matters that would previously have been dealt with by the club secretary, Les Olive, were passed through Edwards' office. The new chief executive decided to improve the club's affairs in matters such as legal advice, administration and accounting. All playing contracts were now negotiated directly by him with the players or, increasingly, with their agents rather than by the new manager, Ron Atkinson. The club's activities were split into separate departments – playing, administration, commercial and catering. The manager of each division was given his own budget and told to report directly to Edwards.

Martin Edwards is a much less interesting figure than his father, 'Champagne Louis'. To many people Louis Edwards came across as a jolly if rather lonely person, and of course at 17 stone or more he could not help standing out. Martin Edwards is dull in comparison – slim, well-dressed, softly spoken, albeit with some charm. He is the typical image of a modern young businessman.

The United manager he had inherited in 1980, Dave Sexton, was, superficially at least, also a rather grey figure. Sexton seems in many ways an unlikely person ever to be a football manager. In his spare time he reads philosophy books, studies the lives of thinkers like

Wittgenstein and Mill and reads the poems of Robert Frost. His approach to football is highly scientific. One of his first acts at Old Trafford had been to buy a video camera and projection screen so that United players could watch and analyse their previous games. Training was largely coaching and tactics, whereas in the Tommy Docherty days it had been mostly games of five-a-side football.

Sexton's period at Old Trafford had been mostly uneventful. Docherty's 4–2–4 team with Steve Coppell and Gordon Hill on the wings had been modified to Sexton's less adventurous 4–4–2 formation. Hill was allowed to follow Docherty to Derby County, as it was considered that he was too selfish and did not contribute enough towards team-work. On one occasion Martin Buchan had clipped him round the ear for failing to help out in defence. Steve Coppell, meanwhile, was played further back.

Indeed, Sexton might have lost his job in 1979 had it not been for United's remarkable FA Cup exploits that spring. While the side had found it difficult to pick up points in the league, in the Cup they knocked out Liverpool in the semi-final after two scintillating games at Maine Road and Goodison Park. The final against Arsenal at Wembley produced what was probably the most exciting finish ever seen in an FA Cup final. Arsenal were winning with just five minutes to go. Then, in the space of two minutes, first McQueen scored and then McIlroy netted an equaliser. Extra time beckoned, and most thought that after such a comeback United were hot favourites. But extra time was never needed. In the euphoria United slackened a little. Graham Rix crossed the ball to Alan Sunderland for the winning goal, seconds before the final whistle.

Thousands crowded the streets of Manchester to welcome Sexton's losing team home the following day. And the excitement of the Cup run overcame any misgivings about how the team had played in general. In the following season, 1979–80, United chased Liverpool to achieve runners-up position – the first time they had come second since 1968 – though a 6–0 defeat at Ipswich just four days after Louis Edwards' death showed that they did not always play championship football.

Martin Edwards formally congratulated the United manager for coming second in 1980. Both Dave Sexton and his assistant, Tommy Cavanagh, were awarded new three-year contracts and their salaries were increased by 50 per cent. Yet early in the following season, 1980–81, relations between Edwards and his manager grew strained. The team had thrown away a money-spinning run in the UEFA Cup by being knocked out in the first round by Widzew Lodz. Edwards was worried about falling crowd figures as United struggled to match the results of the previous season. The team had not lost often, but there had been a succession of home draws against weak opponents. Home matches against Aston Villa and Wolves had attracted gates of barely 38,000, far below the previous season's figures.

Meanwhile, Sexton had spent £1.25 million and a £75,000 signing-on fee acquiring the England forward Garry Birtles from Nottingham Forest. Although £500,000 was immediately recovered with the sale of Andy Ritchie to Brighton, Sexton was told to raise a further £900,000 by selling players to balance the books.

Edwards' financial stringency was part of a more widespread check on the club's accounts, which included several cuts on the playing side. In future the squad would no longer stay overnight at a hotel before home matches. No overseas tours would be made unless the match fees covered the trip's total expenses. The professional squad of players would be reduced, along with scouts and coaches. And the United fourth XI – the B team – would be abolished.

In the months ahead Sexton raised only £90,000 from selling Chris McGrath to Tulsa Roughnecks and Steve Paterson to Sheffield United, just a fraction of what Edwards demanded – and Paterson's £60,000 fee later had to be paid back for medical reasons. Moreover, Garry Birtles found it impossible to score even one league goal by the end of the season. His goal in the FA Cup at Brighton gave a new meaning to the chant 'There's only one Garry Birtles'. Andy Ritchie, in contrast, scored three goals for Brighton against United in four matches that year. United fans joked that when the American hostages were finally released from Iran, their first question would be, 'Has Garry Birtles scored for United yet?'

At one point United went for five consecutive league games without a goal – a club record. The team also drew a record eighteen matches during that campaign – eight of them no-score draws, and eleven at home. It was extremely frustrating for the Old Trafford faithful, and the football was pretty unattractive. By February 1981 it did not look as if Sexton could last much longer.

The manager was asked to explain the team's highly disappointing form before the directors. Martin Edwards quoted to him letters from supporters complaining about United's boring style and bad public relations. The directors even approached David Meek, the *Manchester Evening News* reporter, for advice on creating a better rapport with the press and public. Several journalists had complained of United's

144

unfriendly treatment and of how Dave Sexton would not even give out his home phone number. The frosty reception at Old Trafford contrasted strongly with the warm atmosphere they encountered at Maine Road. Martin Edwards tried to soothe feelings by meeting the local branch of the National Union of Journalists.

What probably gave Dave Sexton a reprieve was a gentlemen's agreement among league chairmen reached on 9 February 1981, right in the middle of United's worst spell. Many clubs had suffered severe disruption from managerial changes in the middle of a season, with knock-on effects on a string of clubs. It was agreed that in future chairmen would not poach each other's managers during the season. Martin Edwards had probably already decided to get rid of Sexton, but had he sacked him then it would have been impossible to find a replacement without breaking the no-poaching agreement almost straight away, or going outside the league. If United wanted a top-class successor to Sexton – and Edwards had Lawrie McMenemy of Southampton in mind – there was little to lose by waiting until the campaign was over.

To Edwards' eventual embarrassment, Sexton ended the 1980-81 season with seven victories in a row, a club record not achieved before or since. He was just two votes away from winning the Manager of the Month award. Yet five days after the final game, Sexton was axed.

Edwards dismissed Sexton because of fans' complaints about United's failure to entertain. 'I felt we'd gone backwards,' said the chairman. 'It was having an effect on gates.' Average home crowds were down by 6,500 on the previous season. Without doubt another reason was Sexton's failure to understand the new financial atmosphere within the club. The £1.25 million spent on Garry Birtles was looking like a waste of money, and Sexton had not managed to recover it.

Of the six directors, Sir Matt Busby is known to have opposed the sacking. Perhaps it was because Sexton had been his recommendation. Busby felt that, because of the bad injuries the previous season and the winning run towards the end, Sexton deserved another year.

But Sexton also suffered from a team of good publicists at Maine Road. City had reappointed Malcolm Allison as their manager in 1979 and then replaced him with John Bond a year later. Whatever their failings with the team, both men were great promoters for the light blues. Similarly, Martin Edwards was himself outshone by the City chairman, Peter Swales, who would go to great lengths to publicise his club. Edwards remarked that United fans were fed up with sports page headlines about City: 'We want a good publicist who can communicate with our supporters – a man with very special qualities.'

Dave Sexton was probably the first United manager since the war to be sacked for commercial reasons. Wilf McGuinness and Frank O'Farrell had been dismissed while their teams were facing relegation. Docherty had been sacked because of a love affair and his personal financial dealings. Sexton went because he endangered the club's profitability.

In 1979 the Annual General Meeting had agreed its first annual dividend since the rights issue. A payment of 5 per cent per share meant a total pay-out of £50,419, compared with a bill of just £312 from a 5 per cent dividend the year before, and indeed similar figures virtually every year since the late 1940s. Dividends of just over £50,000 were paid out again in 1980 and 1981, and as the holders of the majority of shares, Martin Edwards and his relations got a total return in those three years of more than £80,000. Already the rights issue was producing much the effect that Les Olive had predicted. Such dividends in football were then unique: other clubs rarely paid any dividend, partly because so few of them ever made a profit, but largely because most football directors felt that any profit should be channelled back into the team. If other clubs ever did grant a dividend, it added up to only a few hundred pounds – much the same level United's once were. However, Martin Edwards still owed hundreds of thousands of pounds to his bank. To pay off that debt he either had to push up the price of shares by making the business more profitable, or earn more direct returns through his own salary and dividends.

Edwards was also determined to bring sympathetic new blood on to his board. Apart from himself and James Gulliver, every other director – Alan Gibson, Bill Young, Denzil Haroun and Sir Matt Busby – was beyond retirement age. In June 1981 Edwards proposed that his younger brother, Roger, then only twenty-seven, be elected too. The directors readily agreed, but they were not so keen on Edwards' second proposed co-option, Mike Edelson, the Manchester business-man who had bought 15,000 of Edwards' United shares immediately after the rights issue. Edelson, who came from a family of City supporters, had been on the playing staff of Stoke City and Oldham Athletic in the 1960s, but his career had been cut short by a broken leg and he never made either first team. Since then he had taken over his father's multi-million pound fur business in north Manchester, which in 1981 had paid him more than £127,000. Sir Matt Busby opposed the election of Edelson, but this time went along with Roger Edwards. However, for the United president both proposals were yet another sign of the meat family's tightening grip.

When Martin Edwards proposed Mike Edelson again more than a year later, in August 1982, Sir Matt Busby announced that he wished to retire from the board for 'personal and domestic reasons'. Busby was now seventy-three and neither he nor his wife Jean were well. He had suffered a cerebral haemorrhage the year before, while Lady Busby was now permanently in a nursing home. But the main reason was Busby's unhappiness at the way in which the club was now being run. It was no coincidence that his resignation came up around the same time that the latest Edwards' nominee was being put forward to the board, and around the same time that Edwards' salary was increased again, to £40,000. In fact Edelson's election was deferred again and he did not become a director until four months afterwards.

Later Edwards moved to clear the rest of the old guard from the board, directors he felt were unsuited to the increasingly commercial world of modern football. In June 1984 Edwards persuaded vice-chairman Alan Gibson, who had served on board since 1948, and Bill Young, a director since 1960, to resign. As compensation, Edwards explained, they would be made vice-presidents below Sir Matt Busby, who had remained club president after leaving the boardroom.

In their place were elected two younger men. Maurice Watkins was a solicitor with James Chapman and Co., the firm which advised United. Watkins had himself been legal adviser to the club since the Docherty affair in 1977. In time he had also become solicitor to Martin Edwards. Having grown up in Manchester, Watkins had previously worked for the Pilkington glass company and had supported United all his life. He agreed to buy 50,000 shares from Roger Edwards.

The other 'younger' man, though he was soon the oldest member of the United board, was the former United captain and England star Bobby Charlton. After leaving Old Trafford in 1973, Charlton had an undistinguished spell as manager of Preston North End, and later, while serving as a director of Wigan Athletic, had briefly stood in as the Lancashire club's caretaker manager. But he had enjoyed slightly greater success in helping build up several businesses – in travel, providing hampers and jewellery, and in running soccer schools in Britain, the United States, Canada, Australia and even China. Later Charlton was also involved with an organisation called Mundimex which arranged trips for supporters to the Mexico World Cup, but the venture failed to make any money. However, Martin Edwards needed Bobby Charlton as a name on the board after the resignation of Sir Matt Busby, and for his football experience rather than for any business ability. Unlike every other board member elected since the rights issue, Charlton did not have to buy a large shareholding through the Edwards family. And in time United managers would find that Charlton was a strong influence on Edwards when it came to football decisions.

Martin Edwards was soon making an impact in the higher levels of English football. He was among a group of chairmen of leading clubs who were pressing for changes which would make football more commercially minded. They wanted a smaller league and a slimmer first division, as they saw it, to stop the smaller clubs living off the bigger ones. Other demands were that clubs should be allowed to keep all home gate receipts, a reduction in the 75 per cent majority required at Football League meetings, and a better contract with the TV companies. At one point, around 1982 and 1983, Edwards was among those chairmen threatening to form a breakaway super league of the top clubs if football did not mend its ways. 'The danger is that if the present situation persists,' he warned, 'there will be no alternative.'

With no dividends since 1981 Martin Edwards was seeking some way to repay the debts he had built up in buying his stake in United. He had been impressed by the recent decision of Tottenham Hotspur to float the club on the stock exchange in 1983. This flotation had valued the assets of the North London club at more than £9 million. Edwards was convinced that United must be worth more than that, and as the owner of 70 per cent of the shares, he was determined to see if there was any way in which he could get his hands on some of that value.

Yet the current United share price was only about £3. With just over a million shares in all, this valued the whole club at only £3 million. The problem for Edwards was that there was no proper market in United shares. The only people interested in buying them were a few hundred United supporters who generally wanted them only for sentimental reasons. Shares could be bought only through one or two Manchester stockbrokers, such as Joe Stephens and Derek Wall, and even then people who wanted to buy them had to wait until somebody wanted to sell. But if a free, competitive market were established in United shares, Edwards felt that his holding would greatly appreciate in value.

The 3.8 million extra shares that Spurs had issued in football's first stock market flotation in September 1983 had sold out within minutes of coming on to the market. After that the price had initially risen above the opening £1 mark. The operation had made Tottenham's existing shareholders much richer, and in particular Irving Scholar and Paul Bobroff who had bought a majority for just £600,000. It had also raised nearly £3.5 million for the club to spend as it saw fit.

In late 1983 Edwards and his solicitor, Maurice Watkins, arranged for Kleinwort Benson, the merchant bank that had supervised the 1978 rights issue, to investigate the possibility of United taking a public share listing like Tottenham's. They considered both a full listing, like Spurs', or a much simpler listing on the Unlisted Securities Market (USM). A USM listing had in fact already been considered briefly in December 1981, but rejected as being too costly. Yet with a proper market in the shares, prices could more exactly reflect the total assets of the company, the regular annual profit figures and the team's prospects, which after the 1983 FA Cup win against Brighton were looking good.

Kleinwort Benson examined the Spurs flotation and on that basis tentatively valued Manchester United at between £6 million and £8 million. The difference between United and Tottenham was accounted for by the fact that the London club had more than £2 million worth of land at their Cheshunt training ground. Kleinwort's valuation must have been somewhat disappointing to Martin Edwards. Even so, if the club could be floated at a total value of £8 million – including the issue of £1.5 million worth of new shares – existing shares would be valued at £6.50 or so each. Between them his family might then make £500,000 without having to give up control. But if the family were prepared to reduce their share to 40 per cent and take the risk of losing control, it might be possible to make more than £1 million.

Before Edwards could proceed further with the idea, however, he had an even better prospect – a bid to buy United from the multi-millionaire publisher Robert Maxwell. At the time Maxwell's own club, Oxford United, were only in the third division, with division one still a long way off. It was well known that Maxwell had other football ambitions, and in particular was eager to acquire a first-division team. Martin Edwards' version of events is that a gentleman came to see him one afternoon in January 1984 and said that a bid for £10 million was on its way. Then Maxwell phoned in person and, without mentioning money, fixed a meeting in London for two weeks ahead.

It seems that one person acting as a middleman was Andrew McHutchon, a businessman based in North Yorkshire, who specialised at that time in buying football clubs. Later the Football League banned

McHutchon from any involvement in clubs after his work for the notorious Anton Johnson, who had acquired control of three different league sides. McHutchon put out feelers towards United in the middle of 1983, well before Maxwell's bid became public, through the former United goalkeeper Harry Gregg.

Once in contact with each other, however, Edwards and Maxwell appointed as their go-between Professor Roland Smith, the man who advised the Edwards family on the 1978 rights issue and who also had one of the expensive table seats in the Executive Suite at Old Trafford. The publisher never seemed short of money and might have been the answer to the Edwards' money worries – problems which were illustrated by the United chairman's comment at the time: 'I was going to have to do something about my financial situation very soon anyway. The involvement of my brother, Roger, and I in the rights issue five years ago was very costly. . . . We are still very heavily committed at the bank and need to improve our position. So there was going to have to be some kind of flotation in the near future.'

The news that 'somebody' was bidding for United quickly became public through Derek Potter in the *Daily Express* on 1 February 1984. Having been tipped off about the proposed deal, Potter had a private meeting with Edwards before publishing. A figure of £10 million was soon mentioned in the papers. It was another week, however, before Maxwell's name became firm, but there is no evidence that the publisher ever offered this sum. It would have been a rash thing to do straight away for, unlike his Oxford United team, Maxwell claimed to see Manchester United as a financial opportunity. 'I am not a member of the Salvation Army. Football clubs can be a commercial proposition, yielding 10 per cent a year,' he argued.

As might be expected, Maxwell arranged for his own advisers, the accountants Coopers and Lybrand, to look closely at United's finances and make their own serious assessment of what the club was worth. United gave them several years' annual accounts and valuers' reports on the club's properties. But Maxwell's interest soon aroused considerable opposition from ordinary United supporters. An offer to match any Maxwell bid soon emerged from a consortium of wealthy Manchester businessmen, United season-ticket holders and share-holders, led by Peter Raymond who worked for an American chemicals company. Martin Edwards' comment that 'we will listen to any genuine offers as long as the parties prove themselves *bona fide*' seemed to indicate that his interest in Maxwell's approach was more than simple curiosity.

On the morning before meeting Maxwell for lunch in London, Edwards met James Gulliver at the Savoy Hotel and then went with his solicitor, Maurice Watkins, to see Kleinwort Benson in the City. The United men presumably wanted to know if there was any way of increasing the low valuation the bankers had put on the club. Edwards and Watkins then spent two and a half hours with Maxwell over lunch at his London offices. The United chairman reportedly asked Maxwell for £15 a share, a total valuation for the whole club of £15 million. It is not known how much Maxwell was prepared to offer, but it seems unlikely that his own advisers would have valued the club at much more than £8 million. Given his stated desire to run United on a commercial basis, he probably offered a lot less than the widely quoted £10 million, if indeed he made an offer at all.

For the United chairman to have taken less than £10 million, though, after all the speculation in the press, would have made him look silly. Maxwell publicly stated that he was not prepared to haggle over the price of an institution like United. One report has it that the publisher was rather annoyed by Ron Atkinson's comment on television after United's 5–0 victory at Luton the day before, that each goal would increase United's price by £1 million.

Edwards rang Peter Raymond to say that he was now no longer interested in selling his stake in the club to anybody. But the idea of a public flotation was still pursued for several months. Kleinwort Benson eventually concluded that if the club were floated like Spurs, Martin Edwards would gain very little if he wanted to retain a 50 per cent shareholding.

From then on Martin Edwards had to concentrate on other means to reduce and service his large bank overdraft. Fortunately for him, Football Association regulations had eased the limits on the dividends clubs could pay – to 15 per cent of capital per year, so United could now pay out dividends of £150,000 a year. The club made a record profit of £1,731,000 in the year to 1984, and the directors proposed just such a 15 per cent dividend to the Annual General Meeting that November. It produced a total pay-out to shareholders of £151,284 – three times greater than any previous United dividend, and by far a record pay-out for a football club. Martin Edwards received £77,319 of that money. Les Olive cannot have failed to notice that the sum was in fact a few hundred pounds *more* than the figure he had warned about six years earlier, only his prediction had probably come true even sooner than he had feared.

As for Robert Maxwell, his interest turned towards buying the *Daily*

Mirror. Subsequently he boosted his football assets by purchasing Derby County, and in 1987 he unsuccessfully tried to buy Watford from Elton John. Shortly afterwards Maxwell was linked with a 5 per cent shareholding in United owned by a mysterious nominee company, Lancashire & Yorkshire Nominees Ltd. In 1988 rumour had it that Maxwell owned the shares. This seems unlikely since the company is represented by Biddle and Co., solicitors who acted *against* Maxwell in his recent attempts to stop publication of a biography of him. Furthermore, it seems unlikely that Robert Maxwell is about to launch another bid for the club, because 20,500 United shares that Maxwell definitely did own, through his company Publishing and Databank Consultants Ltd, were sold between 1986 and 1987.

The only arrangement Martin Edwards ever did strike with Robert Maxwell involved the publisher's helicopter. After buying the Mirror Group, he made several flying visits to his newspapers' print plant in Manchester. There was no available landing site in the centre of the city, so United agreed to let Maxwell land on the No. 1 car-park opposite the ground – an area which, it so happened, was one of those property assets Edwards had hoped might make United more financially attractive to wealthy investors.

9 CHIEF EXECUTIVE

'Should the United get into the first League they will
speedily become one of the richest and most powerful clubs
in the competition.'

The Book of Football, 1906.

HIS £65,000 suite of offices high above the entrance to United's
ground overlooks the Manchester to Liverpool railway. On the corner
of the building a sitting-room is for relaxation and entertaining
visitors. It is furnished with luxurious white leather arm-chairs, a
matching convertible two-seat sofa, chrome and glass occasional
tables, large pot plants, and mirrors stretching from floor to ceiling and
concealing a television, video recorder and drinks cabinet.

The main office next door, again fitted out with furniture imported
from Italy, is dominated by a large desk and, to one side, a highly
polished conference table for holding business meetings. A glass
bookcase holds volumes of United programmes dating back to the
war, together with virtually every book that has ever been written
about the club. Along one wall, blinds open to reveal a window
looking out on to the Old Trafford pitch and the inside of the stadium.
Next to this window hangs a portrait of the man simply referred to as
'father': Louis Edwards, the chairman whose ambition created this
office, but who did not live long enough to enjoy it. And, symbolically
perhaps, behind the picture is a safe. Just inside the office, a side door
opens on to a bathroom – with a personal WC, wash-basin and a
shower unit. The distinctive United crest is embroidered on each of
the red towels.

On the ground level below, next to the entrance to United's Red
Devil Grill and the Trafford suite, electronically controlled shutters
conceal a double garage. Inside is housed a gleaming company car – a
1989-registered BMW. The driver of the car, Martin Edwards, enjoys
a very different life-style from the directors and part-time chairmen

who presided at Old Trafford in the days when it had only tiny offices and big debts.

The £87,825-a-year chairman and chief executive of Manchester United Football Club runs a business that had a turnover of more than £7½ million in the year ending July 1988. His 160 or so employees include some of the highest-paid sportsmen in Britain; four of them, Bryan Robson, Mark Hughes, Brian McClair and Gordon Strachan, reputedly earn more than £100,000 a year. His football ground is not just host to the million or so people who come annually through the turnstiles. Its directors' box, private boxes, executive suites and window tables are occupied by top businessmen such as Professor Roland Smith and James Gulliver, and former Cabinet ministers such as Stan Orme, Salford MP, and Lord Barnett, deputy chairman of the BBC.

Martin Edwards stands at the centre of one of the most famous institutions in the sporting world. Around him is a complex interlocking network of businessmen and financial deals that have made him a paper-millionaire. The duties of the chief executive of Manchester United are far more glamorous and rewarding than those he once had liaising with Woolworth's store managers in the £11,000-a-year management job in his family meat business.

The man who enabled Edwards' transformation from meat-firm divisional managing director to football tycoon is James Gulliver, a businessman of international stature who had himself risen rapidly during the early 1980s. Both men are children of the Thatcher years, whose rise to power has coincided with the Conservative prime minister's period of office. Like many businessmen of the 1980s they seemed to know more about making money multiply on paper than producing concrete achievements. Yet James Gulliver resigned from the United board in the autumn of 1985, just as his Argyll Group was about to mount its famous and unsuccessful bid for Distillers. The intense scale of his other business activities, and the fact he was now based in the South of England, meant that Gulliver had little time for United matches or board meetings. During his six years on the board Gulliver managed to attend only about a third of the meetings, even though they were monthly not weekly. The Scotsman nevertheless suggested to Martin Edwards that he might like to sell most of his shareholding to him, while carrying on in the job of chairman and chief executive. Gulliver insisted that he himself was not interested in becoming chairman.

Gulliver's offer was rejected, and instead he agreed to sell his

102,000 shares back to Edwards, or rather to Edwards' wife Susan, at £4.05 each. It was not one of Gulliver's most profitable deals, the price being just £1 more than he had paid the Edwards family for the shares six years before: allowing for inflation, they had dropped in price. Part of the arrangement was that Gulliver would be a vice-president of the club, in the same way Alan Gibson and Bill Young had become.

The food tycoon's resignation from the board may partly have been prompted by unhappiness at the way the club was being run, in particular over Ron Atkinson's commercial dealings. 'I think Ron Atkinson's been a good buyer,' Gulliver told *Business* magazine shortly after his resignation, 'but he's a man with no knowledge of the use of money. He's got a blinkered approach. . . . I think he's quite a talented manager, but he needs controlling. . . . I think Mr Edwards has got some toughness, but he's just not able, for various reasons, to handle Ron Atkinson.' Gulliver wrote to apologise to Martin Edwards afterwards, saying that the quotes were highly selective and that he denied having any misgivings.

Martin Edwards admits that he failed to get as much out of James Gulliver's presence as he and his father had hoped when they invited him on to the United board. Above all, the businessman had failed to find a way of creating a fluid market for United shares that would help the Edwards family make money by selling some of their holding. The process of replacing Gulliver on the board, and disposing of his own former shareholding, took Martin Edwards several months.

Earlier in 1985 Edwards had come into conflict with a local twenty-seven-year-old Arab businessman called Amer Mouaffac Al Midani. The cause of the trouble was Edwards' decision to purchase the Warrington Vikings Basketball Club, an episode described in Chapter 12 of this book. Midani was the owner of the rival Manchester Giants team, but the conflict soon turned to an agreement to merge the two basketball sides. Martin Edwards and Amer Al Midani became good friends and, in time, business allies.

Though he was brought up in war-torn Beirut, where he claims to have been the Lebanese junior table-tennis champion, Amer Al Midani actually carried a Saudi Arabian passport until he took out British citizenship in 1985. He first came to Manchester in 1975 as an eighteen-year-old student. According to Martin Edwards, writing in United's 1987 annual report, Midani is a 'graduate of Manchester University and attended the Manchester Business School'. The university, however, has no record of him ever having been on its books, but Midani did take an English language course in Manchester.

The key factor about Amer Al Midani is his father, Mouaffac Al Midani, a Syrian who made his money in textiles and who is reputed to be one of the richest men in the world. A regular visitor to Britain, Mouaffac Al Midani caused something of a stir in the late 1970s when he led a consortium of Arabs who bought the Dorchester Hotel in London, though they sold it again later. Amer Al Midani, assisted by a small share of his father's money, set up a string of companies in the North-west in the early 1980s, operating in various fields. As well as the Giants basketball club, he was involved in property, travel and even in owning racehorses.

Midani's companies belong to one parent body, the AMM Group of Companies Ltd. The company accounts state that this is itself owned by a parent company in Amsterdam, called AMM Development bv, presumably for tax purposes. This Dutch firm is believed to belong to Midani's wealthy father. But, judging from their annual reports, none of Amer Al Midani's firms shows any sign of the 'highly successful business career' Martin Edwards wrote about in 1987. The AMM Group lost between £320,000 and £390,000 in each of the four years between 1984 and 1987.

In May 1986, around the time he agreed to merge the Manchester Giants basketball club with United, Midani agreed to buy 100,682 of the Manchester United shares James Gulliver had sold back to Susan Edwards. In fact they were actually purchased by an organisation based in Lichtenstein called the Philen Establishment. This organisation again belongs to Midani's wealthy father, and Amer Al Midani is described as the firm's British representative. The Philen Establishment's only known UK address is 73 South Audley Street, London W1, at the rear of the Dorchester Hotel in Mayfair, the offices of Gibson, Dunn and Crutcher, Midani's American firm of solicitors. The 100,682 shares represented precisely 10 per cent of United's share capital. The price was £700,000, and so Susan Edwards made a profit of almost £300,000 in the six months since buying the stock from Gulliver.

Amer Al Midani was not actually elected to the Manchester United board until February 1987, some months later. (Coincidentally he was replacing a director, Denzil Haroun, who died in 1985, who also had Syrian ancestry and a background in textiles.) But Midani's share ownership did not become publicly known until Martin Edwards revealed it in answer to a query about the Philen Establishment at the Annual General Meeting in December 1987, eighteen months after the deal with Midani had been agreed. No mention had been made in the 1987 accounts of this link between Midani and the Philen Establishment.

For those who knew him well, Midani's sudden involvement with one of the world's great football clubs came as something of a surprise. Until then he had shown little interest in football. Though Midani is a man of considerable charm, and his father a man of considerable means, it is hard to see what his election as a director has added to the board. Though he has a home in Bramhall, Midani spends much of his time at a health farm his father owns in Majorca called the Marbella Club. He tends to visit Manchester irregularly to take in both a United match and a board meeting. But it is a greater commitment than the man who previously owned his shares, James Gulliver, was able to give.

Midani is also well liked by the players, many of whom have visited the Marbella Club. In the summer of 1988 Martin Edwards was also a guest at Midani's health farm during the period when Tottenham Hotspur clinched the transfer of Paul Gascoigne. Many believe that if Edwards ever decides to sell United, Midani is the most likely buyer.

Bobby Charlton's election to the United board in June 1984 was portrayed as an attempt to improve the club's public relations. It was an area which Martin Edwards had always found difficult, particularly since the resignation of Sir Matt Busby two years earlier, and Edwards felt that his manager Ron Atkinson did not always project the right kind of image for the club. Since then Charlton's influence at Old Trafford has been stronger over playing matters than that of any of the other directors, including at times Edwards himself. The United chairman has been known to defer to Charlton's judgement on matters such as player transfers, and Charlton reportedly had an important role in Atkinson's eventual sacking in 1986. The former United captain was also behind the appointment in 1988 of Manchester Polytechnic lecturer Les Kershaw as chief scout to replace Tony Collins. Charlton's major business interest, of course, is his soccer coaching school, and the tour facilities of Old Trafford are used extensively by the school's weekly batches of summer pupils.

Roger Edwards resigned from the United board in February 1985, after less than four years as a director. He sold his United shares and decided that with that money, together with the proceeds from his Argyll shares, he was now rich enough to emigrate to Majorca and live in semi-retirement as a tax exile. Roger Edwards' own businesses had not been particularly successful, in spite of help from United. His company, Dawn Print Ltd, produced leaflets for the United Development Association, but according to the accounts the business never made much profit.

Martin Edwards arranged to sell 50,500 of Roger Edwards' United shares to an accountant with Price Waterhouse, Oscar Goldstein. It was much the same kind of arrangement that had been struck with the solicitor Maurice Watkins. Like Watkins, Goldstein was not only an adviser to United, but was also employed in a personal capacity by Martin Edwards and became a close friend. Like Watkins, Goldstein was promised a seat on the United board, but the accountant's purchase agreement with Edwards in 1984 also included an arrangement that he could become United's company secretary when Les Olive eventually retired. Goldstein was given two seats in the directors' box in 1984, and he began to accompany the team on foreign tours.

However, the deal was never carried through. In September 1985 Oscar Goldstein pleaded guilty in a Manchester court to falsifying an Inland Revenue form. He was accused of setting up a ring of friends who had all made deeds of covenant to each other in order to cheat the Inland Revenue of hundreds of pounds in tax. Goldstein had originally told the tax men that the deeds had not been made as part of a reciprocal agreement. He was fined £1,000 by the court and subsequently expelled from the Institute of Chartered Accountants. Goldstein had resigned from Price Waterhouse only a few weeks earlier, presumably in anticipation of the court case, and set up in business on his own as a tax adviser. Though Edwards now felt unable to install Goldstein in the United boardroom, the former accountant continued to advise both Edwards and United about tax matters.

A much more recent recruit to the board has been Nigel Burrows, elected in June 1988. Like Mike Edelson, Maurice Watkins, Oscar Goldstein and Amer Al Midani, the deal was that Burrows would earn his directorship by first buying a substantial shareholding. The 50,000 shares Burrows says he bought were those previously held by Oscar Goldstein. When it was clear that Goldstein would not become secretary on Les Olive's retirement in 1988, he took advantage of a clause in his original share purchase contract whereby Edwards had to buy Goldstein's shares back for a minimum of £3 each. It appears, however, that the price Edwards subsequently received from Burrows for the returned shares was more than £5 each. Certainly it was widely known for some time in Manchester that 50,000 surplus shares had been offered to a select group of United's wealthy supporters for £250,000. And the carrot to buy was a place on the

United board. Whether Goldstein received any more than the minimum £3 per share is not clear.

Burrows was only thirty-four when he joined the board. He is the co-founder and director of Analysis Financial Services, a firm based in Harrogate, Yorkshire, and now taken over by the British and Commonwealth Group for whom he is employed on a three-year consultancy fee. Martin Edwards came into contact with him as a member of United's Executive Suite, and a regular patron of the club's Luncheon Club, which has operated since 1986, and the two men had been negotiating their deal since late 1987. Since then Burrows has linked forces with Harold Hassall to take over the name and operations of Delta Sports, the company which used to organise United's corporate hospitality. Burrows claims to be a former Stretford Ender, and describes his election to the board as a 'dream come true'.

Being a United director in the late 1980s is a very different proposition from what it was in times gone by. In 1902 United's four new directors had to pay £500 each to save the club – a considerable sum at that time – and the United president, J. H. Davies, donated £3,000 of his own money for new players. Again, in the 1930s, the club had been saved by funds from the pocket of its latest president, James Gibson. Under FA rules clubs were not allowed to pay directors until 1981, when one paid board-member was allowed for the first time – Edwards, of course, in United's case.

Other rewards come not only from the substantial business contacts one meets at such a large club, but also through generous expenses. United directors get these while carrying out club business, such as attending matches, when in reality of course they are simply furthering their hobby. In 1984 directors' allowances to away matches were as follows: first-class rail fare and cost of taxis; or if travelling by car 28p per mile up to a maximum of £70; meals if not eaten at the team hotel, £20 for dinner and £15 for lunch; an overnight allowance to cover drinks etc. of £15; and an additional allowance of £15 to cover drinks etc. when attending functions.

Since 1984 the expenses have almost certainly been increased. The mileage allowance is now 30p, for example. Directors also get a £20 per day expense allowance while on foreign tours. United fans who spend several pounds on coach and rail fares travelling to Old Trafford, and another £3 to stand on the Stretford End, may be surprised to learn that the wealthy businessmen who serve as United directors actually claim mileage for games at Old Trafford.

After becoming chairman in 1980, Martin Edwards continued to pursue outside business interests. Not only did he remain a director of Argyll Foods until November 1983, but there were other activities too. For instance, he served for several years on the board of Russ Evans Contracting Ltd, a company managed by a Manchester businessman, Ernie Kearns, but which has since gone into liquidation. Much more lucrative was a relationship Edwards began with a firm called Exclusive Cleaning in 1980. Exclusive was the name of several companies, in fact, all part of the multi-million-pound Brengreen Holdings built up by David Evans. Evans, once a reserve player with Aston Villa FC, is also a former Gloucestershire county cricketer, and in 1980 had just recently been elected a director of Luton Town where he later became chairman. He was also embarking on a career in Conservative politics that saw him serve as a councillor, make rousing speeches at the Tory Party conference and in 1987 secure election as a Conservative MP.

In the summer of 1980 Martin Edwards became a non-executive director of David Evans' firm, Exclusive Cleaning and Maintenance Ltd. It was a period when Edwards had no full-time job, and Evans agreed to pay him an annual retainer, an arrangement which lasted until 1985. According to sources inside the company, part of the deal was that Edwards would get commission on all business that he introduced to Photravel Ltd, an Exclusive subsidiary which Manchester United had already been using for some years for most of its club travel.

Photravel's agent, Peter Johnson, the man United usually dealt with, left the company in 1981 to set up his own travel business. At first the United directors voted to move with Peter Johnson, as they felt his service had proved to be 'very satisfactory' in the past. In the following month, February 1982, however, the board changed their minds and agreed that Exclusive could carry on tendering for United's travel.

Martin Edwards also earned commission on cleaning work he introduced to Exclusive. Among his lucrative contacts and contracts were Greenall Whitley, the brewers, Rackham's stores in Leicester and Sheffield, and various branches of both the Midland Bank and the Abbey National Building Society in Manchester and Cheshire. Quite how Edwards went about setting up cleaning contracts for individual building society and bank branches is not clear.

It was a very rewarding sideline for the United chairman. The man who generally liaised with Martin Edwards was the general manager of Exclusive's northern division, Danny McGregor. McGregor, it so happens, had played as a centre-forward in the mid-1950s for United's junior teams and had later appeared briefly for Accrington Stanley before the club folded in 1962. McGregor even sent Martin Edwards a commission payment for work that Exclusive had carried out for United at Old Trafford. Edwards was actually getting a percentage of the money on work he himself was ultimately responsible for commissioning for the club. United's annual reports regularly state: 'No director, either during or at the end of the Financial Period, was materially interested in any contract that was significant in relation to the Group's business.' Clearly United's Exclusive cleaning and travel business cannot have been considered 'significant'.

In July 1985 Martin Edwards advised the United board that the commercial manager at Old Trafford, John Lillie, should be given notice to terminate his contract. Some United directors had been unhappy for some time with Lillie's work, which he combined with running his own business, and it had long been clear that he might have to go. Lillie's replacement as commercial manager turned out to be a former United junior player by the name of Danny McGregor.

Today, from his office at the front of the new administration block, McGregor hustles and haggles for new business for United. The contacts and methods he built up over the years as managing director of Exclusive's northern company provide excellent background for this work. Within United, McGregor is a powerful figure. Yet in an arrangement even more extraordinary than the deal Edwards once had with Exclusive, McGregor was allowed to have an outside arrangement with an organisation called the Delta Group which earned him at least another £600 a month. What is particularly strange about the arrangement is that Delta were responsible for selling advertising space around the ground, and until 1988 also arranged United's corporate hospitality packages.

For Martin Edwards, much more important than outside director-ships and commissions are his substantial investments on top of his majority stake in Manchester United. These include both large shareholdings and property. He owns a luxury flat in Marlborough Road, Sale, which he bought in 1981, and property in Florida in the United States, near to where both his sister, Catherine, and his uncle, Douglas Edwards, now live.

Most of Martin Edwards' share investments were for many years handled by a Manchester securities dealer called Nicholas Baldwin, who lives in the same road as the United chairman – Oak Road in

Mottram St Andrew, a pretty village near Wilmslow. In 1985 Baldwin's firm, Harrison Baldwin, ran into considerable financial difficulties, but he managed to conceal these from Edwards and his other clients. By the middle of 1987 Harrison Baldwin was £1 million in debt, and Black Tuesday in October 1987 finally sent the company over the edge. Harrison Baldwin went into liquidation in January 1988 with debts of around £4 million. Of that, the Edwards family accounted between them for more than £500,000. Martin Edwards was owed only £33,000 of the total, but his mother, Muriel, was owed £383,000 and the trustees of Louis Edwards a further £136,000. Martin Edwards might eventually have expected to inherit a third of the last two amounts.

Since his appointment as chief executive in 1981 on a salary of £30,000 a year, Martin Edwards' income from United has risen rapidly. By 1985–86 he was taking £75,467; in 1986–87 it had increased to £83,611; and 1987–88 saw a 5 per cent increase to £87,675. By July 1988 Edwards had been paid £439,515 by the club in the previous six and a half years. The payments included annual bonus awards, which were decided officially by the United directors. In 1983 the bonus was agreed as 2 per cent of the previous year's profits – £12,700. In 1985 it was agreed that half the bonus would be accounted for by 1 per cent of whatever profits were made on transfer dealings. When this provision became publicly known, there was an outcry. It was argued that Edwards had a direct interest in selling players and not buying them, and the awarding of a bonus on transfer profits was dropped.

But Martin Edwards' remuneration has continued to include a bonus award, fixed by the directors each year. In 1986 the bonus was £25,000 but because of the earlier revelation relating to transfer profits, the awarding of a bonus was a sensitive matter. The ideal solution, of course, would be for Edwards' earnings to be lumped together as an aggregate salary. Possibly because of the fear that this would be seen as a massive percentage increase of around 50 per cent, United still appear to be saddled with the bonus problem. At the annual general meetings of 1987 and 1988, the United chairman stated that his salary had only increased in line with inflation and at the same rate as the incomes of his staff – around five to six per cent.

On top of his salary and bonuses, Edwards has benefited from the large dividend payments over recent years. There were dividends of £50,432 in 1979, 1980 and 1981. Then, after two years with no dividend, he proposed a payment of £151,284 in 1983 and it was followed by dividends of £100,424 in 1985 and £100,464 in 1987. Altogether, by 1987 the 1978 rights issue had cost around £500,000 in extra dividend payments. Of that Martin Edwards had been paid £233,684, and his family, of course, many thousands of pounds more.

Some shareholders argue that the 1987 dividend payment, which cost £100,464, was in fact issued illegally, against the expressed wishes of the 1987 Annual General Meeting. When Edwards put the proposed dividend to a vote, it was rejected overwhelmingly on a show of hands. Edwards then said that he wanted the matter put to a poll whereby votes are assessed according to shareholdings. At that point a shareholder declared that a poll would be unproductive since everybody knew that the dividend would inevitably be accepted because of Edwards' controlling shares. The meeting therefore voted overwhelmingly to reject the idea of a poll, but without rescinding the previous decision by a show of hands against a dividend. Amid the confusion the dividend remained unapproved. Yet shareholders received their dividend cheques only a few days later.

One shareholder, a solicitor called Stephen Elder, who had once worked for Amer Al Midani, even wrote to United pointing out the irregularity and claiming it was a 'serious breach of company legislation'. Elder received a phone call from Maurice Watkins in which the latter stated that it was the only complaint that had been received, and tried to persuade Elder he was mistaken. Yet several other shareholders recall events at the 1987 AGM in just the same way Elder did. When the matter was raised at the 1988 AGM, the board not only refused to accept a proposition that the details be accurately recorded in the company's minutes book and that the original proposal be put to the meeting again, but Martin Edwards denied that any complaint had been received during the intervening twelve months.

In his nine years as United chairman Martin Edwards has used the very size of his own club to become an important figure within English football. Unlike his father and Sir Matt Busby, however, he has never served on the Football League Management Committee, preferring instead to act within an elite group of clubs that have wielded power by their sheer financial muscle. The Big Five, as they refer to themselves – United, Liverpool, Everton, Tottenham Hotspur and Arsenal – accounted for around 20 per cent of league home attendances in 1987–88. Since 1982 representatives of the Big Five have met secretly at regular intervals to plan how to further their own interests. The Five usually get together at the Park Lane Hotel in

London's Mayfair before important meetings of the League or negotiations with the television companies.

Martin Edwards is particularly close to the Tottenham Hotspur chief executive, Irving Scholar, one of the men behind the London club's stock exchange flotation in 1983. Scholar and Edwards meet regularly and the United chairman has often visited White Hart Lane to gather new ideas. In 1988 the relationship was such that Tottenham's publishing subsidiary, Cockerell Books, brought out the official club history of European football, *Red Devils in Europe*. And even United's match-ticket computing system is an offshoot of a Spurs subsidiary. The software is supplied by Synchro Systems, a company which is 75 per cent owned by Tottenham.

Over the last seven years the Big Five have successfully pressed for changes in the League's structure that would give them more power and money. This has inevitably been at the expense of the minor sides within the League. 'The smaller clubs are bleeding the game dry,' Martin Edwards argued. 'For the sake of the game they should be put to sleep.' Among the important changes the Five have successfully lobbied for was the decision in 1983 to end the system whereby away teams got a share of league gate receipts. In 1986 all the first-division sides were given greater voting power and at the same time it was agreed that first-division sides would in future receive 50 per cent of all sponsorship and television money.

Throughout the period the Big Five have not been afraid to apply their ultimate sanction – breaking away to form a 'Super League'. The Liverpool chairman, John Smith, warned of this in 1982. Everton's Philip Carter revealed in 1986 that they had actually carried out a feasibility study. But it was in the summer of 1988 that the Super League warnings by Martin Edwards and his four colleagues from the football elite became most serious. At a meeting of the Big Five at the Park Lane Hotel on 16 June 1988 the clubs' chairmen decided to reject the Football League's arrangements for televised football with the BBC and the new satellite station, BSB (British Satellite Broadcasting). Greg Dyke, director of programmes at London Weekend Television and chairman of the ITV Sports Committee, offered each of the Big Five £1 million every year to allow their games to be televised on ITV. The agreement would run for four years from 1989. This compared with £70,000 they could expect from the proposed deal with the BBC and BSB.

On top of that Dyke wanted to offer five middle-ranking first-division clubs the sum of £2 million to share between them, to join in with the Big Five. The arrangements he proposed would involve twenty live games a season, at least one and a maximum of three from the home ground of each team. Clubs would also receive £50,000 when a match was broadcast live from their ground.

Clause 11 of the ITV proposals was the most explosive. It ran:

> Finally should the ten clubs ever break from the Football League, ITV would be extremely interested in becoming the sponsor of the ITV Super League. We understand this gives you problems with players' contracts but if this could be achieved we think it would be in both your and our interests. In these circumstances it would certainly be in our interests to promote the new League to the best of our ability.

A trawl through the records shows that arguments over television contracts and Super Leagues are nothing new for Manchester United. As long ago as 1947, when only a few thousand people in Britain owned TV sets, the Old Trafford directors told the League that the question of televising games was a matter for the whole League, not individual clubs. A decade later, in 1957, the BBC complained when United sold the TV rights for the European Cup semi-final to ITV for £2,500 without offering them to the BBC. Moreover, the United board had supported the idea of a Super League of top clubs as long ago as 1960. The club wrote to the Conservative MP and former Olympic runner Chris Chattaway when he suggested the idea at the time.

But the proposals to the Big Five in 1988 are the first signs of the inevitable consequence of the commercialisation of the national game into a profit-making business designed to benefit individuals. Martin Edwards came under considerable attack from United supporters in the pages of the *Manchester Evening News* and in phone calls to the club. Edwards and the other Big Five chairmen rapidly had to backtrack, arguing that it was never their intention to form a breakaway league. However, the evidence is that they would have been quite happy to go it alone, and indeed may well do so yet. The hostility shown by the fans in the summer of 1988 reveals how these club chairmen could easily kill, or at least seriously maim, the goose that still lays many of their clubs' golden eggs – the supporters who trudge faithfully through the turnstiles.

10 THE BUILDING OF OLD TRAFFORD

'Old Trafford is the only ground where you can walk out to the centre circle when the place is deserted and it still oozes atmosphere.'

Tommy Docherty.

EDGBASTON, THE famous cricket ground in Birmingham owned by the Warwickshire county side, is not the first place one might expect to find leading officials from a football club, especially in the middle of the soccer season. Yet on the afternoon of Friday, 30 March 1961, the Manchester United chairman, Harold Hardman, along with Louis Edwards, Les Olive and Matt Busby made what proved to be a decisive journey to Warwickshire's home ground. It was a financial visit. They wanted to learn how the men at Edgbaston had, over the previous decade, managed to make so much money. Moreover, they were funds raised not from cricket but, indirectly, from football.

In the early 1950s Warwickshire had realised that the days of great individual cricket patrons, men prepared to subsidise the English county teams, were drawing to a close. The era of company sponsorship, however, had not yet arrived, and the county's officials searched for alternative sources of income. A football pools competition was the answer they came up with, and soon it was producing an annual turnover of more than £500,000 and a yearly profit of £70,000. Warwickshire's army of 4,700 agents looked after a third of a million pools customers, each of whom paid a minimum stake of a shilling a week. With the profits new stands for spectators were erected. Indeed, the ground was improved so much that in 1957 Edgbaston regained its status as a test match venue, after a lapse of twenty-eight years.

Until the 1960s, the finances of English football teams had been fairly simple. Any club knew that its expenditure would be limited by

166

the players' maximum wage of £20 a week. So, according to the number of staff on the books and the level of overheads, it was fairly clear how much any club had to raise every match at the turnstiles. But the 1950s had seen increasing agitation from the Professional Footballers' Association to abolish the maximum wage, a reform that Matt Busby himself supported. By 1960, with footballers under the skilled leadership of Jimmy Hill, it was obvious that limits on players' earnings would not last much longer. Clubs would have to start competing with each other in the money they were prepared to offer. For many clubs it was clear that new sources of income might be needed if they were to stay at the top.

After Munich, Matt Busby and his new director, Louis Edwards, decided that they wanted to develop Old Trafford into the kind of great football stadium they had visited on their Continental travels. Busby's ideal model was a ground at which Manchester United had not in fact played: Barcelona's magnificent Nou Camp stadium in Spain. The United manager admitted at the time, though, that 'we could never pay for it on our gates'.

Five days before Christmas in 1960 the United directors decided to ask the Football Association for permission to run a football pools competition. Without waiting for the FA's reply, they then agreed to go ahead with enquiries: at the following meeting, in January 1961, 'Mr Busby was asked to obtain further information.' Hence the trip to Edgbaston.

Matt Busby and Louis Edwards were keen on copying the Warwickshire pools scheme, but the United chairman, Harold Hardman, felt uneasy. As a Methodist he thought pools were a form of gambling, and he managed to overcome his doubts only when his colleagues promised to shoulder full responsibility. Les Olive made a second trip to Warwickshire, and United tried to persuade the main organiser of the county's pools, Winnie Crook, to come to Old Trafford. She declined. Instead the club took on her assistant, Bill Burke. A former gas board employee, Burke had started off as one of Warwickshire's collectors only a few years earlier, working part-time on commission before joining the operation full-time. United gave him a three-year contract on £1,500 a year.

In July 1961, equipped with nothing more, he says, than 'paper clips, rubber bands and a bottle of ink', Burke set up in a small office formerly occupied by United's assistant secretary. He saw Manchester United as something of a challenge. Could the kind of sudden transformation he had helped bring about at Warwickshire's ground be repeated? Moreover, he felt, at Manchester United any new stands would be filled every other week, instead of only once a year at Edgbaston, whenever they hosted a test match. Burke became secretary and organiser of the new Manchester United Development Association (MUDA), a body which had its own directors – all chosen from the United board – and which had been set up with the object 'wholly to raise funds for the development of amenities for Manchester United Football Club and support of athletic games'. Legally it was a totally separate organisation.

The new man at Old Trafford simply established a football pool modelled on Warwickshire's. The football club lent him £1,000 to get things going, and it was made clear that the Development Association's finances should be run separately from those of the club. Burke recruited his part-time agents by sending out a letter to members of the supporters' club and to all season-ticket holders. Within two years 1,000 United supporters were engaged as agents, earning commission on stakes they collected from the pool's 20,000 customers. As an incentive, agents were also given their own regular prizes. They occasionally received free match tickets too, and priority in the allocation of season tickets. Whenever United were involved in a Cup match where tickets were scarce, agents' names would go into a draw for an allocation. In later years the 'winners' of the Cup ticket draw were almost always those agents whose work was producing the most revenue.

The United pools competition was fairly complicated. In the big national football pools, such as Littlewoods and Vernons, customers have to predict which matches are likely to produce draws, or various alternatives such as selections of home or away wins. But for United to do that would have involved a large amount of work in checking each coupon, and might have annoyed the traditional pools companies. Instead, Burke's pools customers were allocated four numbers corresponding each week to four different Football League or Scottish League matches. Whether people won or not basically depended on the scores in those games. Officially customers could ask to select their own four numbers, but in practice it was difficult to do so, and in effect the contest was one of pure chance. In time the absence of any skill in the contest would cause Bill Burke considerable problems.

In the early 1960s United's new commercial venture was probably unique among English football clubs, though Rangers and Celtic had long run football pools in Scotland. Partly because United enjoyed a monopoly in English soccer, Burke was quickly successful. Many of the quarter of a million members he eventually attracted had no real interest in football and did not identify with Manchester United. Burke says the majority of customers were women who wanted 'a small, regular flutter'.

Under existing pools law, a third of the stake money went in pools tax (nowadays – 42½ per cent) while another third had to be distributed in winnings. After the expenses of running the operation, United aimed for a return of about 12 per cent. By April 1962 Burke had built up a surplus of £5,103 and was able to repay the football club's £1,000 loan. That summer saw the first benefit of the Development Association's work when 1,700 wooden seats were installed at a cost of £5,000 in what became known as E stand at the back of the famous Stretford End terraces. In recognition of their work, development agents were allocated some of the seats in the new stand. Meanwhile, the Development Association's work had grown so much that its offices were soon enlarged.

But the most dramatic innovation arising from Bill Burke's work was the new cantilever stand, on which work began in 1964. Until then the popular side of the ground, opposite the main stand, had consisted of standing terraces which were only partly covered. The ambitious plans for this area – which included the most up-to-date football stand in Britain – ensured that the FA awarded three games in the 1966 World Cup to Old Trafford instead of Manchester City's Maine Road. Since the war City's stadium had arguably been a better ground than Old Trafford; soon United would undoubtedly boast Manchester's top venue.

The new development was inspired by the cantilever north stand at Sheffield Wednesday's ground, Hillsborough, which had been built in 1961. But United's stand, opened in August 1965, was much more impressive as a structure, and it contained a totally new feature in British football. Bill Burke had arranged for the United directors to visit a similar cantilever stand built by the same architects, Mather and Nutter, at Manchester racecourse. In particular he invited them to sit in one of the new private boxes at the top. But the directors did not like the glass barrier which separated them from the action. To convince them, when United's stand was half-built, Burke took the board members up the unfinished concrete terracing to a spot where he had set out a few kitchen chairs. Yes, they agreed, it was a magnificent view out over the pitch. They promptly gave approval for a row of glass-fronted private boxes to be installed above the rows of ordinary seats. The directors decided that the boxes should cost £250 or £300, depending on location, for which the box holder and his four guests would be admitted to every game during the season, but separate arrangements had to be made for the World Cup. Holders were also allowed to add their own television sets and telephones. A bottle of champagne awaited each holder on the day when the boxes opened in September 1965.

Burke hoped to tap a new market for football – local businessmen and companies who wanted to impress clients or reward their staff. One of United's new boxes even housed Albert Finney briefly, during a scene from a famous film of that era, *Charlie Bubbles*, released in 1967. As they sat with their unobstructed view, box holders could order drinks or a simple meal. So as not to lose the crowd atmosphere behind the glass, noise was relayed through a speaker system on which the volume could be adjusted. The boxes not reserved by the directors were so oversubscribed by outsiders that Stretford council had to wait five years before getting one.

The board's initial scepticism about the boxes seemed to disappear completely, for, according to the minutes of one of their meetings, 'each director was allocated three boxes at £300, and one at £250 for disposal to his friends'. The directors' allocation of twenty boxes accounted for nearly half the total. In most cases the directors simply sold the boxes to friends or acquaintances. In spite of the heavy demand, when three boxes were given up by their owners in 1966, one of them was assigned 'for the personal use of the Club chairman' who by then, of course, was Louis Edwards. Edwards was allocated yet another box in 1975, though he actually sat in the directors' box.

When the £325,000 bill came through for the construction of the new stand, most of it was paid directly by the Development Association rather than by the football club. This meant that nearly all the improvements to Old Trafford were being paid for by the surplus from the pools competition, in accordance with MUDA's rules. Consequently, the club's own profits could be devoted to football and acquiring new players. The 1961 Warwickshire trip had provided rapid and impressive results.

A vast new gymnasium had also been constructed by the Association for £30,000 at The Cliff, United's training ground in Salford. About one per cent of the Association's funds was also donated to local sporting causes, which, of course, did much to help United's public image. The Development Association continued to accumulate large levels of funds, waiting for the day when United needed them for ground improvements. And Bill Burke, according to a colleague, was 'a financial wizard' at investing the funds to squeeze out the best return. Money was often placed on overnight markets to earn the last bit of interest.

The pools operation reached its peak around 1969 and 1970, after the excitement generated by the European Cup triumph. A staff of twenty were now employed in the Association's offices by the railway bridge next to the entrance to the ground. A team of 6,000 agents looked after a quarter of a million clients. There were attractive prizes of £4,000 or £5,000, and sometimes Mini cars were awarded to agents. Moreover, both agents and customers were constantly encouraged by the fact that the profits were going towards substantial ground improvements.

In 1970, though, the whole future of Burke's work was put in jeopardy. After a long legal test case, *Singette Ltd and others* v. *Martin*, the House of Lords confirmed the verdicts of lower courts that small pools competitions such as United's were illegal. The deciding factor was that because customers effectively had their numbers chosen for them, no skill was involved. The pools were, in effect, lotteries, and so subject to the much stricter limits then in force on lottery competitions, such as a top prize of only £100.

What initially seemed bad news for United was, however, eventually turned in the club's favour. Fortunately the police seemed to be in no hurry to prosecute. Manchester United quickly banded together with Rangers and Warwickshire and, more importantly, with charities such as the Spastics Society, whose Top-Ten competition ran along similar lines. They lobbied ministers and wrote to every MP. As a result the Government passed the 1971 Pool Competitions Act to help the worthy causes that stood suddenly to lose income. The 1971 Act allowed the existing small pools schemes to continue for another five years, but no new competitions could be established by rivals. From 1976 until 1987 the Act was annually extended by successive home secretaries.

So Burke's successful pools operation was not only allowed to continue, but also, at a time when football was waking up to commercial possibilities, the new law meant that other clubs could not copy the idea and compete. As far as English football was concerned, the Government had granted United a virtual pools monopoly. Bill Burke could give out much higher prizes and turn over much more money than the traditional lottery schemes, and these advantages far outweighed the 33 per cent pools tax that was levied then. A measure of Burke's achievement was the number of officials from other clubs who came to consult him about his work; but the biggest compliment of all was an enquiry from Everton, the club belonging to the Moores family, the owners of Littlewoods Pools.

The Home Office made it clear, however, that it would not carry on renewing the 1971 Act indefinitely, and the exempted organisations were expected to devise alternative money-making ventures. In 1973 the Development Association began a spot-the-ball competition in conjunction with Ladbrokes which, in the brief time it operated, proved to be a bigger money-spinner for United than the pools. Ladbrokes, however, found it not worthwhile and abandoned the venture.

The new 1976 Lotteries and Amusements Act greatly relaxed the previous restrictions on lotteries, allowing much bigger prizes than before. Soon most football clubs and many local councils had set up their own lottery schemes. Bill Burke decided not to jump in straight away; not totally convinced at first that a lottery would be worthwhile. In 1978, however, the Manchester United Lottery was established and it became a sub-division of the Development Association's work. The club sold the familiar scratch cards both on sites at Old Trafford and through association agents. In fact several different lotteries were run at once, some short-term, lasting only a week, and others, with bigger prizes, lasting much longer. But even with the new lottery rules, and free of the 33 per cent pools levy, lotteries could never match the income United's pools competition had once generated.

Yet the old pools were by no means as lucrative as they had once been. Unlike Rangers, for instance, United failed to increase pools stake money in line with inflation. Income therefore declined in real terms. So too did the prize money, and people naturally lost interest. Moreover, the Irish Customs had prevented the large team of agents in Ireland from receiving pools literature, because Irish law is much stricter on such matters. And successive increases in postage rates also added to MUDA's costs.

When Burke retired as organiser of the Development Association in 1981, after twenty years, it was estimated that his work had raised £4 million for United. Most of it had been channelled into paying for the new cantilever stands, which today cover three sides of the ground. Two thirds of that money had come from the work of the Development Association, the rest from other activities initiated by Burke since his appointment as overall commercial manager in 1973. Already, by the time Burke retired, the Association had become much less important as a source of income, and there was much more competition from other clubs' lotteries. Moreover, no proper plans had yet been made for the day when the exemption of the 1971 legislation ended, and United's pools became illegal.

In 1982, shortly after Burke's retirement, United went into partnership with Glasgow Rangers, a club with a brilliant record in the field of prize competitions. Rangers in fact made the first approach; the organiser of their pools, Hugh Adam, was also worried about what to do when the competitions became illegal. The Glasgow club's pools were by then five or six times larger than United's, even though they employed no more staff, and they enjoyed dominance in Scotland among soccer club competitions. Rangers hoped that by going in with United they could take a step further, and gain entry into the much larger market in England.

The result was a contest called Spaceshot, which was designed to use the vast team of agents employed by both clubs. Essentially it was based on the idea of spot-the-ball. Photographs were taken of Rangers and United players against a goalmouth, pretending to take penalties. Customers had to predict where the ball would hit the net, as decided by a team of judges which included Denis Law, Bobby Charlton, the Rangers player Sandy Jardine and the Scottish referee 'Tiny' Wharton. Because the contest involved skill, in as much as customers had to anticipate the judges' verdict, Spaceshot could not be deemed a lottery. This meant that it was not subject to any restrictions in turnover and prize money. A joint company was formed to run Spaceshot, Rangeman Promotions Ltd, and at the time it was widely predicted that the venture would bring both United and Rangers vast wealth.

This did not happen. Spaceshot flopped. Firstly, the competition turned out to be far too complicated for both agents and customers to follow. It was based on two separate photos that had been taken specially – one with a United player and one with a Rangers man – showing them shooting at goal with no goalkeeper or other opponents. People entering the contest had to work out coordinates – 15–27, 21–33, or whatever, on a master grid – to show where in the goal they thought the ball would end up. Customers were then expected to enter both sets of coordinates on a duplicate form. It was so easy, though, for customers to get the photos, and the numbers for the vertical and horizontal axes, mixed up; it would have made things a little simpler if numbers had been used on just one axis and letters on the other. Even Denis Law and some of the staff administering it did not understand Spaceshot fully. Matters became even more

173

complicated when, at around the same time, agents were allowed to pay cash directly into the MUDA and Rangeman accounts through the Girobank transcash system.

Secondly, when Spaceshot was launched in February 1983, it seems that it failed through hostility to operating the scheme, and even religious bigotry, among some of Rangers' agents. Manchester United are regarded as a Catholic club and traditionally have enjoyed close ties with Rangers' arch rivals, Celtic, who, incidentally, were furious about the link-up. Many agents and customers preferred to concentrate on the existing competitions. Some people even tried to enter only one half of the Spaceshot competition and insist the money went solely to whichever of the two teams they supported.

The third reason for the failure of Spaceshot, according to Development Association staff, was that there was even coolness among some senior personnel at Old Trafford to the scheme.

The outcome was that Spaceshot was dropped after just two months, and each club lost £74,000 on the venture. Rangers, however, now run a modified and much simpler version of Spaceshot. It makes what the Glasgow club regards as a modest £250,000 a year, more than United now earns annually on all its competitions. So an excellent financial opportunity may have been lost. Had United run the scheme with Celtic, and made it simpler to enter, it might have made money for Old Trafford too. But then it was Rangers' idea.

As United's competitions – the pools and the lottery – slowly declined, the Development Association found it harder and harder to keep within the rules laid down by the Betting and Gaming Board. In particular the expenses on a lottery must not exceed 25 per cent of the income. In other words each lottery has to achieve an income which is four times greater than its costs. To get round these regulations, lottery expenses were gradually transferred to the football club. Development Association staff suddenly found that they were no longer MUDA employees, but worked directly for Manchester United, though few had any reason to complain. The club was also paying more and more of the Association's administrative costs, such as postage, stationery and staff meals. It meant that the claimed expenses of United's lotteries, as set out in regular returns to the Gaming Board, were increasingly understated and false.

With many different lottery competitions all launched during the course of a season, income from a popular lottery would often be reassigned to an unsuccessful lottery which would otherwise not have met its income target. By juggling with the figures like this, using good lotteries to subsidise the bad ones, it was possible to ensure that the expenses stated on returns to the Gaming Board never went above 25 per cent of the income. On one occasion a lottery for the basketball club, with a car as the first prize, failed to meet its expected sales target of £30,000. So the Development Association's printers, Dawn Print, owned by Martin Edwards' brother Roger, were asked to provide a false invoice. This meant that the basketball lottery's apparent expenses could then be reduced to the permitted level.

Things reached the stage, however, where few of the existing lotteries were making enough money to meet the spending limits, even though they were still just about profitable. Staff in the Development Association offices were spending vast amounts of time playing around with the figures rather than promoting the lotteries themselves. Life was constrained by the fact that Gaming Board returns had to be submitted within six weeks of a lottery finishing. 'At the end,' one former employee recalls, 'it reached a point where there were no longer any good lotteries to pinch money from. So we just pinched money from the lottery that was furthest away in time.'

It got so bad that the absurd situation occurred where United were actually buying their own lottery tickets! To boost the stated income levels on several lotteries Martin Edwards and other club officials actually agreed that United would buy £11,000 worth of lottery tickets at face value from its own Development Association. The money then had to be accounted for. One suggestion was that the £11,000 bill should be presented in United's accounts as a part of the club's expenditure on promotion and advertising. It is not clear whether Martin Edwards and the United staff actually sat down together and rubbed the tickets off to see how much the club had won from itself!

In January 1985 the small pools competition, as permitted by the 1971 legislation, was officially closed down. The Government had finally warned that the exemption of the act would not be extended beyond the next general election. In effect, United's pools operation, with variable prizes depending on the level of stakes and the number of winners, was simply transformed into two linked lotteries with fixed prizes. To most customers it would have looked much the same as the old pools contest.

Since 1978 the Development Association has also been involved in a scheme for agents to sell Christmas hampers. Weekly payments are collected from customers as agents do their competition rounds. Initially the distribution was chaotic, and once several customers had to be reimbursed after their hampers were not delivered in time for Christmas. The hampers were provided by Bobby Charlton Promotions and despatched from a site on an industrial estate in Ormskirk. In 1986 the firm was paid more than £40,000 for hampers. Bobby Charlton's company has also provided jewellery for the Development Association, which was sold to pools customers via agents in a similar way, though it brought much less trade than the hampers.

In 1986 the Development Association's competitions officially made a profit of £350,883 on ticket sales of £942,851. But the figures badly overestimate the true return, since the accounts do not include those large areas of expenditure that are now met by the football club to keep within the Gaming Board's restrictions. Allowing for the subsidy from the club, the 1986 surplus of £350,883 was in fact reduced by more than half to only £158,258. For the same reasons the accumulated development profit of £3,548,659 between 1961 and 1987 must also be an exaggeration. A more accurate figure might be about £2½ million.

Today the Development Association runs a whole series of lotteries – two based on the pools idea, others based on scratch cards – and it continues to sell hampers and jewellery. But the organisation is nothing like the force it was in Bill Burke's day. Burke's successors – John Lillie, the commercial manager from 1981 to 1985, and Barry Moorhouse, who ran the Development Association until 1987, have lacked Burke's ideas, drive and ability. Under Barry Moorhouse, petty rivalries built up between staff involved on the pools competition and those working on lotteries. Morale also fell badly after a series of thefts which lost £8,000 over a four-year period. One Development Association employee was convicted of a small theft and sacked, but afterwards money still continued to go missing.

As Moorhouse failed to find the culprit, or culprits, all his staff fell under suspicion. At one point the assistant manager, Tony Woodward, was arrested by the police, questioned at length, and then cleared completely. Woodward was nevertheless sacked from his job on the grounds, said Martin Edwards, that it would have been intolerable for him to carry on working with Moorhouse. He eventually received £10,000 in compensation following months of legal argument. The money was paid only on condition that Woodward would not take legal action against Moorhouse for defamation of character. He was also obliged to sign United's usual confidentiality clause not to disclose the secrets and internal affairs of the club.

The Development Association, bringing in around £250,000 a year, now accounts for only a small fraction of United's non-football income. Today, with many soccer clubs running lotteries, United faces stiff competition. The 6,000 agents Bill Burke had on the books at the Association's peak in the early 1970s have been reduced to around 1,800.

The absorption of MUDA into Manchester United's financial affairs, which was carried out officially in the early 1980s, means that the relationship between the money MUDA raises and ground improvements is now obscured. The visual incentive that agents and customers once saw growing up all around them in the form of new stands has now become blurred.

The phenomenal success of Rangers in prize competitions paid for the £10 million redevelopment of three sides of their Ibrox ground between 1978 and 1981. The Glasgow club claim that their competitions in Scotland are probably four or five times larger than United's. In generating more than £1 million a year, they have helped make Rangers by far the wealthiest football club in Britain. Manchester United, however, can now make money more easily from other commercial ventures. Both the club sponsorship and shirt deals are now more lucrative. Some of the club's new money earners were, however, actually established with funds raised by the Development Association.

In the 1960s and 1970s Bill Burke and the club directors were determined that as each area of the Old Trafford ground was redeveloped, it should contain ventures that would in themselves generate further income. The private boxes had set a precedent and uncovered further potential. In 1975 a further phase began when the Executive Suite was opened in the main stand for supporters who wanted to eat before matches but could not afford a whole box and might have wanted only a couple of seats. The building contract was awarded to John Lee and Sons, one of whose directors, David Lee, was Louis Edwards' son-in-law, though both Louis and Martin Edwards left the board meeting while the decision was being taken.

By 1987 United's catering facilities had produced more than £600,000 surplus over the previous nine years, making them one of the most profitable parts of the club's business. Old Trafford has two main restaurant areas which during the week cater for the general public, and six different suites which can be hired by individuals and organisations who want to hold dinners, wedding receptions or meetings. They employ forty full-time staff and sixty more part-time. On match days 600 members use the Executive Suite for a fee of £730 each a season. This gives them access to the restaurants and bar, and a seat in an area behind and to the side of the directors' box. The catering staff have been known to prepare more than 800 meals on some days. Less wealthy supporters can use the less luxurious facilities of the Sir Matt Busby Suite next to the ticket office, which provides a cafeteria service.

Twenty years after their installation, the private boxes cost between £4,000 a season for five seats and £15,000 for eight seats, while a four-place window table brings in £6,325 a year. The idea of boxes has been copied at most major football grounds; Arsenal, for instance, have built forty-eight boxes at Highbury's famous Clock End. Both the Arsenal boxes and those being built by Spurs in their controversial development of The Shelf at White Hart Lane have been sold on leases which last several years, while United still prefer to let the Old Trafford boxes annually. In the prosperous South-east the business potential of boxes is now far greater than in the North-west, and for both the North London clubs the recent sale of long box leases provided capital sums of several million pounds. Manchester United still boast more boxes than any other club, however – 103 of them around three sides of the stadium – and in 1987 only two became vacant at the end of the season. But the demand is not as great as it once was, and nowadays United have to go out in search of new occupants.

The area of the large private boxes, restaurants and Executive Suite along the top of the main stand is now filled every match day with businessmen and rich supporters from all over Manchester and the North-west. It is often said that the only way to get hold of the British Aerospace chairman, Roland Smith, is to ring his table at Old Trafford when United are at home. Some occupants of the boxes and the suite use the club's facilities as an extension of their offices. They spend time on the telephone to or meeting friends and business contacts, entertaining and impressing commercial clients, and making money.

The terrace supporter on the Stretford or Scoreboard End or in the United Road Paddock has benefited little from the money generated by Bill Burke and the Development Association. The concrete he stands on and the barrier he leans against are much the same as they were thirty years ago. The refreshment and toilet facilities are spartan in comparison to the executive facilities and in some sections as poor as ever. Even the argument that the ordinary fan has benefited by way of relatively cheap admission to Old Trafford has now lost ground in the wake of United's recent membership scheme. This means that the

Stretford End supporter has to pay more than for many years to support his team from his usual viewpoint. And with season and league match ticket-book holders now forced to become members of the controversial scheme, the cost being incorporated in their substantially increased renewal fee, United have made it clear that loyal supporters are no longer exempt from the drive for profit.

Most of the ground improvements paid for by Bill Burke have benefited a very different class of supporter. The Old Trafford his work helped build is the United of the private box and the Executive Suite: a football ground which, like the club itself, has become a forum for making business deals.

11 PLAYER POLITICS

'It's a rat race, and the rats are winning.'

Alex Ferguson on football agents, 1988.

ON SATURDAY, 11 January 1986, there was great excitement among the press corps at the Manor Ground, the tiny home of Oxford United. But it was not the kind of interest normally associated with a visit by Manchester United. The talk among journalists, which began about two hours before the kick-off, revolved around rumours that Manchester United were involved in a multi-million-pound deal that would mean the departure of their star striker, Mark Hughes.

By the time Hughes volleyed home Gidman's cross in the seventy-fourth minute for yet another of his remarkable goals, the telephone lines between Oxford, London and Manchester were carrying the first reports of his pending departure, soon to be splashed over the back pages of the Sunday morning papers. The speculation would have severe repercussions for United. After winning the FA Cup the previous May, they opened the 1985–86 season with an extraordinary ten consecutive wins and established a ten-point gap at the top of the first division. And Mark Hughes had played a leading role in United's brilliant start. But then form dropped dramatically, and injuries hit the team. Nevertheless, after beating Oxford that day, they still seemed to have some chance of winning the title for the first time in nearly twenty years.

Within days of the Oxford match it was revealed publicly that Mark Hughes' five-year contract with United, signed less than a month earlier, had stipulated that if he left Old Trafford he would cost any buying club £1.8 million. Then it became known that the contract also stated that Barcelona had the right of first refusal if Hughes did choose to leave. When rumours circulated that he had indeed already signed for the Spanish club, United refused to confirm or deny them. The speculation became intense. Eventually, in late March 1986, United announced that Hughes was indeed going to Spain.

It had been a delicate situation for United. Until 1985 Mark Hughes had been badly rewarded by the club. His income had not yet been adjusted to take account of his swift two-year rise from youth team to first team, and he was earning only £250 a week. Had Hughes refused to sign a new contract, he would have been free to seek rich sums abroad. The complicated UEFA multiplier system, based on a player's age and earnings, would have awarded United a meagre transfer fee of around £400,000, just as it had undervalued Joe Jordan when he went to AC Milan in 1981 for £250,000.

For United the near £2 million price tag seemed the only way to guarantee adequate compensation if Mark Hughes chose to leave. Moreover, when the deal with Barcelona was agreed, the Spaniards insisted that it was kept secret, since Hughes' arrival would affect the position of their existing foreign players. So United were unable to put an end to the intense speculation, yet the uncertainty, and Hughes' marked drop in form, seriously undermined the campaign for the league title. In the first half of the season Hughes had scored eleven times. His scoring touch only returned when the speculation about Barcelona was resolved, but by then it was too late. United finished a disappointing fourth for the third time in three years, after a season that had promised so much.

Hughes' contract in Spain was worth around £2 million over five years, but he struggled there as a player. His partnership with the England striker Gary Lineker did not work out, and by the end of his first season he had been demoted to the reserves. When Terry Venables was sacked as Barcelona manager in 1987, Hughes' playing future looked bleak. Only going on loan to Bayern Munich in West Germany revitalised his form and career.

Just over two years later Hughes' return to Old Trafford proved to be almost as remarkable as his departure. On Thursday, 23 June 1988, again after months of press guesswork and gossip, he rejoined Manchester United. The £1.6 million fee was only £200,000 less than United had received when they sold him to Barcelona. As the talks had progressed, and as United fans' anticipation had increased and thus the price of disappointment had grown even greater for Martin Edwards, Barcelona's asking price was reported as having crept up from £1.1 million to £1.3 million, then to £1.5 million and finally to £1.6 million. The figure mentioned publicly, though, was £1.8 million.

Never before in post-war football had any player ever left Manchester United and then returned. Normally those who had left the club in the past found their career going rapidly downhill thereafter, Johnny Giles being perhaps the most notable exception. Equally remarkable was that before his two multi-million pound transfers, Mark Hughes had spent barely two years in the United first team and had made just eighty-nine league appearances.

The 1988 agreement with Barcelona was confidently assumed to have made Hughes the highest-paid player at Old Trafford, far better off than Brian McClair who had just become the first player since George Best to score twenty league goals in a season, and better rewarded than even the England captain, Bryan Robson, whom most would consider a much better player. Robson's earning power, though, is supplemented considerably by his outside activities.

'Sparky' Hughes said he was delighted to be back, but many believed that he had never wanted to go in the first place. A former United reserve player, Joe Hanrahan, recalls Hughes saying to him before he left: 'Has it ever occurred to you I might not want to go?' A similar impression emerged from other remarks Hughes made that winter – one newspaper quoted him as saying that he was being forced out. Later, when he had joined Barcelona, Hughes told guests at Norman Whiteside's wedding that he had never wanted to leave United. Such statements only reinforced the widely held opinion that Martin Edwards and Dennis Roach, who claims he is paid a set fee on any new contract, were more interested in the transfer than Hughes himself.

For ordinary Manchester United fans the Hughes affair greatly increased disillusionment with Martin Edwards and the Old Trafford administration. 'Sparky' was one of their favourite players. After his tremendous partnership with Norman Whiteside in United's youth team, and his introduction to the first team in 1984, he had played a major role in the 1985 FA Cup success, scoring one of his extraordinary goals in the semi-final replay against Liverpool. The details that leaked out in 1986 about Hughes' new contract with United seemed only to anger fans who believed Martin Edwards was simply out to make money for himself. Such opinions were reinforced by the revelation that Edwards received bonuses based upon one per cent of any profit made on transfers during a season.

In the spring of 1988 it was Martin Edwards and Dennis Roach who carried out the negotiations to bring Mark Hughes back to Manchester. And Roach could have expected to be rewarded with around £80,000 for his 'set fee' (based on a modest five per cent) from United, on top of any money from Hughes himself. Remarkably, within a few days of the striker's return in July 1988, the Italian club Juventus offered £2 million for him. Even Martin Edwards would have known that, if the offer were accepted, such a move would be difficult to explain to the fans and would devastate the player. Yet the United chairman may have been tempted by the Italian offer since the money would have been useful in the competition with Spurs to buy Paul Gascoigne from Newcastle. Bobby Charlton's admiration for Gascoigne was common knowledge and he was reported as having been involved in trying to persuade the Newcastle star to come to Old Trafford.

Martin Edwards' close relationship with the agent Dennis Roach leaves him open to criticism of a conflict of interest. For Roach has not just negotiated on behalf of several United players – including Mark Hughes, Gary Bailey, Peter Davenport, Norman Whiteside, Paul McGrath, Jesper Olsen and Johnny Sivebaek – he also works as Manchester United's own agent in arranging overseas tours and friendly matches against foreign opposition. Roach's firm, the Professional Representation Organisation Ltd (PRO), is based in a small office near the cathedral at St Albans in Hertfordshire. It boasts the former Arsenal manager Bertie Mee and the BBC commentator Bob Wilson as its consultants.

United's relations with Dennis Roach go back almost ten years. In 1979 he arranged for Dave Sexton to buy the Yugoslav international defender Nikola Jovanovic for £350,000. Roach's company at that time, the Euroach Agency, registered in Cyprus, had actually bought Jovanovic's registration from his club in Yugoslavia, Red Star Belgrade, and it claimed to own the player. Roach proposed that United should pay his Cyprus company both a transfer fee and a regular service fee while Jovanovic was at United, as well as the player's salary. The Football Association, however, refused to allow such a deal because it involved paying an agent, which was then against the rules of both the FA and the world football body FIFA. When an alternative deal was finally arranged to bring Jovanovic to Old Trafford, he was not a great success, and played only twenty-four games for the club in three years – a cost of well over £15,000 a game.

Another football agency that emerged around the same time was Circle Sports Ltd, based in Essex, which tried to fix United up with two Peruvian internationals – Juan Oblitas and Percy Rojas – from Sporting Cristal of Lima. The proposal came to nothing, but in time United would begin fruitful relationships both with Circle Sports and its owner, Eddie Buckley, and with Dennis Roach and PRO.

After Ron Atkinson succeeded Dave Sexton as manager of United in

1981, the club's relations with Roach began to flourish. He had once played against Atkinson in the Southern League when the United manager was at Kettering and Roach captained Bedford Town. Roach says that he acted as the United manager's personal agent in commercial deals. He had formerly owned a furniture company but in the late 1970s slowly moved into the job of representing star international footballers interested in prospering overseas, including Johann Cruyff, Trevor Francis and Liam Brady.

In 1984 Martin Edwards struck an exclusive agreement with PRO to arrange money-making pre-season foreign tours and friendly matches. In subsequent years Roach has made United hundreds of thousands of pounds from such fixtures, and himself earns 10 per cent on each deal. Until recently most United friendly games against foreign opposition were organised by Roach. The 1987 summer tour to Sweden and Denmark, for instance, made £36,000 for United and £4,000 for PRO. A match in Bahrain in December 1986 made £13,500 for the club and £1,500 for the agent. Roach also organised the Manchester tournament at Maine Road in August 1987 involving United, City, Atletico Mineiro of Brazil and PSV Eindhoven, for which United received a guaranteed payment of £30,000. It was planned to repeat the contest at Old Trafford in 1988, with Gothenburg and Atletico Bilbao as guests, though City would have received a guarantee of only £20,000 compared with United's £30,000. The idea was dropped at a late stage because United said that the newly restored Old Trafford pitch would not be ready in time, but then the club proceeded to arrange another home friendly with Hamburg instead, through another agent. The affair is known to have caused some controversy and it is believed that at one stage Manchester City were even looking to United for some compensation.

When United renegotiated their contract with PRO in 1986, it included additional matches to be arranged during the course of the season and the wording of the contract was changed from 'exclusive' to 'non-exclusive'. The Football Association is quite explicit that the use of exclusive agents is against its rules, and United's previous arrangements with Roach were contrary to the regulations. Dennis Roach is just one of the many football agents who now inhabit top-class European football. His PRO agency is probably the biggest of them all and Manchester United have, at various times, been involved in several other of Roach's money-making ventures.

Nowadays nearly all United's first-team players employ agents of their own to negotiate with the club. Up until about a decade ago

ABOVE Norman Whiteside scores the second goal against Brighton in the 1983 Cup final replay – becoming the youngest player ever to score in a Wembley FA Cup final. (*Manchester Evening News*)

BELOW United players posing for the FA Cup winners' traditional photo after beating Brighton 4–0. (*Syndication International Ltd.*)

LEFT Club president Sir Matt Busby and his right-hand man Jimmy Murphy. Over forty years ago they set about the task of building Manchester United into football's most famous club. (*Harry Goodwin*)

BELOW Decision time as the directors meet for their monthly board meeting in 1984. On the agenda this time is a warm welcome for the newest members, Bobby Charlton and Maurice Watkins. Others in attendance are (left to right) Roger Edwards, Denzil Haroun, secretary Leslie Olive and chairman Martin Edwards. (*Manchester United Supporters Club*)

RIGHT Ron Atkinson with his second batch of signings, in 1984 – Jesper Olsen, Alan Brazil and Gordon Strachan. Brazil says he was not suited to receiving crosses from the two wing men. (*Syndication International Ltd.*)

LEFT Peter Beardsley was signed for £250,000 by Ron Atkinson, but played only one match before being transferred back to Vancouver. (*Manchester United Supporters Club*)

RIGHT United chairman, Martin Edwards, in front of the stadium his father built into one of Britain's top football grounds. (*Manchester Evening News*)

Room at the top. Martin Edwards' luxury penthouse accommodation in the main administration block contrasts starkly with the windowless first floor office of Sir Matt Busby. (*Manchester United Supporters Club*)

LEFT Another new signing? No, just another way in which Old Trafford is utilised, this time to promote a famous brand of whisky. (*Paul Francis Photography*)

RIGHT Martin Edwards and ⸱shi Mitsuda of Sharp Elec⸱onics conclude another ⸱tension to the club's sponsor⸱ip deal with the Japanese ⸱m whose contracts since ⸱82 have brought United over ⸱million. (*Manchester United ⸱pporters Club*)

LEFT A whole new ball game saw United branch into basketball when they took over the Warrington Vikings on New Years Eve 1984. It proved a financial disaster and was sold three years later. (*Manchester United Supporters Club*)

RIGHT United's 'Red Devils' ⸱sketball team is launched at ⸱e Stretford Sports Centre in ⸱85, (left to right) Rick Taylor ⸱eneral manager), Maurice ⸱atkins, Ron Atkinson, Joe ⸱helton (coach), Martin ⸱dwards and Bobby Charlton. ⸱*Manchester United Supporters ⸱ub*)

ABOVE FA Cup winners 1985. United won their last major honour with Ron Atkinson as manager and the cup takes pride of place at the pre-season photocall of 1985–86. (*Manchester United Supporters Club*)

BELOW Fergie's Furies. Alex Ferguson and his players pose for a new team photograph shortly after his arrival as manager. Of the twenty-two players pictured, only nine were still with the club two years later. (*Manchester United Supporters Club*)

Sir Matt presents captain Bryan Robson with the winners' trophy at the end of the Manchester international tournament, held at Maine Road in August 1987. In the background is Dennis Roach, the agent involved in many of United's deals. (*David Smith Sports Photography*)

BELOW Shortly after Norman Whiteside's transfer request was announced, this poster appeared on a billboard in the centre of Manchester. (*David Smith Sports Photography*)

LEFT Jim Leighton and Mark Hughes were signed in the summer of 1988 for £2 million. (*David Smith Sports Photography*)

BELOW Match-day host Vince Miller (centre) presents United's senior officers to members of the Europa club at the beginning of the 1988-89 season. From the left are club directors Nigel Burrows, Bobby Charlton, Amer Midani and Maurice Watkins; Martin Edwards (chairman), Sir Matt Busby (president), Danny McGregor (commercial manager) and director Michael Edelson. (*Manchester Evening News*)

players would talk directly with the manager about contracts and salaries. Now the discussions are between the chief executive and a player's personal representative who, in some cases, may receive 20 per cent of what he agrees for his client.

Three other developments in the last thirty years have radically changed the relationship between a top league club and its players, and have had a particularly far-reaching effect on United's affairs. First came the abolition of the maximum wage in 1961. Until then most United first-team players would be on the maximum wage, which before abolition was £20 a week during the season and £17 in the summer. Benefits on top of that were few. Players might receive occasional bonuses if they won a trophy, and at the end of five- or ten-year-year periods they would get a lump-sum benefit payment of a few hundred pounds. Because of the restriction United could not use its wealth to attract top stars since they would get no more at Old Trafford than elsewhere. It meant that Matt Busby's early dealings with his players had been relatively simple.

The second development was the introduction of freedom of contract in the late 1970s. Until then players remained on the books of a club even if their contract came to an end and they no longer had any wish to play for the side. This meant that clubs had a considerable hold over players. Now, though, when a contract finishes, a player is free to move as he pleases. His previous club is compensated only by a transfer fee agreed between the sides or, more often, fixed by an independent tribunal which is rarely generous in its estimates. It is therefore in a club's interests to keep all its players on contracts so as not to lose them without much compensation. But this inevitably costs teams like United more in higher and longer lasting wage agreements, and involves the club constantly in negotiating contract renewals.

The third important change has been the destruction of foreign barriers to transfers over the last ten years. The process began in a marked way with the arrival of the Argentinian World Cup stars Osvaldo Ardiles and Ricky Villa at Spurs in 1978. Since then United have taken on several foreign stars – Nikola Jovanovic, Arnold Muhren, Jesper Olsen and John Sivebaek – and have negotiated for many others. Yet foreign clubs have also succeeded in luring away top United players at the peak of their careers – Joe Jordan, Ray Wilkins and Mark Hughes. Until the late 1970s it was unknown for a top player to leave United until the club had decided that he was no longer of much further value.

At Old Trafford these trends have been responsible for a marked shift in power away from the manager. In Matt Busby's day he would have conducted any negotiations over players, though the board would have taken a close interest. Now his successors as manager have neither sufficient time nor enough business experience to do all the work; nor could they commit the club to the large sums of money involved. Instead players' contracts are now largely the responsibility of Martin Edwards, who will often be assisted and advised by Maurice Watkins.

The financial climate for top British footballers began to change radically in the late 1970s. It was exemplified perhaps in the summer of 1980 when Dave Sexton tried to sign the Arsenal player Liam Brady. Arsenal wanted £1.5 million for him, but Brady himself was also demanding an annual salary of £90,000, guaranteed bonuses of £20,000 and a signing-on fee of £50,000. The figures were extra-ordinary by the standards of the time. The United board would offer Arsenal only £1 million and Brady a salary of only £50,000 plus a £100,000 signing-on fee spread over three years. Even though the payments were much less than the Arsenal player wanted, they were far higher than any United player received at the time – Steve Coppell, for instance, was earning only £33,800 a year. But the terms were not enough to stop Brady going to Juventus of Italy instead.

When Garry Birtles joined United from Nottingham Forest in October 1980, his contract involved a £1,250,000 transfer fee, wages of £800 a week (£41,600 a year), and a signing-on fee of £75,000. Meanwhile, negotiations to keep Joe Jordan at United collapsed the following summer when the Scottish striker refused a £15,000 fee to sign a new contract and turned down wages of £750 a week, and higher in subsequent years. Jordan left for AC Milan after demanding sums that would have brought him £97,000 a year – almost £2,000 a week. But Jordan would have been happy to stay at Old Trafford if United had been a little more flexible and at least discussed a compromise.

The UEFA mutiplier system awarded United only £250,000 for losing Jordan, while the replacement signing by Ron Atkinson – Frank Stapleton – not only cost the club £900,000 (a fee fixed by the League tribunal which Arsenal considered absurdly low) but he was also paid around £1,000 a week. Bryan Robson was given a similar salary on joining United a few weeks later.

The era of players' agents, high wages, arguments over contracts and high signing-on fees had truly begun. Sometimes players' agents managed to negotiate into their contracts limits on the amount the club could get if the player was subsequently transferred again. Jesper Olsen, who cost £800,000 from Ajax of Amsterdam in 1984, insisted that United could ask for no more than £450,000 if they wanted to get rid of him, and that if he chose to return to Denmark they would get no fee at all. By the time Dennis Roach negotiated his transfer to the French club Bordeaux in November 1988, the fee was only £375,000.

Brian McClair was promised a signing-on fee of £100,000 when he joined United from Celtic in 1987, though it was to be paid over four years. The Scot joined the club only after long, secret negotiations over the previous season. Alex Ferguson and Martin Edwards met McClair secretly in both Glasgow and Carlisle before they managed to secure his transfer, and Ferguson's successor as Scotland manager, Andy Roxburgh, complained about them holding a meeting with the player in the Scotland team hotel.

The rewards for players and their agents are made all the more complicated by United's sophisticated bonus systems which become more lucrative every season, though some might argue that they have little effect on results. When bonuses began in the 1950s and 1960s, they generally involved payments simply if the club finished at a certain position in the league. In 1965, for instance, the players shared £6,500 between them when they won the league championship. One United bonus agreement, made just after the abolition of the maximum wage in 1961, even offered players extra amounts according to the home crowd figures. During the post-Munich period when gates at Old Trafford fell badly, the players were promised £1 each for every 1,000 spectators above 37,000 and £2 for every 1,000 above 45,000.

By the early 1980s the bonus system was even more complex, with extra money for each league point won, and progressively more money as more points were accumulated. But United's system of reckoning was particularly confusing in that the club continued to award only two points for a win, even after the league itself introduced three points for a win in 1981. In the 1986–87 season players received £100 per point for the first thirty-five points, £200 for each of the next ten points, £300 for the next ten and £400 for any points thereafter. It was difficult for the players to understand on a week-to-week basis, but once the last threshold had been passed in the latter stages of the season, each subsequent victory was worth £800 to each player.

The inadequacy of this system was highlighted in the last ten matches of the 1987–88 campaign when United claimed eight wins and two draws. Based on the previous season's bonuses, those who played in all ten games would have received an extra £5,200 each. Such was the absurdity that the team's 2–1 win over Wimbledon in the last match of the 1987–88 season would have awarded each player an £800 bonus, including substitute Lee Martin who was then earning around £130 a week in basic wages. The result would have cost the club £10,400 in bonuses, yet the match itself was almost completely meaningless. United were already assured of being runners-up, and the official gate was only 28,040 – the real attendance was lower still. In contrast, had the players beaten Liverpool in the highly important match at Old Trafford earlier in the season, instead of drawing 1–1, they would have earned only £100 each in bonus money, because the season had not yet reached the high levels of bonus payment.

Some would attribute the famous end to the 1980–81 season – the seven successive victories which were followed by Dave Sexton's controversial sacking – to such cumulative bonuses. Yet the argument that players perform well only with such incentives seems unconvincing. More often United have squandered vital points at the end of a season, and it does not account for the tremendous start in 1985–86 which would have earned only meagre bonuses.

Since 1988 United have operated a much simpler bonus system, paying £100 for each actual league point won. There is no progressive element, but the system is slightly more generous overall than before and the £50,000 extra bonus for winning the title has been doubled to £100,000.

Bonuses differ substantially from club to club. At Highbury, for example, payments are better than United's if Arsenal are high up the league, but are not so good for Cup games. Liverpool players are paid £125 a point but only £5,000 each for winning the title itself compared with a £7,692 title bonus at Old Trafford. Liverpool players also get much lower rewards in the Cup competitions.

In terms of basic wages the spread among the United first-team squad is surprisingly wide, and probably wider than ever before. Long-serving defenders have often been badly rewarded in comparison with star forwards. In his last season, for instance, Kevin Moran was paid a basic salary of only £41,600 after ten years' service with the club. The 1986–87 basic salaries for Bryan Robson (£98,000), Gordon Strachan (£78,000) and Jesper Olsen (£85,000) reflected their star quality and high transfer fees, though in Strachan's case his contract was renegotiated when he threatened to move to France just before the 1988–89 season. Norman Whiteside (£45,000) and Paul McGrath (£39,000), who did not arrive via expensive transfers, got relatively small rewards. Perhaps the most surprising figure was that of Brian McClair who, with his signing-on fee, was receiving only £65,000 a year before bonuses in 1987–88 – the season he scored thirty-one goals. His salary may have reflected his previous pay at Celtic who are notorious for how little they pay their staff. In November 1988 McClair's contract was renegotiated to bring him in line with Mark Hughes.

Life on the fringes of the team seems particularly unrewarding. Salaries earned in the 1986–87 season by Liam O'Brien (£13,000), Gary Walsh (£9,100), Billy Garton (£18,200) and Clayton Blackmore (£20,800) reflected the fact that most ordinary footballers cannot expect vast incomes even in the modern game, though Walsh received an additional £75 in appearance money for first-team games. The sums may still be higher than what most people earn, but in comparison with the rest of the entertainment industry, and allowing for a footballer's short career span, being an ordinary player, even at Old Trafford, does not make you a rich man.

On top of their salaries most of United's first-team squad have club cars. The club meets insurance and tax on the vehicles, but the players are expected to service them. And in the past, ten of the top players had the extra perk of living in club houses for which they paid a rent of £1,000 a year – well below the economic charge. They could also buy their homes at any time during the period of their contract, and at a cost of just 5 per cent in excess of the original purchase price, which normally meant a good bargain. United have always provided club houses for players, though as time has passed the club's modest suburban semis in Sale, Davyhulme, Old Trafford, Urmston and Chorlton have been replaced by much larger properties, worth £150,000 or more, in the leafy Cheshire lanes around Bowdon, Hale and Wilmslow.

Manchester United's elaborate system of rewards for its players and officials was perhaps an obvious case for scrutiny by the tax authorities, especially at a time when the Inland Revenue is meant to be gunning for big names to set an example to the ordinary public. When the tax men launched an investigation into United in late 1987, it was dismissed by Martin Edwards as routine. 'This is not a big concern for me or Manchester United,' he said when news of it reached the press in February 1988. But four months later a different story emerged when it was revealed that the club had confessed to having avoided tax on payments to players, and the Inland Revenue accused United of holding 'sham' board meetings.

The investigation looked into a string of tax-free, lump-sum amounts that United had made to players and club officials dating back to 1980. Most of the payments had been made on advice from Martin Edwards' close associate Oscar Goldstein while he was a partner with Price Waterhouse.

United admitted that the sums of £25,000 to Lou Macari, £10,000 to Martin Buchan and £4,000 to Mickey Thomas had been wrongly declared as tax-free 'ex-gratia' payments. The Revenue also queried the tax liabilities of £60,000 paid to Arnold Muhren when he left United, £60,000 of a £104,750 insurance payment to Steve Coppell when he was forced to retire through injury, and £15,000 to Garry Birtles.

The inspector, Mr. Tillmanns, made reference to other examples (£50,000 to Sammy McIlroy and £25,000 to Jimmy Nicholl) of compensation having been first negotiated and then dressed up with such phrases as 'ex-gratia' and 'mark of personal esteem' in what he called 'prima facie, sham letters' and board meetings.

Payments made to Frank Stapleton through an off-shore trust account were also under investigation and it was revealed that former manager Ron Atkinson was paid £115,000 when he was sacked, with his assistant, Mick Brown, receiving £45,000. Aberdeen were given £60,000 as compensation for Alex Ferguson who replaced Atkinson as manager.

In March 1988, possibly in response to the tax enquiry at Old Trafford and similar investigations at other clubs, the Football League, the Professional Footballers Association and the Inland Revenue issued new guidelines about tax-free payments to players. All such payments linked with transfers are now clearly liable to tax, though amounts paid in the case of injury or retirement which are not part of a contract are not always taxable. The agreement also granted clubs an amnesty over most previous payments.

Player transfers too have become a complex business nowadays. It should be stressed, though, that the figures given in the press are in fact only estimates of the fees that change hands. In most cases the figures are pretty accurate, but not always. When the Scotland goalkeeper Jim Leighton joined United from Aberdeen in May 1988, a decision may have been taken to exaggerate his price. The figure quoted in the press was £750,000, but the real amount was only

£450,000, and United have done nothing to correct any newspaper's mistake. It was perhaps in United's interest to make out that they spent more than they did, and in Aberdeen's to let their supporters think they received more than they did. Similarly when Ray Wilkins joined United in 1979, the price was only £700,000, though the figure most often given in public was £825,000. In contrast, when United signed the seventeen-year-old Torquay player Lee Sharpe in May 1988, the official fee was £65,000, yet journalists talked of £30,000. Sixty-five thousand pounds was a large sum for a teenager who had appeared only fifteen times in the Torquay first team. Moreover, United agreed to pay Torquay a further £60,000 when Sharpe made a first-team competitive appearance – which occurred in September 1988 – and another £60,000 after thirty first-team competitive games – £185,000 in all. A further condition was that United would play a friendly match at Torquay, for expenses only, at some future date.

The most complex deal of all must be that which brought John Sivebaek to Old Trafford from Vejle Boldklub of Denmark. At one point it looked as though the move had collapsed because of fears about a pelvic injury that had shown up on the player's medical examination, but United eventually agreed to pay the sum of £285,000 in three separate instalments. An initial fee of £150,000 was to be followed by a further £75,000 eighteen months later, and another £60,000 twelve months after that, so long as the player was passed fit to play a minimum of twenty-five matches during the 1986–87 season. Had the playing conditions of the agreement not been met and Sivebaek chosen to return to Denmark, there would have been no fee involved and only if he was then transferred to a club outside Denmark would United have been able to claim back their initial £150,000. As it happened Sivebaek made a total of 31 appearances in 1986–87 before being transferred to St. Etienne at the beginning of the 1987–88 season for £227,000. United also agreed to play a friendly against Vejle at Old Trafford or to pay £10,000 if the game could not be arranged.

Friendly fixtures are a common aspect of transfers nowadays, especially for players from lower-division sides and foreign clubs. United played St Patrick's Athletic in 1983 after buying Paul McGrath, and Brandon United in 1988 after acquiring Paul Dalton from them. Outstanding fixtures against Aberdeen (Alex Ferguson) and Cologne (as settlement of the dispute over Gordon Strachan) have yet to be played.

Alex Ferguson, the United manager at the time of going to press, has long been worried, however, by the extra burden that meaningless friendly games arranged as part of some financial deal, or by agents such as Dennis Roach, place upon players. He argues that the fans rightly expect their players to be fresh. The reduction of the first division to twenty clubs and the disappearance of four league fixtures should help a little.

When Alex Ferguson arrived at Old Trafford in November 1986, he inherited a squad from Ron Atkinson that was demoralised and indisciplined. In fact the lack of discipline among the players was one of the reasons why Ron Atkinson was sacked after being the longest-serving manager since Sir Matt Busby. Atkinson had not been the first choice for the job in 1981. Lawrie McMenemy, Bobby Robson and Ron Saunders all rejected Martin Edwards' approaches first – a sign partly of how difficult people realised the United job to be and partly of disquiet at the way in which Dave Sexton had been sacked. Atkinson was the first of Busby's successors not to have been chosen by Sir Matt himself, although Busby did suggest that the appointment be kept in-house and recommended Harry Gregg for the job.

Atkinson's first season, 1981–82, saw more than £3 million spent on new players – including £900,000 on the striker Frank Stapleton from Arsenal and £2,000,000 on the midfield players Remi Moses and Bryan Robson from West Bromwich Albion. Robson was to become the most complete English footballer of the 1980s, and soon assumed the England captaincy from his injured United team-mate Ray Wilkins. In his all-round ability Robson had everything – tackling, passing, running, vision, stamina, goal-scoring and sheer domination of a game. He would perform superbly in defence if needed, and yet could be relied on to score almost as frequently as the forwards. The only drawback for both United and England was that, throughout the Atkinson years, Bryan Robson suffered persistent hamstring and shoulder injuries and was absent for long and important periods.

Under the leadership of Atkinson and Robson, United reached three Wembley finals – the FA Cup finals of 1983 and 1985, and the Milk (League) Cup in 1983. Twice the FA Cup came back to Old Trafford with red and white ribbons. In 1983 beating Brighton required extra time in the first game, which ended 2–2, and a Wembley replay before United marked up a 4–0 victory. Two years later the reds prevented Everton chalking up a remarkable treble of league championship, FA Cup and the European Cup-Winners Cup. Norman Whiteside scored in extra time when United were down to ten men after Kevin Moran had rather unjustly been sent off.

The Atkinson years also saw the resparkling of United's old European tradition. In the Cup-Winners Cup in 1984 Barcelona, one of the strongest teams on the Continent, were beaten 3–0 on an incredible night at Old Trafford after United had gone down 2–0 in the first leg in Spain. But Atkinson's injury-striken team were defeated by a last-minute goal from Juventus's Paolo Rossi in the second leg of the semi-final in Italy.

Yet United never managed to emulate their exciting Cup success in the league championship. Season after season the club seemed within reach of Liverpool or Everton, the two sides that had now come to dominate the English game, and yet, after chasing the leaders throughout the campaign, never managed even to finish runners-up. In 1983 United came third. Then three years running, in 1984, 1985 and 1986, after being in serious contention each time, they had to settle for coming fourth in a two-horse race! Something was badly missing from the United make-up, as seen so dramatically after the collapse that followed ten consecutive opening wins in the 1985–86 season.

Frequently the United players displayed their best form only against top teams. Liverpool secured just one league victory over United during Atkinson's five seasons, while United went unbeaten at Anfield. Against lesser sides, however, the players often struggled. After a 3–0 defeat at Southampton, the United manager threatened to put 'kids in place of the international stars if their application isn't 100 per cent all the time. . . . I consider it an honour to be manager of Manchester United,' Atkinson complained; 'I think players should have that same pride. . . . If you're getting well-paid for it, you've got to sweat blood and tears sometimes. All we're sweating at the moment are tears.'

Apart from United's extraordinary inconsistency, Atkinson, like Dave Sexton before him, was ultimately condemned by several unwise financial moves during his last two seasons. Not only had he brought the future England striker Peter Beardsley to United and then let him return to Canada after only half a first-team game, but he spent vast sums on other forwards who seemed overawed by Old Trafford. Alan Brazil cost £700,000 from Spurs but never got a proper chance in the first team and quickly lost confidence. Atkinson later swapped him, together with £350,000, for Coventry's Terry Gibson, who proved an even greater failure, scoring just one goal in twenty-three games. Neither Brazil nor Gibson was the type to make use of the balls sent across by Atkinson's two wing-men, Jesper Olsen and Gordon Strachan. Another striker bought by Atkinson, Peter Davenport from Nottingham Forest, also found it difficult to hit the target. In the new profit-and-loss world of Old Trafford, a manager cannot afford to make such mistakes, or to throw away comfortable leads at the top of the first division. And Old Trafford attendances were slowly dropping.

The United manager found himself increasingly in conflict with Bobby Charlton on the United board. Ron Atkinson attended fewer board meetings than any previous post-war United manager except Wilf McGuinness who was not invited. In his absence Martin Edwards would often defer to Bobby Charlton. Atkinson, for instance, wanted to buy the England defender Terry Butcher from Ipswich for £700,000, but Charlton argued that he would not be a worthwhile investment.

Atkinson's final season at United began badly when he fined seven players for an after-hours drinking session on a pre-season trip to Holland. Then Jesper Olsen was involved in a fight with Remi Moses that ended with the Dane needing eleven stitches in hospital, missing a Littlewoods Cup match and causing big headlines. Initially Atkinson denied that there had been any trouble, calling it simply a 'clash of heads'. When the truth came out, it only undermined Atkinson's credibility. Moses was also in trouble for getting medical treatment in Holland without club permission and then presenting United with a bill for several thousand pounds.

Such incidents only hastened Atkinson's departure. So too did his failure to achieve much of a rapport with supporters, who considered him too 'flash' and would sing, 'He's big, he's round, he's worth a million pounds,' in derision rather than admiration. The axe finally fell after a 4–0 defeat in the Littlewoods Cup at Southampton in November 1986. Before sacking Atkinson, however, Martin Edwards made sure that there was a good replacement.

The story told by Martin Edwards and his new manager, and accepted by the official United history published in 1988 by David Meek and Tom Tyrrell, is that Atkinson and his assistant, Mick Brown, were dismissed first, and then Martin Edwards flew to Aberdeen to persuade the Aberdeen manager, Alex Ferguson, to replace him. Ferguson himself told one of the authors that the call from Edwards after Atkinson lost his job came as a complete surprise. The Aberdeen chairman, Dick Donald, was convinced, however, that the deal had been arranged before Martin Edwards phoned him officially to ask permission to come and talk to his manager. One would give Edwards and Ferguson the benefit of the doubt had not the United chairman made secret arrangements for himself and Maurice Watkins to meet the Aberdeen manager at Glasgow Airport on the evening *before* Atkinson was dismissed.

The new man found Old Trafford a much harder job than he had expected. Results did not improve much and the disciplinary problems continued. Four players, Gordon Strachan, Billy Garton, Paul McGrath and Kevin Moran, were fined heavily for arriving late for the team bus in Dublin in March 1987. Then, on a tour to Malta in May 1987, Norman Whiteside and Paul McGrath were reported as having spent all night drinking, and arrived late at the airport the next day. They were fined a week's wages. The club's troubles continued on a mid-season visit to Bermuda in December 1987, when Clayton Blackmore was accused of raping a woman. The resulting legal bill was sent to Blackmore himself.

In Alex Ferguson's first full season, 1987–88, the team finished second, nine points behind Liverpool. It was only the second time since 1968 that United had even been runners-up. And though the number of league defeats – five – was the lowest since 1906, and Brian McClair scored more than twenty league goals, United did not look likely champions. Ferguson was unhappy with the attitude of many of his squad. Indeed, by the end of the season there were few players who had their manager's full confidence. Apart from those he had bought – Brian McClair, Viv Anderson and Steve Bruce – the only players he seemed contented with were Mike Duxbury and Peter Davenport, though he later sold Davenport to Middlesbrough. Following United's FA Cup defeat at Arsenal in February, the reds' manager admitted: 'The players are playing for their futures. They have a duty to perform with total commitment in every game, with every kick, until the end of the season.' Secretly, Ferguson was looking to replace the likes of Chris Turner, Gordon Strachan and Jesper Olsen, and by March had drawn up a list of priority signings, which included Jim Leighton, Mark Hughes, Trevor Steven, Gary Pallister and Paul Gascoigne. As back-up, names like Paul Stewart, Craig Johnston, Kevin Drinkell and Colin Clarke were also mentioned.

So when two of United's top stars Norman Whiteside and Paul McGrath publicly asked for transfers in April 1988, Ferguson told the board that they should be allowed to leave. A fee of £900,000 was expected for McGrath and £1.5 million for Whiteside. Publicly Ferguson's stance was that United could not afford players who did not want to play for the club, but privately the reasons behind the requests were more complex. In fact, Ferguson is thought to have considered selling Whiteside for a while because of worries about the player's behaviour, and McGrath had asked for a transfer as long ago as the previous October. In January 1988 McGrath was banned from driving for being found drunk after a crash, but alcohol was only part of his problem. The biggest concern was his persistent knee injury. Whiteside too enjoyed a drink, and reports from the changing rooms at The Cliff that alcohol could be smelt on his breath each morning at training did not endear him to a puritanical manager who greatly admires teetotallers like Viv Anderson.

United were even said to be prepared to get rid of the biggest United player of them all, the England captain Bryan Robson, who was also banned from driving after being caught over the alcohol limit. Indeed, when Martin Edwards spoke to Newcastle United in April 1988 about Paul Gascoigne, he said that they could consider any United player in exchange for Gascoigne, including Robson.

While the United manager wanted to clear out most of his first-team squad, long contracts signed before his arrival prevented him from doing so. Eventually, though, Turner moved to Sheffield Wednesday early in the 1988–89 season and Olsen to Bordeaux. Ferguson agreed to keep his former Aberdeen player, Gordon Strachan, for a further year, but his plans were almost upset in August 1988. Strachan declined to sign a new contract and suddenly announced that he was joining the French club Lens, but then signed a new agreement to stay at Old Trafford for another season.

Ferguson's problem was that, unlike Terry Venables, a manager in a rather similar position at Spurs, he was heavily restrained by his chairman in what he could spend on new players. Martin Edwards recalled only too well the costly transfers of Ron Atkinson's last two years when almost £2 million had been wasted on Alan Brazil, Terry Gibson, Chris Turner and Johnny Sivebaek. Ferguson was not helped either by the presence of Atkinson's much cheaper acquisitions. Players such as Mark Higgins and Peter Barnes had restricted the progress of the club's own promising youngsters, and also commanded high wages. Ferguson, on a four-year contract, clearly had more immediate priorities than Edwards, who might own the club for life. Yet he boasted a highly successful buying record at Aberdeen. The financial tensions between the two United men were revealed publicly after Ferguson had been at Old Trafford for about a year. The United manager stated after one board meeting:

> If we buy now it will mean going into the red. I am not saying we can't buy but we have got to be prudent. We cannot afford to get it wrong. We got £1.8 million for Hughes, but that money had already been spent on new players before we had even received the fee. . . . We still have a big squad on high wages, so there are limits to which we should go.

For Ferguson the resources he had been allowed at Old Trafford clearly did not match his expectations:

> I came here thinking I would have the luxury of buying players. I have done a lot of hard work at youth levels but to win the league we need to buy. I'm disappointed I haven't had that kind of money. Liverpool have bought the best and what sticks in my gullet is the difference between us and them. I respect them but I don't like being second.

He was hardly veiled in his criticism of Edwards:

> He is now facing two very tough choices between having a very good team and balancing the books. It is impossible to have both at present. All I can say is that at Aberdeen I bought twelve players and had just one failure, and I felt that badly. I have a respect for money.

The best example of the financial tensions between Ferguson and Edwards, though, came in the summer of 1988 over Paul Gascoigne, the young midfield player who had made it clear that his horizons lay beyond Newcastle United. United had originally met Gascoigne's advisers at Old Trafford in late 1987 to discuss possible transfer arrangements.

To have met Paul Gascoigne's extraordinary personal terms would have required a vast outlay – far more than was being paid to either Bryan Robson or Mark Hughes. Firstly, Gascoigne wanted a £100,000 signing-on fee. Then his required salary on a four-year contract would have averaged out at £125,000 a year. On top his new club would have to pay £5,000 for every England cap he won. The Football Association would not have been too pleased to learn that the club that acquired Gascoigne had a considerable interest in his *not* playing for England. He was to get a £15,000-club car, a £200,000-new house and a huge slice of any transfer profit at the end of the period. They were among the most demanding terms ever made in the history of

English football – higher in some ways than what Liam Brady had requested in 1980 – and particularly bold for a twenty-one-year-old player who had yet to play for his country.

For Martin Edwards, the majority shareholder whose dividend payments are dependent upon his club's finances, it would have been difficult to sleep at night with a £4 million overdraft, a figure which might easily grow to £5 million by the end of the 1988–89 season after high interest payments. Edwards must have doubted that the club would ever get the money back, particularly since nobody seemed to be showing interest in the transfer-listed Whiteside and McGrath. Even Manchester City's transfer debts in the early 1980s had never been greater than £3 million.

Gascoigne's transfer took place, or rather did not take place, while Alex Ferguson was on holiday in Malta. With Tottenham about to complete the deal, Edwards went for a week's holiday at Amer Al Midani's Marbella Club and the player agreed to join Tottenham Hotspur. Early the following season he won his first cap for England.

Edwards subsequently stated that he could not understand what had happened, and claimed, 'The indications were he would join us. We did table a bid which we believe was as good as Tottenham's.' But Alistair Garvie, Gascoigne's adviser, totally refuted the suggestions, insisting: 'Martin Edwards is talking a load of rubbish and he knows it. It was in their power to match Tottenham's offer and the fact is they didn't.'

Alex Ferguson's enthusiasm for buying Paul Gascoigne was ultimately thwarted by Martin Edwards' reluctance, and this time not even Bobby Charlton tipped the balance. United's accumulated debt at the start of the 1988 season remained at £2½ million, a sizeable sum. But perhaps with Gascoigne the extra crowds and team success would have made it easier to pay off, in much the same way as Liverpool had cleared their debt despite their considerable outlay for Peter Beardsley and John Barnes. Even the acquisition of Ian Rush on the eve of the 1988–89 season left the Merseysiders in the black, thanks partly to the greatly increased support for the club (they had now overtaken United as the best supported club in Britain).

So, after Manchester United had bought Anderson, McClair, Bruce, Leighton and Hughes for an outlay of more than £4 million, it had become clear that there could be no further big deals until money was brought in from the sale of players. Ferguson was stuck in his options. He was desperate for certain players to leave so as to replenish the transfer account and ease the wage bill. Deals were set up for Graeme Hogg, Clayton Blackmore and Peter Davenport, but all were reluctant to leave even if to stay meant reserve football at United, though Hogg eventually left for Portsmouth in 1988 and Davenport for Middlesbrough. The Davenport income was used to buy Luton's Irish defender Mal Donaghy. Ferguson could only rebuild his side as players gradually left the club.

Remarkably few clubs seemed interested in Norman Whiteside or Paul McGrath, two of the fans' favourites, who in the public view were worth more than £1 million each. Norman Whiteside did talk with two clubs before the 1988–89 season, but nothing resulted, and then injury kept him out for several months. Paul McGrath proved equally difficult to sell, largely because of worries about his physical condition. When a transfer was set up with Spurs in September 1988, the London club was so worried about McGrath's injury that payment partly depended on how many games he eventually played: on top of a basic £450,000, United would later receive £100,000 for every thirty games up to a maximum of £300,000. In the end the deal fell through.

Manchester United kicked off the 1988–89 season with their hopes depending very much upon the new forward partnership of Brian McClair and Mark Hughes. Yet initially the two strikers found it difficult to operate together, and could not produce a single goal between them in the first five games. By the end of November McClair had scored just two league goals. A succession of easy autumn games that should have ended in victory produced single-point draws as United languished in mid-table. It looked like being yet another of those disappointing seasons.

Over the Christmas holiday period, however, United's fortunes changed dramatically. First Nottingham Forest were beaten 2–0 at Old Trafford on Boxing Day, then arch-rivals Liverpool were defeated 3–1 on the very first day of the new year. The new form continued into January and February. United had suddenly been rejuvenated by several young players whom Alex Ferguson had been forced to pluck from the reserves and youth teams. Defenders Tony Gill and Lee Martin; midfield players Russell Beardsmore, Lee Sharpe, and David Wilson; forwards Mark Robins and Deiniol Graham all had yet to celebrate their twenty-first birthdays. For the fans it rekindled memories of the time when Manchester United were famed for their youth policy.

FA Cup wins over QPR, Oxford and Bournemouth led to a quarter-final tie against Nottingham Forest, while in the league United remained only eleven points behind the leaders Arsenal at the end of January, despite the many lethargic displays in the first half of the season. The fact was, however, that no first division side had performed particularly well, and both Merseyside clubs were playing well below their usual form.

United entered 1989 with hopes still glimmering thanks also to another player who had once starred in the United youth team. Mark Hughes had returned from Spain and Germany with an extra dimension to his game – he now used the ball unselfishly, and yet after his barren start, had by early February claimed thirteen league goals in twenty-three matches – in line with Brian McClair's notable scoring-rate the year before.

Although the youngsters provided stability that the side had seemed to lack when Alex Ferguson had juggled with his regular well-paid stars, most of them lost their places as the more senior players recovered from injury.

Yet it was only because of the financial stringency forced upon the United manager that the youth players had ever been given a chance. Apart from Lee Sharpe, who had made a few appearances in the fourth division with Torquay, the new breed of Babes had begun life at Old Trafford as YTS trainees. Like hundreds of their keen, raw predecessors in the United A and B sides, they might easily have left Old Trafford disappointed – discarded to make a living in front of small crowds in the lower divisions of the football league. Indeed, with the exception of Mark Robins, all the new home-grown players had begun the 1988–89 season with fewer than twelve months left on their contracts. In most cases there had been no expectation that they would be kept on the following May.

The Busby Babes in the 1950s were part of a conscious effort to develop a youth policy – nurtured and encouraged until they were good enough to wear first team shirts. The latest crop of young players got their chances almost by accident, despite Ferguson's own long-term plans to improve the youth system. Significantly, when United's title chances finally evaporated in a 2–1 defeat at Norwich in February 1989 only one young player, Lee Sharpe, had been in United's starting line-up.

Amid the hopes that were once again aroused as the club approached the end of the 1980s, Alex Ferguson must surely have known from studying the records of previous managers how dangerous high expectations can be at Old Trafford if they are dashed. As he began his third year in charge of the team, the pressure on Ferguson to win the first division championship was, of course, greater than ever.

12   A DIFFERENT BALL GAME

'Manchester United had the opportunity to become one of
the top basketball clubs in Europe, and it didn't happen. It
was a missed opportunity.'

Rick Taylor, General Manager
Manchester United Basketball 1985–87.

THE SEVEN men who gathered in October 1907 to sign the
memorandum of association of Manchester United Football Club Ltd
clearly had high ambitions for their new company. Article 4, item 2 of
the memorandum set out the sporting objects of Manchester United:
'To promote the practice and play of Football, Cricket, Basketball,
Lacrosse, Lawn Tennis, Hockey, Polo, Bowls, Cycle and Motor Riding,
Running, Jumping, the physical training and development of the
human frame . . .' For a further eight lines the item continued to set
out the club's possible sporting activities.

For nearly eighty years Manchester United confined itself to the
very first of the sports laid down in the company's memorandum,
football. Then, towards the end of 1984, Martin Edwards began
negotiations for United's involvement in the fourth sport on the list,
basketball. It wasn't the first occasion on which interest had been
shown in extending the club's activities in this direction. In 1980–81
there had been tentative discussion about taking over the Manchester
Giants basketball team, which at the time was owned by an Eric
Atkinson. The deal eventually fell through and the Giants were
in the end bought by an Arab businessman by the name of Amer Al
Midani.

In November 1984 the new United director Maurice Watkins was
approached by the FSO Warrington Vikings Basketball Club. They
were having financial problems, and wanted to know if Manchester
United might be interested in buying the club. United's directors were
certainly interested. Watkins had been to one or two Vikings games as

a guest of one of their directors, Nigel Roden. The United chairman had, of course, played basketball at Cokethorpe. His friend Dennis Roach was the owner of the Polycell Kingston basketball club in London, one of the country's top sides, and had taken him along to see several matches. Edwards was also aware that many leading European football clubs, such as Real Madrid, Barcelona and Bayern Munich, also ran strong basketball teams. He soon had what he calls the basketball 'bug'. A meeting was arranged with the Vikings' directors on the evening of Tuesday, 27 November 1984.

FSO Warrington were one of the country's top basketball sides, and near the top of the first division of the National Basketball League. At the time of the approach to United they had also been playing in European competition, and were already in the semi-finals of basketball's national cup competition. Warrington had run into money problems, however. Their home ground, the Spectrum Centre in Warrington, held only 1,200 spectators. The venue could not cope with the public demand, yet the club was losing money.

It was a time when Manchester United's football future was looking extremely rosy. After four years with Ron Atkinson in charge, the team looked set to add more trophies to the FA Cup they had won in 1983 and they were regularly playing in Europe. Edwards saw a basketball team as a natural step forward. With weekly television coverage on the new Channel 4, basketball looked as if it might enjoy an explosion of popularity in the same way that snooker had done. Martin Edwards was also keen to be seen to further relations within the local community.

His interest aroused, the United chairman quickly began going to local basketball games and, in particular, to Vikings matches. He met officials from the English Basketball Association, who soon agreed for the basketball club's name to be changed to Manchester United. Trafford Council were happy to let the team use the main hall at Stretford Leisure Centre on Chester Road, only a few hundred yards from the Old Trafford football ground. But the Stretford hall was barely larger than the Spectrum Centre in Warrington and could hold only 1,550 people. For future years Martin Edwards hoped that he might be able to use the new Greater Manchester Exhibition complex, the G-Mex Centre, which was currently being built on the site of the old Central railway station in the city centre. In the meantime, other ways would have to be found to stem the basketball team's continuing losses.

Sharp Electronics, which had sponsored United's football team since 1982, were approached for a similar deal on the new basketball operation. An extension to the existing Sharp agreement was due shortly and it was felt that they might agree to include basketball in the new sponsorship deal. Edwards met representatives of Warrington's existing sponsors, FSO, at the Royal Lancaster Hotel in London and they were happy to support the new club for the time being. With the likely prospect of Sharp taking over sponsorship in the long term, a contract to buy Warrington Vikings was finally signed on New Year's Eve 1984. The new FSO Manchester United Basketball Club was officially launched at a press conference on 3 January 1985.

United invested £7,000 to acquire a 75 per cent stake in their new acquisition, and it is thought that they paid off £40,000 of the Vikings' debts. A new company was set up, Manchester United Basketball Ltd, whose board comprised both United directors and two former members of the Vikings board who had agreed to transfer their bank guarantees to the new operation. Almost immediately, though, United's plans hit a problem. Top-class basketball was, of course, already being played in the Greater Manchester area, just 6 miles along the Chester road in Altrincham, by the Manchester Giants. The Giants' owner and chairman, Amer Al Midani, was not happy about United transferring the Warrington club to Manchester. He regarded it as the Giants' catchment area for basketball support and fund-raising. In view of his father's wealth, Midani would be a tough opponent.

The Arab businessman quickly issued a writ against United. Rather than get involved in a long, expensive, legal tussle, Edwards and Midani met to try to resolve the differences. Midani dropped his action on the understanding that United would not organise any basketball fund-raising activities, such as lotteries, for the next fourteen months. The two men also agreed to consider the idea of jointly building a brand-new sports arena to house both basketball clubs and to promote other events. United would assist the Giants in trying to secure equal television rights over the coming year, and there would be two pre-season friendly matches between the rival sides.

The Vikings had actually been purchased through United's Development account, MUDL, referred to internally as 'Muddle'. It was the same account that had been used two years earlier for the disastrous Spaceshot project with Glasgow Rangers.

Officially, United's full involvement was not due to start until the beginning of the 1985–86 basketball season, but the team's success in winning the 1985 basketball championship play-offs was seen as the first trophy for the new Red Devils. With the regular television coverage Sharp Electronics happily agreed to pay £250,000 to sponsor the club for three years.

Martin Edwards was delighted at the success of his new team. He had watched most basketball home games up to the end of the season and witnessed the basketball side's triumph at Wembley, which preceded the football team's FA Cup triumph there only a few weeks later. Edwards' enthusiasm for his new basketball team was similar to that of a small boy with a new toy. Indeed, there were some who wondered whether his interest was now greater than it was for the United football side.

Overall, Manchester United basketball matches attracted a very different kind of audience from the football club. Families often went together, and a survey has shown that 47 per cent of British basketball spectators are female. At Stretford Leisure Centre there was little of the aggressive hostility towards opposing fans seen at soccer matches. Supporters of both teams happily sat side by side, egged on by the young American-style female cheer-leaders, and a running commentary. Very few of those who went to watch Manchester United basketball went to the football too. Many United football fans resented their club's involvement in the new sport, arguing that it detracted from the football team. The basketball team, now called Sharp Manchester United, won the National League in 1986 and so qualified for the European Cup – at a time when United's football team were banned from Europe after the Heysel disaster.

Meanwhile, Edwards was also keen on building a new 'activity centre' to cater not just for basketball but other sports too, as well as pop concerts, exhibitions and religious events. This idea had indeed first been mooted by his father in the late 1970s. It would be built on the No. 3 car-park, land United had bought opposite the scoreboard end of the Old Trafford ground. In August 1985 the club's architect, Ernest Atherden, attended a United board meeting with plans he had prepared for a building with 9,000 seats on two tiers and which would cost £3½ million. But now Edwards was beginning to have doubts about the idea. The European football ban, together with the Football League's failure to reach a deal with the TV companies over television rights in the coming season, would mean that United could expect to lose a substantial amount of income. The club could make £200,000 from each round of European competitions, and as much as £1 million from a good European season. Without television United lost not only a share of the money from the TV deal itself, but also large sums from ground advertising. A decision on Atherden's plans was deferred, but the directors allowed the architect to carry on with a feasibility study at no extra cost.

The basketball team itself was also adding to Edwards' financial worries. At United's 1985 Annual General Meeting, he had to report a loss of £107,000 on the basketball over just six months. When asked about the loss in 1986, the chairman revealed that this had been £253,000 in less than two years, but predicted that the deficit would be only £30,000 in the year ahead. Despite the large losses, the basketball club's general manager, Rick Taylor, had managed to raise more than £100,000 a year in match-day sponsorship on top of the £83,000 they were receiving each year from Sharp. He also argued that some of his original sponsors had defected to the football team, though many others had come from the football in the first place.

Edwards' friendship with Amer Al Midani grew to the stage at which, in May 1986, the two men agreed to merge their two basketball teams. The result was one of the strongest basketball sides in Europe. Although the Giants had lost around £½ million in recent years, United paid nearly £100,000 for the operation. Martin Edwards told his fellow football directors that he would nominate Midani as a director of United, though an opportunity to do so at the 1986 AGM was passed over and he did not finally join the board until February 1987.

The United chairman had not abandoned his plans for United to move into other sports. Edwards, Danny McGregor and Bobby Charlton made several visits to the big European clubs to develop their expansionist ambitions; Edwards visited Real Madrid after a European Cup basketball tie between United and the Spanish club in the autumn of 1986; and Bobby Charlton and Danny McGregor made a special trip to Barcelona in October 1986. They reported that the 109,000 members at Barcelona paid about £32 a year each for which they got free admission to basketball and handball matches and could use several sports facilities, including an ice-skating rink. Members could even obtain preferential rates of interest at local banks and book tickets for matches over the bank counter. Barcelona also had a waiting list to join.

At the same board meeting at which the directors heard about the Spanish visits, Martin Edwards reported that he had also been involved in negotiations with Salford City Council, who wanted to use the Manchester United name on many of the sports teams they ran. United had recently become involved in a scheme being tried out by the Professional Footballers' Association called 'Football in the Community'. Run by the former United forward Brian Kidd, this programme was designed to allow members of the public in the Manchester area to use the facilities of six local football clubs at times when they were not required by the clubs themselves. Professional footballers would also get involved in coaching in local schools and at youth clubs. The Salford scheme, however, offered a much wider opportunity than the PFA scheme. Moreover, Salford provided a much simpler option for United than copying the big Continental clubs by building brand-new facilities, which would have been expensive. In April 1987 the then Sports Minister, Richard Tracey, helped Edwards launch a scheme in conjunction with Salford, with the clumsy name of Manchester United Salford Sports Systems. In future 10,000 Salford schoolchildren would participate on a team basis in soccer and eight other sports – athletics, gymnastics, swimming, basketball, volleyball, handball, trampolining and even artistic roller-skating – playing under the name of Manchester United Salford. A joint trust was set up between United and Salford Council, and a company was established to administer matters. Sponsorship worth £40,000 was arranged with Homeowners Financial Services.

For £2.50 any citizen of Salford can now join the 'Triple S' scheme as it is known. In theory sports formerly run solely by the council now receive regular support from the football club, though in practice the support often seems to be nominal. Leading United players have been designated presidents at each of Salford's six sports centres and hand out prizes. There have, however, been soccer training sessions at The Cliff for Salford schoolboys with United players involved in the coaching. Because of legal complications in setting up the joint Salford-United trust, the scheme started slowly and it was almost a year before it was regularly mentioned in United's match-day soccer programme. Recently, though, volleyball and handball teams have competed abroad under the Manchester United name.

By 1987 the basketball club's losses were becoming intolerable. Sharp Electronics had made it clear that now that basketball was no longer getting regular television coverage, they were not prepared to renew their sponsorship when the current three-year contract ended. The main cost was wages. Although the players were all part-time, the basketball wage bill was £131,000 a year – including £110,000 for the players – and Edwards decided that he had either to trim the squad or cut their pay. The United chairman reconciled himself to the idea of having a much weaker team if it meant cutting losses and United basketball surviving a few more years. The team's general manager Rick Taylor was told that he could spend no more than £80,000 on players' wages.

The finances of the Manchester United basketball team were tiny in comparison with those of the football team. The operation involved both amateurs and part-time professionals. Even Alton Byrd – the most entertaining player in the league – earned only £22,000 a year. In spite of attempts to cut the wage bill, no way could be found of balancing income with expenditure. By November 1987 Martin Edwards was having strong doubts about whether to carry on with the basketball. The losses for 1986–87 had worked out at £67,000, more than twice as much as the United chairman had promised share-holders the year before, and he was no longer a regular attender of matches. In an effort to save the venture an alternative venue was sought and at one stage it seemed that it might be possible to move matches to Eccles, where Salford would make available a hall seating 3,000 at a cost of just £50 a game, compared with £450 at Stretford.

But at the 1987 AGM Edwards, a man who hates the slightest criticism, got just what he had feared. A shareholder called Anderson, who had protested at the basketball losses in 1986, continued his attack:

> I think we agreed at the meeting last year, you and I, that this money is coming out of the pockets of the people who pay at the turnstiles to watch football. Now in view of the fact that the manager has said publicly very recently he is not able to get all the money he wants to buy necessary players, do you think it's right we should continue to throw money down this bottomless well?

Martin Edwards, having to defend a policy he no longer believed in, announced that the club would persist with the venture for one more year. He argued that there were no basketball teams anywhere in Europe which made a profit and said that it was seen as a promotional thing.

Having experienced shareholders' hostility for the third year running, Edwards immediately took steps to rid himself of the club. What had made matters worse was Rick Taylor's decision to accept a lucrative and secure job in America as assistant director of athletics at San Diego University. Taylor says that his main reason for leaving was not being allowed to extend his commercial activities into the football side of United, as Edwards had initially suggested to him. 'There was nowhere for me to go up in the organisation,' Taylor explains. 'I got the results but for some reason they didn't follow through.'

Yet Edwards knew it would now be almost impossible to find anybody as good as Rick Taylor at raising money for basketball. He referred to Taylor's expertise as 'selling fresh air'. The club was no nearer getting a basketball sponsor to replace Sharp, and finding one would be even harder now that it was known United might be involved for only another year. What made the situation even worse was that after recent modifications the possible new Eccles venue could hold no more spectators than the Stretford Leisure Centre.

Coincidentally Edwards had been involved in discussions on football matters with David Kay, a Manchester businessman, who ran a sports agency with the former England rugby union captain, Richard Greenwood, called People Management Ltd. The company employed the star United basketball player Alton Byrd, and had heard about Edwards' problems with basketball. Kay and Greenwood saw a good opportunity and offered to find a new sponsor for Edwards. But as United's commitment to basketball became less certain, this quickly grew into an agreement around Christmas 1987 for the company to buy the whole basketball venture.

In January 1988 People Management Ltd agreed to pay United £50,000 – in three instalments – for their 75 per cent shareholding in the club. No credit was given to People Management to allow for the remaining sponsorship money United had already received from Sharp. The individual directors who guaranteed the club's bank account had settled the club's overdraft.

The People Management director Richard Greenwood argues that soccer and basketball were 'uneasy bed-fellows', and that British sport is not familiar with Continental-style multi-sports clubs such as those of Barcelona and Real Madrid. He also felt that United had treated basketball very much as a 'sideline'. It is true that after attending nearly all his team's early matches Martin Edwards' interest soon waned, and big United names like Bobby Charlton and Bryan Robson were seen far less frequently at Stretford Leisure Centre.

People Management stated initially that they expected the basketball team to be breaking even within a year. By the spring of 1988 this looked fairly improbable. It was obvious that with United's name no longer linked with basketball many of the sponsors would choose to end their association with the team, and this largely seemed to happen.

One man who cannot have been too happy with United's decision to pull out of basketball was that ubiquitous sports entrepreneur, Dennis Roach. For while his ally Martin Edwards was negotiating for his club to withdraw from the game, Roach's hopes of trying to sell his own club, Polycell Kingston, to Tottenham Hotspur were finally ended. When Manchester United had moved into basketball three years before it was predicted that several other top soccer clubs would move into the new up-and-coming sport, but only Portsmouth had actually done so. It had become obvious it was not a profitable area to become involved in and Roach was forced to look elsewhere. Instead Glasgow Rangers agreed to buy Kingston in the summer of 1988, and they moved the team and franchise to Scotland. It was another sign that the Scottish club, and not United, are now the wealthiest football club in Britain.

The sale was not just a financial humiliation for the Old Trafford club. In the spring of 1988 their former basketball team was given a new name, Manchester Eagles, chosen after a competition held in the *Manchester Evening News*. A name change had in fact been part of the agreement to sell the club, but David Kay and Richard Greenwood argued that it was necessary anyway. The name of Manchester United, they said, conjured up the wrong kind of image.

13 SELLING UNITED

'You can see the changes. Business people come in, not many with any experience of football. It has become a business organisation.'

Sir Matt Busby on United, 1986.

'ATTENTION PLEASE!' the loud-speakers boomed out before each game. 'Will somebody please remove Read's sausage van from outside the players' entrance.'

'My dad was no fool,' Al Read, the Manchester comedian who died in 1987, often told his audiences. Having deliberately parked his meat van right outside Old Trafford, 'he knew damned well that sooner or later' the announcement would come. Often he might wait for a second request before actually going out to move the van. Two messages like that, Read calculated, broadcast to the 25,000 or so who watched United in the period around the First World War, were excellent free advertising for his sausages. And it cost no more than a few pence turnstile money. Herbert Henry Read was, perhaps, in his own small way the first man to appreciate the true commercial potential of Manchester United Football Club. It would take the son of another Salford butcher to exploit it fully.

Right up until the late 1960s few football directors paid much attention to making money beyond the ordinary turnstile and transfer receipts. In 1948, for instance, Oxo offered to pay Manchester United £20 a season for the right to run refreshment bars selling their famous hot drink at reserve games played at Old Trafford – the first team were still playing at Maine Road. The United directors were so keen, however, that supporters out on the largely uncovered terraces should be able to warm themselves with steaming Oxo that they asked for only a 'nominal rent of £5', a quarter of what the company had offered. The United board was similarly generous the following year. When the new British Railways Board asked for an advertising hoarding alongside their station next to the main stand, the directors allowed them to put one up for nothing.

Even in the era of the 1968 European Cup win Manchester United did practically nothing to exploit the club crest and name commercially. At that time anybody could use United's club badge to sell their own products, without fear of legal action. When United looked into the matter, they found that the existing crest, based on the City of Manchester coat of arms, could not be copyrighted, and eventually designed a new one on which they declared a copyright and so could sue anyone who breached it.

Today, however, few areas of Old Trafford are not exploited to full commercial advantage. In the late 1980s home match gate receipts of around £4 million a year account for only two thirds of United's total income – the rest comes from a whole range of other activities. The ultimate aim is to get that outside income up to 50 per cent.

The best-known of Manchester United's current commercial arrangements, though actually not the most lucrative, is with Sharp Electronics, the Japanese company which has its British headquarters in East Manchester, within only a few yards of the site where United began playing as Newton Heath more than a hundred years ago. Sharp's relationship with United began in 1982, shortly after Martin Edwards became chief executive.

United had in fact been rather slow to acquire a club sponsor. Liverpool and Everton, for instance, had arranged sponsors as early as 1979, and wore the logos on their shirts. One drawback initially had been that the television companies refused to allow shirt advertising in televised games, and a high proportion of United games were on TV. At its launch in 1982 United's three-year contract with Sharp was described as the biggest sponsorship deal in soccer, and was worth £750,000. By the time the current fourth contract expires in 1990, United will have earned nearly £3 million from Sharp. Officially much of the money has been allocated to specific development projects, such as the new administrative block at the northern end of the main stand. In reality it simply boosts United's total income.

The present sponsorship deal, agreed in March 1987, is worth £800,000 to the club. Publicly neither side ever reveals the amount paid, though both sides have been happy to let others refer to the slightly underestimated figure of £750,000, £50,000 below the true amount. For their large outlay Sharp get their name on United's shirts and tracksuits, especially attractive now that the TV companies allow shirt displays. It particularly helps that United's red shirts are the same

211

colour as Sharp's corporate red. The club are also expected to provide Sharp with considerably more than the prominent logos on the team members' chests.

Indeed, the extra benefits Sharp get are themselves worth well over £100,000 a year. United provide an eight-seat box for Sharp's guests at every game, together with meals. They are also given twelve seats at the back of the directors' box, and twenty-four seats in the Executive Suite for every home match. Then, for two matches every season which are chosen as Sharp family days, the firm is given a further 2,500 seats. On top of that they automatically get 100 ordinary seats for every game, as well as 100 extra places in the Executive Suite for four matches during the course of a season. In addition United must provide Sharp with ten seats at every away game, 100 seats for every Cup semi-final the team is involved in, and 200 tickets if United reach any Cup final.

In terms of extra advertising, Sharp get two pages in every match-day programme, including the back cover, and their logo on the front cover. There are regular announcements on the electronic scoreboard and the public address system, two advertising hoardings outside the ground, and six boards around the pitch. The latter are in the most prominent positions – by the half-way line directly opposite the television gantry, behind the goals and next to the corner flags.

United players are also meant to promote Sharp and its products. Photos showing members of the squad with Sharp microwave ovens and photocopying machines are taken each season and used in the firm's advertising. Two players are expected to have a drink with Sharp's guests after each game and pose for photos with them. Under Ron Atkinson, deciding who was going to fulfil the unpopular Sharp suite chore became something of a ritual. Names would be drawn from a hat at the team hotel before the match, or on the coach during the ride to the ground, and the unlucky 'winners' were derided by the rest of the party. Players are also expected to make regular promotional visits to Sharp's factories in Manchester and Wrexham.

Sharp's former UK chairman, Toshi Mitsuda, became a fervent United fan, but rather than use his firm's private boxes he preferred to go out in the rain and mud to take photographs by the touchline.

The company believes that the United association has helped get the Sharp name recognised in Britain. At times, though, Sharp have been strict, and United are not allowed to take any sponsorship or advertising from Sharp's electronics competitors. When their Japanese rivals, Canon, began sponsoring the Football League Championship in

1983, Sharp expressed concern. Canon's sponsorship of the competition was barely mentioned in the match-day programme thereafter and, unlike other league clubs, United did not give Canon a full-page advertisement. Similarly, in 1982 Sharp were very angry with a photo on the front of a programme showing a United game against Arsenal. The problem was that Sharp's logo could barely be seen anywhere in the picture, but the logo on the Arsenal shirts was quite prominent – and it belonged to Sharp's rival, JVC.

Commercial operations at Old Trafford did not really get going properly until 1973, when Bill Burke, the man who had set up the Development Association, was appointed commercial manager as well. One of his first moves was to end Shell and BP's monopoly of advertising boards around the edge of the pitch, for which they paid just £10,000 a year, a sum that also covered a full-page advertisement in each programme. The petrol companies were getting a remarkable bargain at a time when around two thirds of United's home matches were shown in recorded highlights on television. Within a year of terminating Shell's contract, Burke was receiving £22,000 from perimeter advertising, and the figure rose steadily thereafter.

Of course, advertising boards have been a feature at English soccer grounds for as long as Oxo has been around, but recently at Old Trafford the boards have moved upwards. Today on the roof above the Stretford End is a 'Wonderfuel Gas' sign; the money British Gas paid in the first year went towards new lavatories at that part of the ground. In direct competition, two neon signs at the other end of the stadium state 'This is a . . . Plug for Electricity'. Previously a clever sign for the Mortgage Point changed from red to white to yellow to green and back to red every few seconds and made £2,500 in 1986–87. The new corner Family Stand, for children accompanied by parents, proclaims that it is sponsored by Panini Stickers – the football stickers children collect and put in special albums – and earned £10,000. In recent years boards around the field have encouraged spectators to fly with three different airlines and drink two brands of whisky!

In 1986 the selling of advertising around the edge of the pitch was contracted out to Delta Sports Ltd, based in Bolton and run by Harold Hassall, the former Wanderers and England international. United received 85 per cent of all the revenue from the perimeter adverts and from the posters on six huge hoardings on the number one car park. Nowadays this work is contracted out to Bermitz Farmer Ltd, based in Hull, who bring in even more money from ground advertising as a result of new television agreements with ITV and the BBC for live coverage of league and cup games. Even more lucrative, though, are those matches that are now shown live in Scandinavia on a regular basis. United have always enjoyed strong support in Denmark, Norway and Sweden and when chosen as the 'live' match hoardings in the various languages are erected around Old Trafford. The money to be earned from ground advertising on these occasions can sometimes be almost twice that received for matches broadcast to a home audience – a reflection perhaps of the current state of English football.

But, despite the huge fee United receive, from ITV in particular, when a home game is shown live in the UK, there will no doubt be some disappointment expressed at the reduced revenue for ground advertising should a Saturday broadcast to Scandinavia be cancelled to accommodate ITV's *The Match* on a Sunday afternoon – as was the case when Tottenham Hotspur visited Old Trafford in February 1989. Since 1987 United have added to their advertising revenue by hosting the Rugby League premiership finals, which are broadcast by the BBC. The return from the sale of ground advertising in 1986 – the sum of £170,000 – is almost certain to increase to around £200,000 by the end of 1988–89.

From 1985 Delta Sports also sold corporate hospitality packages for United and what is known as 'match sponsorship'. From this work United received a guaranteed £50,000 a year, or 50 per cent of Delta's gross income after expenses, whichever was the greater. Delta's corporate hospitality packages were designed for the new breed of business football supporter. They included a night's hotel accommodation, tickets to the match, a champagne reception beforehand, a tour of the ground, lunch, entertainment hosted by former player Pat Crerand, free drinks, travel and even a photographer to record the occasion. It used to cost £98 a person. Since 1988, however, United have organised the hospitality packages themselves. Matches are now graded into 'A' games, 'B' games and 'C' games, depending on the calibre of the opposition, and each costs a different price.

Alternatively firms can 'sponsor' a particular match, a different thing from Sharp's sponsorship of the club over several years. For a fee of £5,750 upwards match sponsors can buy 'hospitality' at a game for forty or more guests, as well as advertising in the match programme, on the electronic scoreboard and over the public address system. They also get several advertising displays, including two 20-foot boards by the pitch, positioned near corner flags to catch television cameras. United's ventures into the world of corporate hospitality are, of course, part of the growing trend in British sport. From Wimbledon to Cheltenham, Wembley to St Andrew's, companies use sporting occasions to reward staff and entertain clients – though often, it seems, customers have little interest in the events they are invited to.

The most blatantly commercial of all their arrangements, however, must be the one United have for their playing strip with the world-famous sports manufacturer Adidas. Exploiting the popular Manchester United kit was one of the first moves made by Bill Burke when he became commercial manager, at a time when manufacturers were beginning to realise the potential. Until then one red and white football outfit was much the same as another – United's plain red shirts with white trimmings, plain white shorts and plain red socks were identical to several league sides'.

Burke first agreed a deal with the manufacturers, Umbro International, whereby they would design a distinctive United kit with a club badge and enjoy the right to produce it under licence. This meant that replicas could be made and sold in shops. United were granted a royalty of 10 per cent on each kit. In 1975 United's kit contract was switched to Hurst and Cooke of Leicester, who later became Admiral. The new suppliers guaranteed United a minimum of £15,000 a year for three years, although the overall royalty was only 5 per cent. Admiral also agreed to pay extra bonuses if the team achieved certain playing targets – £10,000, for instance, for reaching the FA Cup final, and another £6,000 if they went on to win the Cup. For Admiral the extra television exposure and prestige of a Wembley appearance would make the money worthwhile.

In 1980 Admiral signed a new four-year contract with the club, but then went bankrupt within only a few weeks – the two events were unconnected, it seems. A new deal for a similar period was quickly agreed with the German firm Adidas, who, after Admiral's demise, had become the main manufacturer of English league kits. As part of the arrangement the players received £15,000 to share between them. The Adidas contract was renewed in 1983, ahead of schedule, and again in 1987. But on the second occasion United actually received a more favourable offer from Hummel, the kit manufacturer that is a subsidiary of Tottenham Hotspur. Hummel promised a minimum of £1.6 million over four years, while Adidas was offering only £1.5 million over the same period. Martin Edwards went back to Adidas and they agreed to improve their bid.

United's present deal with Adidas is worth a guaranteed £350,000 a year and lasts for five years, not four as originally proposed. United get an extra 10 per cent royalty once sales go beyond £750,000 in any one year. Adidas enjoy sole rights to manufacture and market the strip, which sells for about £40 in the shops. It brings Adidas an annual turnover of about £1 million, so United can expect some royalties on top of their guarantee.

Nowadays the design of football strips is a fine, calculated business. Each set of shirt, shorts and socks is carefully planned to generate the maximum revenue for the sole manufacturer and the club. As part of every kit deal since 1973, including the current five-year contract with Adidas, the two parties agree to change small details of the strip every two years, a deliberate move to regenerate demand at regular intervals. And each part of the kit – shirt, shorts and socks – has to be changed. In 1984, for instance, white bands, looking like shoulder-straps, were added to the shirt; red pinstripes appeared on the white shorts; and white bands were added on the top of the black socks. 1986 saw equally small changes. The white shoulder-straps were replaced by two white stripes down each arm of the shirt; the shorts' red pinstripes gave way to three black and red stripes down the side; and the white bands on top of the socks fell to half-way down. The new strip introduced in 1988 included the letters 'MUFC' subtly marked in the texture of the fabric, rather like a watermark on paper. Few adult supporters notice or care about such small details, but their ever-demanding children certainly do. United's deal with Adidas is the most lucrative commercial arrangement of all at Old Trafford. Sharp actually guarantee a larger annual payment, but allowing for the numerous extra benefits Sharp get, such as free boxes and hospitality, the Adidas deal is in fact more profitable.

United's match-day programme, the *United Review*, is another major source of income. Carrying advertising copy from all the club's major sponsors, it plays an important role in the commercial operations. The programme is among the most popular in the league. It used to sell to around 96 per cent of every home crowd, partly because of the tokens inside which fans collect to get priority for tickets for big matches. At 60p the programme is among the cheapest in the country and, helped by a small amount of advertising that actually pays, it generates a profit of well over £100,000 a season – as high as £190,241 in 1986 for instance. The publication became so burdened with advertisements from United's many commercial ventures that in 1988 the number of pages had to be increased to thirty-two. As well as Sharp's two pages, single pages are devoted to Adidas, the Football League sponsors, Barclays Bank, and each particular match-day sponsor. There have also been regular advertisements for the Club-Call (the recorded telephone message service), Red Devil Lager and United's recent leisurewear enterprise.

A much less successful publication was *Man-U-News*, a newspaper launched by Danny McGregor in September 1987. It was based on monthly newspapers which had already been successfully produced for Chelsea and Portsmouth by Hayters, a sports news agency run near London's Fleet Street by Frank Nicklin, a former sports editor of *The Sun*. Hayters hoped to finance the paper through advertising, and United received 50,000 free copies each month to sell at 30p each. But distribution through major outlets was unsuccessful. Poor circulation hit advertising revenue. Nicklin could not make the publication pay and it folded after three issues.

A quite profitable activity in the last few seasons has been the sale of video tapes of United games. Dave Sexton originally bought the club's video equipment in the late 1970s to film every match for analysis in coaching. It has since developed into a business and fans can buy compilations of matches and goals, and there have even been plans to sell the videos in the shops of away teams that have come to Old Trafford and won! United were also expected to earn lucrative royalties on the BBC video, *The Official History of Manchester United FC*, released in 1988.

Diaries and books bring in further revenue. The *Manchester United Diary*, published every year, earns United a guaranteed £2,500. Other money is earned from in-house events, such as the club's own version of the *Miss Manchester United* contest, which, together with fashion shows, was budgeted to realise £4,000 in 1986–87. Charity Dinners and Fun Day events, an extension of another successful venture first initiated by the supporters' club, were expected to earn £4,000. The original fans' 'Family Day' was run in conjunction with the Variety Club of Great Britain and helped provide a mini-bus for under-privileged children.

There are limits, though, to the extent to which matches at Old Trafford, space inside the stadium and the United name can be sold commercially. Bill Burke's latest successor, Danny McGregor, believes that those limits have nearly been reached. He sees his task now as finding new ways of exploiting the magic of the Manchester United name beyond Old Trafford. Already that has meant United joining in projects involving other British clubs.

One of the most controversial recent ventures was Red Devil, supposedly United's own lager, which caused a minor outcry when it was launched in 1987. The scheme, set up with a firm called Team Advance, also involved Liverpool and Everton. Red Devil drinkers who collected a certain number of ring-pulls from the cans could obtain tickets and team souvenirs. A total of 640 ring-pulls could be exchanged for one ticket to Old Trafford, though after that amount of lager the police might not allow one into the game. For John Smith, chairman of Liverpool and the Sports Council, Philip Carter, chairman of Everton and the Football League, and United's Martin Edwards to launch a club lager was perhaps a little strange when alcohol is banned from football terraces and drink is blamed for much football violence. But such considerations – and indeed the unhealthy linking of alcohol and sport – came second to the expected profit. In fact, Team Advance failed to market the lager successfully, and little mention of the scheme is made these days. As far as is known, nobody ever collected the necessary 640 ring-pulls!

Red Devil lager failed despite the publicity generated by the controversy. The launch even warranted an edition of the Manchester United Club-Call, a daily recorded telephone message put out by British Telecom's Supercall department. Fans can dial for the latest information about United – scores, match reports, interviews, ticket news and so on. A team of journalists in London, backed up by stringers in Manchester, keeps the service up-to-date. United guarantee to give the Supercall journalists reasonable access to players and officials for interviews. In return United expected to earn £20,000 in 1986–87. Today it is probably worth nearer £100,000.

Club-Call's editorial standard is quite high, though overall it contains little you could not find in the press. But costing 46p a minute at peak hours and 23p off-peak, up to a maximum of three minutes, the service cannot endear itself to the parents of young fans who could spend £5 a week if they called every day. Manchester United's is among the most popular of all Supercall's forty soccer lines. Around 1,000 calls are received every day, averaging a minute and a half in length, and the figure rises to 2,400 when United are playing a distant away game. Calls also reached a peak on the day Ron Atkinson was sacked in 1986; and so, with the subsequent extra royalties, United recovered a little of Atkinson's £100,000 severance cheque!

Supercall even introduced its own 'man of the match' award at the end of the 1987–88 season. They hoped that fans would actually be keen enough after a game to pay for the privilege of phoning to nominate their best United player. The award was quickly dropped.

The Red Devils Souvenir Shop next to the railway bridge on Warwick Road is United's most public commercial enterprise. For more than twenty years it has sold pens, underpants, lampshades, mirrors, cigarette lighters and hundreds more items all sporting the Manchester United badge. After opening in 1967, it quickly became the most successful souvenir shop at any league club, with a range of more than 200 items. On match days the trade was once so heavy that there were long queues outside an hour and half before kick-off. The people had to be marshalled by a commissionaire, and smaller branches were opened around the ground.

Yet the fact that Sir Matt Busby had owned the lease on the shop became widely known only in 1979 when somebody asked a question at the first large-scale Annual General Meeting of the club, though a previous revelation in a Sunday newspaper had passed almost unnoticed. By then Sandy Busby had in fact taken over the day-to-day running of the business. The shop proved to be so successful over the years that by 1986 it had an annual gross profit of around £100,000 and employed eight staff. The £5 rent that Sir Matt Busby originally agreed to in 1968 had been increased voluntarily to £75 a week by the mid-1980s.

Almost since becoming chief executive in 1982, Martin Edwards had been trying to persuade Sandy Busby to give up the lease. In particular he was keen to include shop profits within the club accounts at a time when he wanted to make United more attractive for public flotation. It was only in 1987, however, when the lease had nearly expired anyway, that Sandy Busby agreed to sell the remaining two years. Busby knew that if he stuck it out until the very end, United would take the freehold back and he might end up with nothing.

The price was reported as being more than £200,000. It seems a generous sum but Martin Edwards admitted at the 1987 annual general meeting that it included over £100,000 worth of stock that Busby had bought over the years. And a large proportion of the money was paid by way of an annual consultancy fee to Sandy Busby, but on one important condition. He had to agree not to reveal to outsiders any information about the souvenir shop or United as a whole, or indeed anything learnt about the club even after he left. Busby also had to agree not to run a business selling sports souvenirs within 10 miles of Old Trafford for the next five years.

Sandy Busby would have been happy to continue running the shop, even on very different terms from those his family had previously enjoyed – as a United employee, for instance. Instead the shop was leased to Circle Sports Promotions Ltd, part of Maybank Press Ltd, based in Ilford, Essex, and run by Eddie Buckley. United had enjoyed various dealings with Buckley over the previous ten years, including the publication of six *Manchester United Annuals* between 1977 and 1982 and the production of other items such as club calendars, a poster magazine, duvets and bed-linen, on which the club received various royalties.

The new Circle Sports management, however, ran the operation somewhat less efficiently and attractively than the Busbys. Their window displays were drab, dusty and full of rubbish dropped by customers. In January 1988 the window still showed a poster for a programme fair that had occurred two months earlier. In the spring of 1988 Circle Sports went into liquidation, and in August 1988 United began direct management of the Red Devils Souvenir Shop.

The summer of 1988 also saw the club launch out in a new retail venture – leisurewear. United's new venture involves selling simple everyday clothes in modern designs – shirts, trousers, pullovers, jackets and so on, from a new fashion shop next to the Red Devils Souvenir Shop. But unlike previous garments sold by the souvenir shop, many do not display the United name prominently, and few are in United colours. Some carry United's small, distinctive, stick-man logo, made up from the letters MUFC. A glossy catalogue showing United players modelling the new leisurewear was sent out to all club members, and the intention is that many of the sales will come from mail-order business.

The takeover of the souvenir shop from Sandy Busby in 1987 was perhaps symbolic of a process that has been going on at Old Trafford now for twenty-five years. It marked the final phase in the transfer of power at Manchester United from the Busbys to the Edwards. Sandy Busby, the son earmarked by the creator of the modern United to continue his influence at Old Trafford, had finally been evicted by Martin Edwards, the son of the man Busby had brought to United, who had bought the club for next to nothing and started his own dynasty.

CONCLUSION

'THIS SEASON we mean business' a slogan on the back of the *United Review* has claimed – for the past two seasons! It was one of two advertisements from Sharp Electronics in alternate home programmes, playing on the link between United and their official sponsors. 'One team,' says the other advertisement 'will be there or thereabouts by the end of the season.' Or thereabouts? The words seem to have been added as an afterthought by a copywriter who felt more realistic than confident about United's prospects. In a way both slogans sum up the state of Manchester United Football Club twenty years after Sir Matt Busby first announced his retirement; it is a football club that has become a business without reaching its previous heights.

The magic of Manchester United is rapidly disappearing. It is a hard thing for United supporters to accept, but arch-rivals Liverpool are now challenging what Manchester United were for so long – the team with the aura and magic, the side that everyone wants to watch. Until very recently Liverpool's phenomenal playing success had failed to generate the kind of affection enjoyed by United, even though the Merseyside club has amassed many more trophies than the Manchester reds. For so long the Anfield team was mechanical rather than entertaining, scientific rather than artistic, and respected rather than loved. Despite sustained success, Liverpool's home crowds were usually many thousands below United's – 11,000 fewer on average, for instance, as recently as 1985–86, the year in which Liverpool won the league and Cup double.

Yet in 1987, with £4 million worth of new forwards – John Barnes, Peter Beardsley and John Aldridge – and improved further in 1988 with the return of the £2 million Ian Rush, the Merseyside team added a new excitement to their play and achieved a new level of popularity. Away to Charlton Athletic, for instance, in January 1988, Liverpool drew 28,095 spectators: not a large crowd by most standards, but extraordinary for the poorly supported South London

221

club and nearly four times the average for Charlton's other home matches that season. At one time only Manchester United could have boosted London crowds like that, yet the reds' visit to Selhurst Park the previous August had pulled in only 14,046, half the Liverpool figure. And by the end of the 1987–88 season Anfield was for the first time in fifteen years housing the best supported club in English football.

At Old Trafford, meanwhile, the crowd has lost its famous old roar, with its ability to frighten opponents. Under the new membership scheme large gaps have appeared on the most vociferous side of the ground, the Stretford End. To United supporters positioned around the half-way line, the visiting fans crammed into their pens at the Scoreboard End often seem to make more noise than the once-legendary Stretford Enders. The home crowd comes to life only briefly to celebrate a United goal, or to rally the players in the moments after the opposition has scored. Sadly, the large repertoire of amusing United songs has diminished to a handful of inane chants, such as the famous 'Here We Go' and, increasingly, 'What a Load of Rubbish'. And, as they grow impatient for success, spectators at home games seem ever more inclined to pick on individual players like Colin Gibson and Ralph Milne. The heart is fading from this once-great club.

As the 1988–89 season drifted through autumn and into another year of apparent mediocrity, a home match one November night against Sheffield Wednesday summed up United's plight. The reds performed abysmally. Hopes rose briefly when Mark Hughes put United into the lead with only seven minutes left, but within ninety seconds Wednesday had equalised. It was the fifth league draw in a row and each had been against mediocre sides who should have been beaten easily. Remarkably it was the eighth consecutive match in which United had thrown away a lead. The Old Trafford malaise continued.

The official attendance against Wednesday, albeit on a cold and misty night, was just a fraction over 30,000; the real figure, however, was many thousands fewer, since United's figures, unlike many clubs', include season-ticket holders who do not turn up. Until recently such a low turn-out would have been unthinkable so early in the season against such well-supported, local opponents. But after twenty-one years without the league championship, the fans' patience is disappearing quickly. 'Will we ever win the league?' sang the Stretford End in mocking despair – the most original chant for months. 'Fergie out!' shouted the more blunt of the brethren.

Four days later United drew yet again in a live television match at Newcastle. It was their sixth consecutive league draw – a club record – and though the chants of 'Sack the board' came from the disillusioned Geordie fans and were directed at their own club's directors, many of the Manchester United supporters in attendance were having similar thoughts about the control of their own club. If Alex Ferguson had failed to restore United's fortunes quickly, in terms of entertainment as well as success, the pressure would have grown to the point where Martin Edwards had to announce the sixth dismissal since Busby. Yet it is perhaps inevitable that in time 'Fergie out!' would be followed by 'Taylor out!', should Graham Taylor, as just one possible replacement, be the next in line, or 'Charlton out!', 'Clough out!', 'Bloggs out!', or whoever else fails to grapple with the United problem.

Even the world's most brilliant football manager could not deal with Manchester United as long as the club is run from the chairman's office in the way it is. Continuing to appoint and dismiss United managers will be a fruitless and expensive exercise. Only drastic changes in the way the club is administered will make any difference. The businessmen who run Old Trafford must be more sympathetic to the Matt Busby tradition than the Edwards family have been since they took control of Manchester United. Louis Edwards simply hoped to transfer his activity and investment from the meat factory of Miles Platting to the football stadium 4 miles westward. Sir Matt Busby, the man who must so regret inviting Louis Edwards in, could not possibly have envisaged the carve-up that has resulted.

Of course, it was only correct that football clubs in the 1970s and 1980s should apply a more stringent, commercial approach to running the ailing national game. The two most successful sides in recent years, Liverpool and Everton, are run on excellent business lines. But neither the Liverpool chairman, John Smith, nor his Everton counterpart, Philip Carter, reward themselves with large dividends and salary bonuses – although their teams' successes would make them more deserving cases than Martin Edwards. At Anfield and Goodison the money generated is almost all ploughed back into football.

Manchester United have also ignored one of the important lessons of Sir Matt Busby's success – family continuity. At Old Trafford, after the relative failure of the inexperienced Wilf McGuinness in 1970, such continuity was abandoned far too swiftly. United has thus suffered as each subsequent manager from outside has come and introduced his own ways.

However, the millions of United faithful around the world need not despair. The legend that has been betrayed could be resurrected if control of the club was restored to directors prepared to represent those people who helped Sir Matt Busby build United – the fans. Manchester United is owned and run by one man, and whatever one might argue, if the chairman is also the majority shareholder, the mere fact that he has installed himself as chief executive must lead to a conflict of interests. But, ultimately, even the present owner will have to recognise that it cannot be a choice between the magic of United and the money. It has been shown since he took control that if the red magic is suffocated beneath a pile of cheque books, bonus payments and dividend slips, so too is the cash it can generate.

APPENDICES

APPENDIX A:
MATCH ATTENDANCES 1946–88

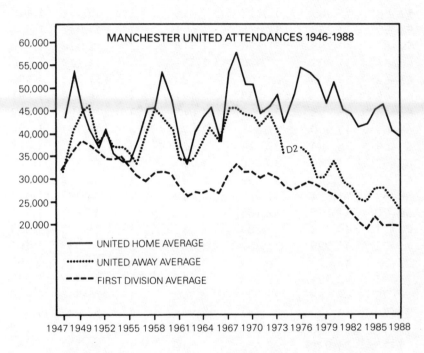

MANCHESTER UNITED ATTENDANCES 1946-1988

The following table sets out United home and away attendances since the war, together with annual ratios between United's average attendance and the first division average.

Year	Home Average	Division One Average	Ratio	League Position	Away Average	Ratio
46–47	43,615	32,479	1.343	4	31,364	0.966
47–48	53,660	36,217	1.482	3	40,493	1.118
48–49	46,023	38,776	1.187	3	44,720	1.153
49–50	41,455	37,400	1.108	7	46,172	1.235

Year	Home Average	Division One Average	Ratio	League Position	Away Average	Ratio
50–51	37,159	36,102	1.029	9	38,091	1.055
51–52	41,870	34,871	1.201	4	40,945	1.174
52–53	35,737	34,740	1.029	8	37,068	1.067
53–54	33,637	34,967	0.962	10	37,096	1.061
54–55	34,077	32,656	1.044	9	35,865	1.098
55–56	38,880	30,539	1.273	3	32,872	1.076
56–57	45,192	29,877	1.513	1	39,772	1.332
57–58	45,583	31,317	1.456	1	45,352	1.448
58–59	53,258	31,878	1.671	1	44,028	1.381
59–60	47,288	31,150	1.518	2	41,026	1.317
60–61	37,807	27,980	1.351	3	34,139	1.220
61–62	33,490	26,106	1.283	5	33,964	1.301
62–63	40,317	27,035	1.491	4	34,894	1.291
63–64	43,753	27,027	1.618	3	38,697	1.432
64–65	45,990	27,508	1.672	1	41,377	1.504
65–66	38,456	27,014	1.424	3	38,171	1.413
66–67	53,984	30,828	1.751	1	45,577	1.478
67–68	57,759	33,094	1.745	1	45,802	1.384
68–69	51,121	31,569	1.619	1	44,295	1.403
69–70	51,115	32,183	1.588	1	43,997	1.367
70–71	44,754	30,204	1.481	2	41,695	1.380
71–72	45,999	31,352	1.467	2	44,085	1.406
72–73	48,623	30,299	1.605	1	41,171	1.359
73–74	42,721	28,292	1.510	1	35,337	1.249
74–75	48,388	27,301	1.772*	1	25,556	0.936*
75–76	54,750	28,331	1.932	1	37,037	1.307
76–77	53,710	29,540	1.818	1	35,357	1.197
77–78	51,938	28,692	1.810	1	30,424	1.060
78–79	46,687	27,499	1.697	1	30,498	1.109
79–80	51,562	26,327	1.958	1	34,101	1.295
80–81	45,055	24,660	1.827	1	29,849	1.210
81–82	44,685	22,556	1.981	1	27,214	1.207
82–83	41,583	20,120	2.066	1	25,294	1.257
83–84	42,534	18,856	2.256	1	24,936	1.322
84–85	43,010	21,129	2.035	1	27,884	1.320
85–86	44,422	19,562	2.270	1	28,204	1.442
86–87	40,625	19,794	2.052	1	25,221	1.274
87–88	39,155	19,272	2.031	2	23,041	1.196

* Second division season – ratios compared with first division average.

NOTES

1. All official attendance figures are extremely unreliable. Clubs often understate their crowds for financial reasons, though this is probably less prevalent since clubs stopped paying away teams a percentage of gate receipts. Unlike many clubs, Manchester United include season ticket and league match book holders at Old Trafford for matches even if they do not turn up. Most clubs include only people who are at the game. During periods of disillusionment, or lack of interest at the end of a dull season, when season ticket holders often do not use their tickets, the Old Trafford figures are overstated significantly.

2. Figures since 1983 are also distorted by live television games. United played one live home league game in the 1983–84, 1984–85 and 1985–86 seasons, two home TV games in the 1986–87 season, and one in 1987–88.

APPENDIX B:
PLAYER TRANSFERS 1945–88

TRANSFER FEES quoted in the press are usually only rough estimates, based on information supplied by the club. Most of the figures below, however, are the actual fee. They do not include VAT or the additional 5 per cent levy payable to the Football League when players are signed.

SIR MATT BUSBY (1945–71)

Arrivals			*Departures*		
1945–46					
J. Delaney	Celtic	£4,000	J. Smith	Blackburn	£3,000
1946–47					
J. Dale	Witton	£1,130	T. Breen	Glentoran	£600
			N. Tapken	Darlington	£530
1947–48					
J. Ball	Wigan	£2,000	J. Walton	Preston	£12,000
			J. Dale	Port Vale	£1,000
			H. Worrall	Swindon	£1,000
1948–49					
J. Downie	Bradford PA	£20,000	J. Hanlon	Bury	£5,500
B. Stenson	Altrincham	£500	J. Morris	Derby	£25,000
			R. Burke	Huddersfield	£15,500
1949–50					
T. Bogan	Preston	£3,500	J. Anderson	Nott'm Forest	£8,000
R. Wood	Darlington	£6,000	E. Buckle	Everton	£6,500
R. Allen	QPR	£11,000	H. Williams	Witton	£500
T. Ritchie	Bangor	£750	R. McMorran	Walsall	£1,000
1950–51					
E. McIlvenny	Philadelphia	£1,700	I. Feehan	Northampton	£525
H. McShane	Bolton	£5,000	J. Ball	Bolton	*exchange*
(& J. Ball *exchange*)			C. Hughes	Leeds	£1,250
			J. Delaney	Aberdeen	£3,100
			S. Lynn	Bradford PA	£3,500
			T. Bogan } T. Lowrie }	Aberdeen	£8,000
			J. Warner	Oldham	£150

230

1951–52

J. Berry	Birmingham	£25,000	C. Mitten	Fulham	£16,200
E. Bond	Leyland M	£250	L. Cassidy	Oldham	£450
			B. Birch	Wolves	£6,000

1952–53

T. Taylor	Barnsley	£29,999	W. McGlen	Lincoln	£3,000
			H. Killin	Lincoln	£1,250
			E. Bond	Carlisle	£5,000
			T. Ritchie	Reading	£3,250
			F. Clempson	Stockport	£2,000
			R. Hampson	Reading	£300

1953–54

			J. Downie	Luton	£9,500
			S. Pearson	Bury	£4,000
			F. Mooney	Blackburn	£600
			H. McShane	Oldham	£750
			T. McNulty	Liverpool	£6,000

1954–55

			H. Cockburn	Bury	£1,250

1955–56

			D. Gibson	Sheff Weds	£8,000
			E. Lewis	Preston	£9,000
			J. Scott	Grimsby	£1,500

1956–57

			P. Kennedy	Blackburn	£2,000
			W. Whitehurst	Chesterfield	£750

1957–58

H. Gregg	Doncaster	£23,000	T. Barrett	Plymouth	£1,000
S. Crowther	Aston Villa	£23,000	J. Doherty	Leicester	£6,500
E. Taylor	Blackpool	£8,000	J. Whitefoot	Grimsby	£8,000
T. Heron	Portadown	£7,000			

NB: Jimmy Murphy was responsible for signing Stan Crowther and Ernie Taylor immediately after Munich.

1958–59

A. Quixall	Sheff Weds	£45,000	C. Webster	Swansea	£6,000
W. Bradley	Bishop Auck	£100	R. Wood	Huddersfield	£1,500
			E. Taylor	Sunderland	£9,000
			S. Crowther	Chelsea	£10,000

1959–60

K. McDowall	Rhyl	£1,000	R. Harrop }	Tranmere	£4,000
M. Setters	West Bromwich	£30,000	G. Clayton }		
T. Dunne	Shelbourne	£6,000	E. Holland	Wrexham	£1,750
			F. Goodwin	Leeds	£15,000
			E. Jones	Wrexham	£2,250

1960–61

N. Cantwell	West Ham	£29,500	A. Scanlon	Newcastle	£17,500
			J. Carolan	Brighton	£9,000
			I. Greaves	Lincoln	£2,000
			T. Spratt	Bradford PA	£1,750
			K. Morgans	Swansea	£2,000

1961–62

D. Herd	Arsenal	£40,000	R. Cope	Luton	£10,000
D. Law	Torino	£115,000	D. Viollet	Stoke	£24,000
			A. Dawson	Preston	£20,000
			W. Bradley	Bury	£2,500

1962–63

D. Sadler	Maidstone	£750	N. Lawton	Preston	£11,500
P. Crerand	Celtic	£56,000			

1963–64

G. Moore	Chelsea	£35,000	F. Haydock	Charlton	£10,000
J. Connelly	Burnley	£56,000	J. Giles	Leeds	£34,000
P. Dunne	Shamrock	£10,000	M. Pearson	Sheff Weds	£17,000
			S. McMillan	Wrexham	£6,000
			P. Chisnall	Liverpool	£25,000

1964–65

			A. Quixall	Oldham	£3,300
			M. Setters	Stoke	£30,000
			J. Nicholson	Huddersfield	£1,000
			I. Moir	Blackpool	£10,000
			R. Smith	Scunthorpe	£3,000

1965–66

			E. Dunphy	York	£4,000
			G. Moore	Northampton	£15,000

1966–67

A. Stepney	Chelsea	£52,000	J. Connelly	Blackburn	£40,000
			W. Anderson	Aston Villa	£20,000
			P. Dunne	Plymouth	£4,000

1968–69

W. Morgan	Burnley	£105,000	F. Kopel	Blackburn	£9,000

1969–70

I. Ure	Arsenal	£80,000	J. Ryan	Luton	£20,000
			D. Givens	Luton	£15,000

1970–71

			N. Stiles	Middlesbrough	£22,500

NB: Wilf McGuinness neither bought nor sold any players during his six months as team manager in 1970.

FRANK O'FARRELL (1971–72)

Arrivals   *Departures*

1971–72

M. Buchan	Aberdeen	£125,000	F. Burns	Southampton	£40,000
I. Moore	Nott'm Forest	£180,000	A. Gowling	Huddersfield	£60,000

1972–73

W. Davies	Manchester C	£60,000	J. Aston	Luton Town	£30,000
E. MacDougall	B'rnem'th	£200,000	J. Connaughton	Sheff Utd	£15,000
T. Anderson	Portadown	£20,000			

TOMMY DOCHERTY (1972–77)

Arrivals			Departures		
1972–73					
G. Graham	Arsenal	£120,000	E. MacDougall	West Ham	£170,000
A. Forsyth	Partick T	£100,000	P. Edwards	Oldham	£13,000
L. Macari	Celtic	£190,000	C. Sartori	Bologna	£45,000
J. Holton	Shrewsbury	£91,000	W. Davies	Blackpool	£14,000
M. Martin	Bohemians	£25,000			
R. O'Brien	Shelbourne	£20,000			
G. Daly	Bohemians	£22,000			
1973–74					
P. Roche	Shelbourne	£15,000	D. Sadler	Preston	£20,000
S. Houston	Brentford	£45,000	J. Rimmer	Arsenal	£36,750
J. McCalliog	Wolves	£60,000	R. O'Brien	Notts County	£40,000
S. Pearson	Hull	£200,000	P. Fletcher	Hull	£33,000
1974–75					
R. Davies	Portsmouth	£43,000	G. Buchan	Bury	£10,000
S. Coppell	Tranmere	£60,000	B. Kidd	Arsenal	£85,000
			G. Graham	Portsmouth	£35,000
			T. Anderson	Swindon	£25,000
			J. McCalliog	Southampton	£40,000
			W. Morgan	Burnley	£30,000
1975–76					
G. Hill	Millwall	£85,000	M. Martin	West Brom	£20,000
1976–77					
A. Foggon	Middlesbro	£25,000	A. Foggon	Sunderland	£30,000
C. McGrath	Tottenham	£30,000	J. Holton	Sunderland	£64,000
J. Greenhoff	Stoke	£100,000	G. Daly	Derby	£170,000
A. Grimes	Bohemians	£40,000			

DAVE SEXTON (1977–81)

Arrivals			Departures		
1977–78					
J. Jordan	Leeds	£350,000	G. Hill	Derby	£275,000
G. McQueen	Leeds	£450,000			
1978–79					
T. Connell	Coleraine	£20,000	D. Bradley	Doncaster	£5,000
T. Sloan	Ballymena	£32,500	J. Clark	Derby	£50,000
M. Thomas	Wrexham	£300,000			
1979–80					
R. Wilkins	Chelsea	£700,000	M. Rogers	QPR	£5,000
N. Jovanovic	RS Belgrade	£350,000	S. Pearson	West Ham	£200,000
			D. McCreery	QPR	£170,000
			B. Greenhoff	Leeds	£350,000
1980–81					
A. Whelan	Bohemians	£30,000	A. Ritchie	Brighton	£500,000
G. Birtles	Nottm Forest	£1,250,000	C. McGrath	Tulsa	£30,000

RON ATKINSON (1981–86)

Arrivals			Departures		
1981–82					
J. Gidman	Everton	£355,000	J. Jordan	AC Milan	£250,000
F. Stapleton	Arsenal	£900,000	M. Thomas	Everton	£450,000
R. Moses	West Brom	£500,000	S. McIlroy	Stoke	£350,000
B. Robson	West Brom	£1,500,000	J. Nicholl	Toronto	£235,000
P. McGrath	St Patrick's	£60,000	T. Connell	Glentoran	£37,000
1982–83					
P. Beardsley	Vancouver	£250,000	P. Roche	Brentford	£15,000
			G. Birtles	Nottm Forest	£275,000
			P. Beardsley	Vancouver	£250,000
1983–84					
A. Brazil	Tottenham	£700,000	A. Grimes	Coventry	£200,000
A. Graham	Leeds	£65,000	S. McGarvey	Portsmouth	£85,000
J. Olsen	Ajax	£800,000	R. Wilkins	AC Milan	£1,400,000
1984–85					
G. Strachan	Aberdeen	£600,000	D. Platt	Crewe	£50,000
			A. Graham	Bradford C	£10,000
1985–86					
C. Turner	Sunderland	£275,000	S. Pears	Middlesbro	£85,000
C. Gibson	Aston Villa	£312,000	A. Davies	Newcastle	£65,000
P. Barnes	Coventry	£55,000	A. Brazil	Coventry	£280,000
T. Gibson	Coventry	£630,000	M. Hughes	Barcelona	£1,800,000
P. Davenport	Nottm Forest	£600,000			
J. Sivebaek	Vejle	£285,000			
J. Hanrahan	UC Dublin	£30,000			
M. Higgins	Everton	£58,500			
1986–87					
L. O'Brien	Bohemians	£72,500	M. Dempsey	Sheff Utd	£4,500

ALEX FERGUSON (1986–)

Arrivals			Departures		
1986–87					
			F. Digby	Swindon	£25,000
			P. Barnes	Manchester C	£15,000
			M. Higgins	Bury	£10,000
			M. Russell	Norwich	£25,000
1987–88					
V. Anderson	Arsenal	£250,000	S. Ratcliffe	Norwich	£40,000
B. McClair	Celtic	£850,000	T. Gibson	Wimbledon	£200,000
S. Bruce	Norwich	£825,000	J. Sivebaek	St Etienne	£227,000
P. Dalton	Brandon	£5,000			
L. Sharpe	Torquay	£125,000*			
J. Leighton	Aberdeen	£450,000			
M. Hughes	Barcelona	£1,600,000			

1988–89

M. Donaghy	Luton	£650,000	G. Hogg	Portsmouth	£150,000
R. Milne	Bristol C	£170,000	C. Turner	Sheff Weds	£175,000
G. Maiorana	Histon	£30,000*	P. Davenport	Middlesbro	£700,000
			J. Olsen	Bordeaux	£375,000
			L. O'Brien	Newcastle	£275,000

* Additional payments are due subject to appearances.

A breakdown of the transfer dealings of United's managers since the war is as follows:

	£ Purchases	£ Sales	£ Loss
Sir Matt Busby	833,179	631,505	201,674
Frank O'Farrell	585,000	145,000	440,000
Tommy Docherty	1,249,000	902,750	346,250
Dave Sexton	3,482,500	1,585,000	1,897,500
Ron Atkinson	8,048,000	5,841,500	2,207,000
Alex Ferguson	4,955,000	2,217,000	2,738,000
Totals	19,152,679	11,322,755	7,830,424

Although no United manager has made a transfer profit during his period in charge, the Busby era must rank as the most impressive in terms of the number of years involved and the success achieved. Since his retirement in 1971 his five successors have failed to win the First Division Championship and though it is often claimed that over £18 million has been spent in chasing the dream, over two-thirds of the money has been recouped by outgoing transfers. The true cost over the past seventeen years has averaged out at less than £500,000 a season.

APPENDIX C:

THE EDWARDS FAMILY TREE

LOUIS ROCCA

JOSEPH EDWARDS

LOUIS PANIZZA

ROBERT JENKINS

LOUIS ROCCA 1859-92

JOSEPH ROCCA b. 1872

JOSEPH CHARLES EDWARDS b. 1853

CAROLINE LOUISA PANIZZA b. 1854

CATHERINE JENKINS b. 1882

M. 1875

LOUIS CHARLES PANIZZA EDWARDS 1876-1943 — LCE Founder

LOUIS ROCCA 1882-1950 — MU Assistant Manager

JOSEPH ROCCA 1897-1963

M. 1926

BEATRICE LOUISE EDWARDS 1904-83

M. 1902

KATHLEEN EDWARDS

LOUIS CHARLES EDWARDS 1914-80 — MU Director 1958-80 / MU Chairman 1965-80 / LCE Co-Chairman

MURIEL BULLEN 1920-

M. 1944

DOUGLAS JOHN EDWARDS 1916- — LCE Co-Chairman

M. 1944

① EMMELINE HASLAM d. 1964
② VALERIE BARLOW-HITCHEN
M. 1973

MARGARET (PEGGY) EDWARDS 1919-65

DUDLEY DENZIL NAMAAN HAROUN 1913-85 — MU Director 1964-85

M. 1964

MARGARET (MAGI) HAROUN 1948-

JOHN EDWARDS 1945- — LCE Director

PETER EDWARDS 1947- — LCE Director

JOHN LEE — John Lee & Sons

CHARLES MARTIN EDWARDS 1945- — MU Director 1970- / MU Chairman 1980- / LCE Director

ROGER LOUIS EDWARDS 1953- — MU Director 1982-5

CATHERINE ANNE LINDEN EDWARDS 1947-

M. 1969 DIV.

① DAVID ANTHONY LEE b. 1945
② RAY KETAY

SUSAN LLOYD JONES 1944-

M. 1968

EILEEN JONES

M. 1983

LUCINDA JANE EDWARDS 1972-

JAMES LOUIS EDWARDS 1969-

KEY
MU = Manchester United
LCE = Louis C. Edwards & Sons Ltd.
M = married
b = born
d = died
DIV = divorced

236

BIBLIOGRAPHY

Arthur, Max, *The Manchester United Aircrash* (Aquarius, London, 1983).

Atkinson, Ron, *United To Win* (Sidgwick & Jackson, London, 1984).

Ball, Peter, and Shaw, Phil, *The Book of Football Quotations* (Stanley Paul, London, 1984).

Best, George, *Where Do I Go From Here?* (Queen Anne Press, London, 1981).

Best, George, *Best of Both Worlds* (Pelham Books, London, 1968).

Bird, Alex, *The Life and Secrets of a Professional Punter* (Queen Anne Press, London, 1985).

Busby, Matt, *Matt Busby's Manchester United Scrapbook* (Souvenir Press, London, 1980).

Busby, Matt, *My Story* (Souvenir Press, London, 1957).

Busby, Matt, *Soccer at the Top* (Weidenfeld and Nicolson, London, 1973).

Cantwell, Noel, *United We Stand* (Stanley Paul, London, 1965).

Charlton, Bobby, *Bobby Charlton's Most Memorable Matches* (Stanley Paul, London, 1984).

Clarke, Alf, *Manchester United FC* (Convoy, London, 1951).

Coppell, Steve, *Touch and Go* (Collins Willow, London, 1985).

Crerand, Pat, *On Top With United* (Stanley Paul, London, 1969).

Docherty, Tommy, *Call the Doc* (Hamlyn, London, 1981).

Dunphy, Eamon, *Only a Game? The Diary of a Professional Footballer* (Kestrel Books, London, 1976).

Ferguson, Alex, *A Light in the North: Seven Years with Aberdeen* (Mainstream, Edinburgh, 1985).

Finn, Ralph, *Champions Again: Manchester United 1957 and 1965* (Robert Hale, London, 1965).

Fitton, Peter, and Keith, John, *Manchester United FC Official Annual 1978* (Circle Publications, Ilford, 1977).

Fitton, Peter, and Keith, John, *Manchester United FC Official Annual 1979* (Circle Publications, Ilford, 1978).

Foulkes, Bill, *Back at the Top* (Pelham Books, London, 1965).

Gallacher, Ken, *Jock Stein: The Authorised Biography* (Stanley Paul, London, 1981).

Gowling, Alan, *Football Inside Out* (Souvenir Press, London, 1977).

Greaves, Jimmy, *Taking Sides* (Sidgwick & Jackson, London, 1984).

Green, Geoffrey, *There's Only One United* (Hodder & Stoughton, London, 1978).

Gregg, Harry, *Wild About Football* (Souvenir Press, London, 1961).

Harris, Norman, *The Charlton Brothers* (Stanley Paul, London, 1971).

Hodgson, Derek, *The Manchester United Story* (Arthur Barker, London, 1979).

Hugman, Barry, *Rothmans Football League Players' Records* (Queen Anne Press, London, 1981).

Inglis, Simon, *League Football and The Men Who Made It* (Collins, London, 1988).

Inglis, Simon, *The Football Grounds of England and Wales* (Collins Willow, London, 1983).

Keith, John, *Manchester United FC Official Annual 1981* (Circle Publications, Ilford, 1980).

Law, Denis, *An Autobiography* (Queen Anne Press, London, 1979).

Law, Denis, *Living For Kicks* (Stanley Paul, London, 1963).

Liversedge, Stan, and Keith, John, *Manchester United FC Official Annual 1982* (Circle Publications, Ilford, 1981).

Liversedge, Stan, and Keith, John, *Manchester United FC Official Annual 1980* (Circle Publications, Ilford, 1979).

Macari, Lou, *United – We Shall Not Be Moved* (Souvenir Press, London, 1976).

McCartney, Iain, and Cavanagh, Roy, *Duncan Edwards: A Biography* (Temple Nostalgia Press, Nottingham, 1988).

Macdonald, Roger, *Manchester United in Europe* (Pelham Books, London, 1968).

McIlroy, Sammy, *Manchester United: My Team* (Souvenir Press, London, 1980).

Matthews, Tony, *Manchester United's Who's Who 1945–85* (Breedon Books, Derby, 1985).

Meek, David, *Anatomy of a Football Star: George Best* (Arthur Barker, London, 1970).

Meek, David, *The Manchester United Football Book, Nos 1–15,* (Stanley Paul, London, 1966–80).

Meek, David, *Manchester United Football Book No. 16 and Official Annual 1983* (Circle Sports, Ilford, 1982).

Meek, David, *Red Devils in Europe* (Cockerell Books, London, 1988).

Meek, David, and Tyrrell, Tom, *Manchester United: An Official History* (Hamlyn, London, 1988).

Mellor, Keith, *Heathens and Red Devils: Pictorial Milestones of Manchester United* (Temple Nostalgia Press, Nottingham, 1987).

Miller, David, *Father of Football: The Story of Sir Matt Busby* (Stanley Paul, London, 1970).

Morrison, Ian, and Shury, Alan, *Manchester United: A Complete Record 1878–1986* (Breedon Books, Derby, 1986).

Murphy, Jimmy, *Matt . . . United . . . and Me* (Souvenir Press, London, 1968).

Manchester United Supporters' Yearbooks (Manchester United Supporters' Club, Manchester, 1972–1988).

Neill, Terry, *Revelations of a Football Manager* (Sidgwick & Jackson, London, 1985).

Parkinson, Michael, *Best: An Intimate Biography* (Hutchinson, London, 1975).

Radford, Brian, *Through Open Doors* (Harrap, London, 1984).

Reed, Al, *It's All in the Book* (W. H. Allen, London, 1985).

Roberts, John, *George Best: Fall of a Superstar* (Manchester, 1973).

Roberts, John, *The Team that Wouldn't Die* (Arthur Barker, London, 1975).

Robson, Bryan, *United I Stand* (Pelham Books, London, 1984).

Rothmans Football Yearbooks 1970–1989 (Rothmans/Queen Anne Press, London, 1970–88).

Stepney, Alex, *Alex Stepney* (Arthur Barker, London, 1978).

Stepney, Alex, *In Safe Keeping* (Pelham Books, London, 1969).

Stiles, Nobby, *Soccer My Battlefield* (Stanley Paul, London, 1968).

Taylor, Frank, *The Day a Team Died* (Souvenir Press, London, 1983).

Thornton, Eric, *Manchester United: Barson to Busby* (Robert Hale, London, 1971).

Tyrrell, Tom, *Manchester United* (Hamlyn, Feltham, 1984).

Tyrrell, Tom, *The Manchester United Annual 1989* (Hamlyn, London, 1988).

Tyrrell, Tom, *The Red Devils Disciples* (Kaye and Ward, London, 1970).

Williamson, Stanley, *The Munich Air Disaster* (Cassirer, London, 1972).

Young, Percy, *Manchester United* (Heinemann, London, 1960).

INDEX